# SCOTTISH
# RAILWAY WALKS

D1260135

*Remains of Tongland Viaduct*

# SCOTTISH RAILWAY WALKS

## M. H. ELLISON

CICERONE PRESS
MILNTHORPE, CUMBRIA, ENGLAND.

© M. H. ELLISON 1989
ISBN 1 85284 007 2

*Tailpiece sketches by R.B.Evans*

*Bridge over River Tay at Ballinluig*

# CONTENTS

*Carron Station - Dufftown to Ballindalloch,*
*Grampian Region*

# INTRODUCTION

The two rusty poles which once supported the station nameboard, point defiantly upwards from the variegated green carpet. Brambles send out exploratory shoots in their never ending efforts to colonise more land which once formed the platforms of a now abandoned country station. Where once railway staff tended their prize winning station gardens, only a few clumps of roses, which have reverted to wild briar stock, remain. The walker enters an open door leading to the inner sanctum of the ticket office, whilst a sheep scampers from the waiting room, startled by a sudden sound. Empty racks which once held tickets for family outings to the big city or for the Sunday School outing to the seaside, cling defiantly to the wall. Papers are strewn all over the floor, a special traffic notice is picked up and read. Did Mr Jones ever get his coffin back, hopefully empty, which did not turn up on the 1.13pm local? Emerging from the buildings, the walker scans the abandoned trackbed which curves its way through the hills. Overhead a buzzard watches the same countryside, looking for its next meal. A sudden flash of brown as it swoops and an unsuspecting vole, which was attempting to scurry across the trackbed, becomes the bird's repast.

The days have long gone when the border hills would echo to the beat of an A3 Pacific hauling heavy freight on the long climb to Whitrope. A Jones Goods no longer basks in the summer sun having brought its train over Dava Summit. Motorists no longer have to wait for a Caley tank engine to cross the bridge at Connel Ferry with the branch train to Ballachulish. The British Rail map no longer marks the location of places like Riccarton Junction, Auchtermuchty, Glenfarg and Strathpeffer; all lost to the railways in the name of progress.

Railway rambling, the art of following the dashed line marked on many Ordnance Survey maps as "cse of old rly" is the only means to follow these abandoned routes. Where the map marks a clear route it may well turn out to be a tangle of gorse and brambles. The thin blue thread becomes a clear winding burn, generally too wide to jump, but great for a paddle to ease tired and throbbing feet, where anglers no longer have to curse at the clanking engine as it crosses the bridge and disturbs their sport. Walking these routes gives an opportunity to admire the countryside without having to dodge the omnipresence of the motor car. At their best the trackbeds provide a green haven where all the family can enjoy the pleasures of walking.

Railway development in Scotland started in the early eighteenth century with the opening of the Tranent Wagonway, carrying coal down to the coast from inland collieries. Initially development was slow, until the middle of the nineteenth century, when the railway mania saw a rapid growth in the network. Gradually five major companies emerged: the Caledonian, the North British, the Glasgow and South Western, the Great North of Scotland and the Highland Railways. Even as late as the start of the First World War, these companies were still opening new lines and expanding their empires. In 1923 the grouping of the railways saw the independent Scottish Railways divided between the London and North Eastern Railway and the London Midland and Scottish Railway. This grouping, together with the increased competition of the motor bus and tramcar, saw the closure of several lines in the 1930s.

The heyday of the network was over, as passenger services were withdrawn on the Wanlockhead branch, the Forth and Clyde Junction Railway, the Slamannan Railway and countless other lines. The outbreak of the Second World War saw a decline in the closure rate as the railways were called upon once again to assist in the country's war effort. At the onset of "peace" the railways were "nationalised" on the 1st January 1948, to form "British Railways", which combined all the Scottish lines under the aegis of the Scottish Region.

Although the railways were now owned by the public, they were still being closed. During the 1950s the suburban lines which served Edinburgh and Glasgow reluctantly offered their first victims for the ritual sacrifice. No longer would it be possible to travel above the banks of Loch Earn from St. Fillans to Lochearnhead, whilst in the borders several branches of the network were removed. In the 1960s, amidst great publicity, Dr. Beeching announced his plans for the reshaping of British Railways and the wholesale slaughter of the Scottish Railway System began. Nature was allowed to reclaim her ownership of routes from as far apart as Forres to Aviemore, Dunblane to Crianlarich, Edinburgh to Carlisle via Hawick and along the coastline of Fife. The many years' efforts spent on construction and maintaining the iron roads were cast aside by the stroke of a red pen. Whole counties were left without a railway station: Roxburgh, Clackmannan, Peebles, Selkirk, Berwickshire – although some still had a railway passing through them.

Once a line has been closed, rails, sleepers and other equipment are removed for use elsewhere or for sale on the enthusiast market. Bridges, viaducts and tunnels may be removed, blown up or filled in to either make them safe or remove the responsibility for their mainte-nance. The trackbed is then made available for purchase whilst it is left in the tender care of mother nature. British Rail try to secure a quick sale, to ensure the greatest financial benefit, passing on to the new owner obligations for maintenance of fences, drainage, civil engineer-ing structures etc. In some cases this sale may be nothing more than a transfer of ownership either to a local authority or to the original owner of the land. Generally ownership of a disused trackbed falls into one of three different categories: local authorities, landowners or British Rail.

Based on a 1966 government circular, some far-sighted authorities have purchased sections of railway for conversion (or future conversion) into footpaths and bridleways. With substantial grants available for the purchase and conversion, this is perhaps the best use of these trackbeds. In other cases the purchase has been for road building, rubbish dumping or more ignominiously, car parking. When the local authorities do not want to purchase the trackbed, it may be offered to the adjacent landowners. Whilst this allows for the land to be reclaimed for agricultural use, it does destroy the linear nature of the railway. In a good agricultural area, a short stretch of line may be sold to several different owners. The walker is then presented with a multitude of owners in the course of an expedition.

If the adjacent landowners do not want to buy, the trackbed may be purchased by any interested party. This generally happens with former station sites, where the buildings can be converted into private dwellings or for industrial premises. Alternatively a trackbed may be used as a caravan site because of its good drainage and relatively level nature.

Those sections of closed lines which attract no purchaser remain the property of the British Rail Estates Department. Whilst this department is theoretically responsible for the maintenance of such sections, mother nature is largely left to assume the role of care and maintenance. Fencing slowly decays, whilst a rich assortment of wild flowers grow, unmolested by modern agricultural chemicals. The railway buildings slowly decay, visited only by the intrepid walker. Consequently in attempting to walk a particular route, the walker has a very difficult task in tracing the ownership of the line. The BR Estates Department generally only record the original purchaser; if a section has been subsequently resold, this is not recorded by BR. In these cases, a tangled web of sales has to be traced, hopefully ending with the current owner of the trackbed. A note of caution should be raised where the land remains in the tender care of British Rail. Even when the trackbed is completely disused, it is a criminal offence to trespass (under the Railway Regulations Act of 1860 and the British Railways Act of 1965) upon an abandoned trackbed. It is therefore possible for those who trespass to be fined; fines being lower on disused lines than on used lines. Permission to ramble on disused railway lines may be obtained from the British Rail Board.

Whilst the walker is advised to seek the owner's permission, the situation in Scotland tends to be more favourable for an impromptu ramble. Many of the abandoned routes pass through open country grazed only by sheep or cattle, this in conjunction with the greater freedom available under the Scottish trespass laws, generally allows the walker to follow the deserted route, seeking permission where required on the spot. This delicate freedom should be cherished by the rambler by following the country code and respecting the property owned by unknown individuals. In asking for permission to ramble you may be refused, more likely you will find a kindred spirit who may relate to you images of days when trains passed along the trackbed. You may even be lucky to be given a cherished memento of a railway ticket, a station master's whistle or some other form of memorabilia.

*Please note, however, that the inclusion of a route in this book does not mean there is automatic right of access.*

The difference between a happy ramble and an exhausting slog is often as small as a missing bridge, an ill fitting piece of equipment or a misread bus/train timetable. Careful preparation prior to the walk should tackle three main areas: the route, the walker's equipment and the availability of public transport. Whilst it is possible to walk the railway "blind", a little reading about the history of the route adds a great deal to the enjoyment of the walk.

Examples abound. A mound of bricks basking under the warm summer sun becomes the remains of a station which once was famous for its floral displays. A lofty viaduct suffered a major collapse during its construction, with the loss of life of several of the navvies employed. An ornamental bridge façade resembling a romantic castle gateway had been built as a condition of the local laird giving his permission for the railway to traverse his land. This reading gives some insight into the human side of the railway which helps to make it different from any other trackbed.

With equipment, the rambler should be prepared for all kinds of conditions underfoot. Many trackbeds are liable to flooding in sections, even during the driest of summers. Cuttings which blocked the lines for periods during heavy snowfalls, still collect the snow after the last train has long since departed. By striking a balance between heat and cold, wet and dry the walker should be able to cope with most conditions encountered on the walk. Starting with the feet, a pair of fell-walking boots are probably the best type of footwear. These give the necessary support for the rough going whilst offering reasonable protection in waterlogged sections. Many trackbeds still have the knobby ankle-turning ballast left in situ even though the track has been dismantled. Boots with rigid anti-slip soles are suited for this type of walking, whilst stopping the smaller stones from entering the boot and protecting the ankle against the ever present danger of a twisting turn on the unyielding ballast.

Moving up the body, the walker should protect his/her legs against the thorns, gorse, nettles and brambles which thrive on disused railway lines. But there is nothing worse than sweating in heavy duty trousers on a hot sunny day. A pair of comfortable trousers strikes the right balance, with waterproof overtrousers for protection against the sudden shower. The upper storey requires similar protection, several layers of thin clothing being more practicable than a few layers of heavy clothing. Ideally the clothing should have either button, velcro or zip-up fronts to allow the garment to be opened as the walker warms up along the walk. A waterproof anorak or cagoule should be carried, offering protection against wind and rain with a zip-up front and large pockets for holding maps and other equipment. Whilst high visibility colours may be selected, a neutral olive green blends into the surrounding landscape and does not advertise the walker's presence to local wildlife or landowners.

Apart from clothing, the walker will probably need to carry a map which marks the route of the railway being followed. The map is kept in a convenient pocket or it is slung round the neck in a plastic mapcase. Sold in most outdoor shops, the best mapcases incorporate a velcro strip across the opening to protect the contents against the vagaries of the weather. Even the standard OS 1:50,000 maps show the route of the railway in some detail, depicting bridges, tunnels, viaducts, embankments and cuttings along with some lineside buildings. They also show the terrain of the surrounding countryside and can be useful in making a detour when the trackbed becomes blocked by missing bridges, fences or impenetrable undergrowth. Larger scale maps can be useful in following railways which have been closed for a long period of time or served some industrial concern. However these maps cover a smaller ground area, requiring the walker to carry additional maps for a given walk.

Whilst not essential, the walker may want to take a camera to record anything of interest seen on the walk, or a pair of binoculars to observe the wildlife, a notebook, pencils, reference books and sundry other items to make the walk more enjoyable. Festooned with such a plethora of equipment, the rambler may often ask what was it that made him/her take up railway walking in the first place. However, at the end of the day, footsore and weary, the pleasures of the walk far outweigh the "minor" difficulties encountered on the way.

The final item that should be checked before the walk is details of transport to/from the walk. Even if a private car is used, the walker will probably rely on public transport at one stage of the walk. Whilst obtaining information about the train timetables is relatively easy, the bus timetable presents another problem.

In Scotland, tourist offices produce travel guides to the Borders, (the land lying between Berwick, Edinburgh, Glasgow and Carlisle) and to the Highlands and Islands (the land to the north and west of a line from Glasgow and Inverness). Outwith these regions, the problem of finding out bus times becomes more difficult. No longer is it possible to easily obtain timetables which cover all services operated by the various subsidiaries of the Scottish Bus Group, or the local authority. Instead, separate leaflets for each service are produced, which are not much use if you are not sure of which services you will be interested in. However, patient inquiry at a major city bus station or tourist office will usually allow the walker to discover the relevant information.

So the great day dawns, underneath a blazing sun and a clear blue sky, the walker stands at the start of the trackbed about to be conquered. Armed with the relevant equipment and a good supply of optimism, a quick check on the right direction and off into the brave new world. Sounds idyllic, but it may just be the walker's lucky day; he could be meeting up with a blinding swirling mist, torrential downpour or even a marked lack of trackbed. Sadly, all too often the walk starts in an urban area where either the trackbed has been landscaped out of all recognition or it has been turned into an official/unofficial rubbish dump. In these cases a spell of map reading is required to select an exit to a more rural area where the trackbed may be discovered. Eventually the walker reaches the promised land as the feet come in contact with the hallowed ground. Conditions underfoot vary from hard ballast chippings through grass covered ground to a close approximation of a semi-watered canal.

The trackbed becomes a linear nature reserve, where plants and wildlife can exist without having to worry about the deadly presence of mankind. Flowers grow in great profusion, gentle orchids, foxgloves, various campions, dandelions and the doyen of the abandoned railway, the Rose Bay Willow Herb. A lightweight guide to wild flowers proves an invaluable companion to identify the more unusual species. On the way the walker may encounter a variety of obstacles, from minor inconveniences like fences and gates to major problems like dismantled bridges or private property. Although the walker does not like making detours, they are often required to ford rivers or avoid private housing etc. which occupies the trackbed. *Think before you act – it is often safer to make a detour and this should be the adopted policy whenever there is the slightest doubt.*

Lunchtime may be alfresco on the trackbed or on the better days at a quiet pub, drinking and listening to the conversation of locals who remember the railway in happier days. One of the pleasures of railway *walking is the ad hoc* conversations which add the human touches to the bare bones of the recorded railway history. The burn becomes the one from which water was taken in buckets to refill the empty tanks of the 1.35 that hot summer's day when the locomotive ran out of water. The river crossing is where the anglers were "splashed" by an unwanted piece of slag thrown out of the tender of the pick-up freight by a fireman in mischievous mood, a ragged rosebush becomes the once proud remnant of the stationmaster's garden, whilst a few wooden posts mark the site of the once busy cattle dock. Maybe the walker will be lucky enough to discover a relic of the bygone railway age, though unfortunately very few items can be carried far due to their weight. Those which can be carried are generally nondescript and would not warrant the effort in carrying them home. Better a photograph of the rust-encrusted milepost, leaving the original in situ for the next walker to discover.

Gradually the hours progress and the miles diminish as the rambler approaches the end of the line for the day. Hopefully the frustrating sight of the last train or bus heading away over the crest of the hill into the setting sun will not be the vision that greets the walker. In contemplating the successes and failures in the day's walk, one may wish to consider joining the company of fellow travellers. A nationwide organisation, "Railway Ramblers", aim to record the state of all of Britain's disused railways and provide a programme of day and weekend walks along disused railways throughout the country. The address of this organisation and other related organisations is given in an appendix at the end of this book.

*West portal of the CR tunnel at Peebles*

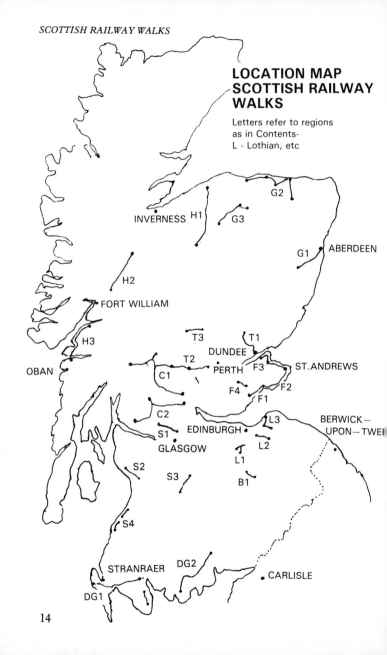

**LOCATION MAP
SCOTTISH RAILWAY
WALKS**

Letters refer to regions
as in Contents-
L - Lothian, etc

INVERNESS  H1  G2  G3

G1  ABERDEEN

H2

FORT WILLIAM

H3

OBAN

T3  T1
T2  DUNDEE
C1  PERTH  F3  ST.ANDREWS
F4  F2
F1

C2

S1  EDINBURGH  L3  BERWICK—
GLASGOW  L2  UPON—TWEE

L1

S2  S3  B1

S4

STRANRAER  DG2  CARLISLE

DG1

# I:
# WALKS IN
# BORDERS REGION

## Railways to Peebles

One of the most attractive border towns is Peebles. It was once a flourishing railway centre with two stations, which served the local population with trains of the North British Railway to Edinburgh and Galashiels, and the Caledonian Railway westwards to Symington. The citizens of Peebles were incensed with the opening of the Hawick Railway in 1849, from Edinburgh to Hawick via Galashiels, which bypassed the town. Plans were laid for constructing a line from Esbank southwards to Peebles, which was opened by the Peebles Railway Company on 4th July 1855. The company made a profit of over £990 during the first eight weeks of operation. It had to extend the length of several of the station platforms within three months of opening, due to the need to lengthen its trains, because of the higher than expected passenger traffic.

On November 5th 1860, the Symington, Biggar & Broughton Railway was opened from Symington to Broughton. Taken over by the Caledonian, this line was extended to Peebles on February 1st 1864. In October of the same year, a single track line was opened from Peebles to Galashiels. The Peebles Railway Company was taken over by the NBR on August 1st 1876, leaving the two companies glowering at each other, on opposite sides of the River Tweed. A short spur joined the two lines, but it was only used for occasional exchange of traffic and was never used as a regular service. Passengers trying to travel from Galashiels to Symington via Peebles, a theoretical possibility, had to face up to the bitter rivalry between the two companies determined to prevent easy exchange of passengers in the town.

Both companies provided prestige services to Edinburgh, the NBR train from Galashiels took only 53 minutes for its morning journey to the capital, the same time as that taken by the evening return service. The Caley service, which had a longer mileage took one and three quarter hours to travel from Peebles to the capital and two hours for the evening return service. After the 1923 grouping, the services remained much the same, the rural tranquillity being disturbed only when fire damaged the engine shed in 1930.

Nationalisation came and shortly thereafter the passenger service was withdrawn from Peebles West (the CR station) to Symington on June 5th 1950. Goods services were maintained from Peebles to Broughton until June 7th 1954. What was claimed to be Scotland's first diesel service started running from Galashiels to Edinburgh via Peebles on July 11th 1956, the service being operated by two-car diesel units. The increased demand for the new service caused BR to introduce two extra trains on the service. However the increased demand and cheaper running costs proved to be a temporary phenomenon. The axe fell on the passenger service from Hawthorden Junction via Peebles to Kilnowe Junction (Galashiels) which was withdrawn on 3rd February 1962.

The final service left Edinburgh Waverley at 11.01 pm, following the route taken earlier in the day by a steam hauled farewell tour. The final train, a Saturday only service from Edinburgh to Galashiels, arrived at Peebles shortly before midnight, and left a few minutes later on the Sunday morning laden with people saying farewell to their line.

So the train picked its way along the winding valley of the Tweed for the last time. The passengers had a long walk back home from Galashiels, perhaps hearing the final cry of a steam whistle echoing in the hills, to aid them on their journey.

*Mileages*

| | | |
|---|---|---|
| PEEBLES | 0.00 miles | |
| LYNE station | | 3.00 miles |
| CARDRONA | 3.50 miles | |
| INNERLEITHEN | 6.50 miles | |
| WALKERBURN | 8.25 miles | |
| THORNIELEE | 12.00 miles | |
| CLOVENFORDS | 15.25 miles | |
| GALASHIELS | 18.50 miles | |

*Ordnance Survey 1:50,000 map number:– 73*

*Public Transport*

Peebles, Cardrona, Innerleithen and Walkerburn are all served by an hourly bus service from Edinburgh to Galashiels. The frequency of this service is reduced on a Sunday. Details of this and other services in the area may be found in the public transport timetable, issued by the Borders' Regional Council.

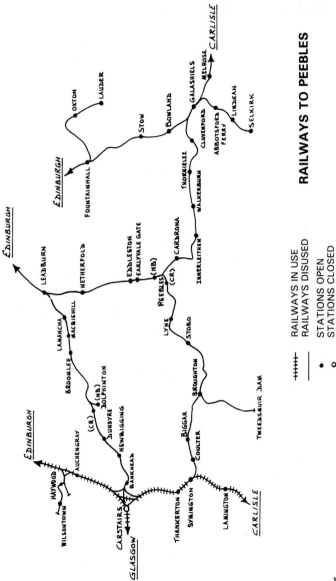

**RAILWAYS TO PEEBLES**

RAILWAYS IN USE
RAILWAYS DISUSED

STATIONS OPEN
STATIONS CLOSED

# I/1: Peebles to Walkerburn

Although the walk starts at the site of the Caledonian Station, a detour to view the tunnel and Tweed Viaduct in the grounds of Neidpath Castle, provides an interesting start to the walk. The station site has now become a housing estate which is gradually creeping westwards, requiring one to detour along a well used riverside path before the trackbed is gained, near to the eastern portal of the tunnel. Wooden gates protect both of the entrances to the tunnel, although they are often open. The tunnel is "S" shaped, requiring the use of a torch to guide the walker through its dark interior. Internally, the tunnel is in good condition, with very few signs of water penetration. Beyond the western portal the trackbed crosses the River Tweed on a 12 arched stone built viaduct. Presumably its close proximity to the castle resulted in it being built with mock castelations and ornamental iron railings.

Returning to **Peebles West**, the trackbed of the link to the NBR, survives as a grassy embankment separating the river from a car park and toilets. Whilst the bridge over the Tweed has been removed, the northern abutment can still be observed, along with a short section of trackbed as it heads through private gardens, to link up with the ex-NBR route. **Peebles East**, the NBR station, has been converted into a car park. A small goods office remains in use as the car park attendant's accommodation. The NBR line through the town, now lies buried beneath a by-pass, allowing traffic to avoid the awkward and narrow roads through the town centre. The railway walker faces a roadside walk, to the site of the town's gasworks, before a walkable trackbed can be regained. The gasworks were situated to the south of where the railway passed beneath the A72, one mile to the east of the town.

Several buildings still remain in situ, providing an interesting relic of the days when most towns had a small gas-works, producing gas from coal before the advent of North Sea Gas. A path, cantilevered out from the railway, provided a means of access for the workers. The gasworks had been served by rail in its heyday, traces of which can be discerned to the east of the gasworks. Beyond the gasworks, the trackbed makes a sharp turn eastwards at the base of spoil tips, to become a pleasant riverside path. On one side flows the Tweed, on the other fields of cattle are protected by avenues of mature deciduous trees, which shelter them from winds funneled through the high sided valley. Conditions underfoot are generally good, the use of the line as a diversionary route for the Waverley Line, resulted in it being well maintained and ballasted with stone chippings instead of the ash ballast commonly used for branch lines.

The ruins of a tower house acts as a reminder of the troubled history of the border area, as the walker approaches the site of **Cardrona Station**. Immediately before the station, the trackbed crosses over the Tweed, from the north to the south bank, by means of a low, bow sided girder bridge. The bridge has now been converted into an access road, which has replaced the original ford, allowing the walker to reach the station site with dry feet. Since there is no other bridge in the locality, one is left to wonder how the station was reached by foot passengers from the nearby houses on the north bank of the river. The station is well worthy of inspection, the wooden buildings still remain largely intact on the single platform. It would appear that the station buildings have only recently been abandoned, internally much of the original pannelled woodwork remains in a good state of preservation. Nearby are the remains of the small signal box and assorted lineside huts, including a standard pre-Beeching Elizabethan version built in reinforced concrete. Beyond the station, the trackbed can be followed to the site of the next bridge over the Tweed.

In places the path is a narrow track, one "cutting" being formed by large cylindrical bales of straw, that bear a close resemblance to an outsized version of a well known breakfast cereal, Nearing the bridge site, the trackbed has been seeded with a spruce plantation, although a path can still be followed through the young trees. unfortunately the bridge has been removed, along with any traces of the abutments and presumably the piers in the river. Consequently, unless a parting of the waters can be performed, a detour back to the earlier bridge is required, followed by a roadside walk to reach a path from the cottages of Woodend, which allows access to the trackbed on the north bank of the river.

As a reward for this detour, the trackbed reveals two intact underbridges, still proclaiming their original numbers of 42 and 43. The rails were supported on planking resting on flimsy "I" section girders, with braced rail sections provided to support the original running rails. Beyond the second bridge, the trackbed has been ploughed into the adjacent fields leaving a stony path to mark the route of the railway. Only as the walker reaches the outskirts of Innerleithen, does the trackbed return to a more recognizable form. Before reaching the station, the line passes alongside a whisky bond, once rail connected as traces of the original sleeper positions remain within the fenced-in enclosure.

**Innerleithen Station** has been converted into a private house. The enforced detour through the village may provide an excuse to sample the products of Traquair House Brewery, in the local hotel, thus fortifying the system for the final miles to Walkerburn. The line is regained, to the east of the town's gasworks, near to a caravan site and prior to its next crossing over the River Tweed. Fortunately this bridge is still intact, although it is in a poor state of repair.

Beyond the bridge the trackbed can be traced as a faint level path through the rich pasture. Nearing the site of Walkerburn station, it disappears beneath further ploughing operations. Whilst **Walkerburn Station** has been converted into a private house, the goods yard appears to be used by a haulage contractor. However, from the enforced roadside detour, there seems to be no road access to the yard site. This raises an interesting question about how the lorries get into the yard. Although the station had a passing loop, there was only the single platform. The station building now forms the basis of a very attractive private house. The original buildings having been extended by the filling-in of the original canopy structure. On the opposite side of the tracks, what was presumably the original station master's accommodation remains in use as a private dwelling house.

Whilst the trackbed continues towards Galashiels, two miles from Walkerburn another bridge has been removed which once spanned the River Tweed. Consequently the lengthy detour is a good reason for making Walkerburn the end of what has been an attractive, thought provoking walk. The village has an interesting museum depicting the history of the woollen industry of the Borders, which is worthy of a visit before possibly catching the hourly bus service back to Peebles, the starting point of the day's walk.

*Walkerburn Station*

# II:
# WALKS IN
# LOTHIAN REGION

## Railways of the North Esk Valley

The first railway to penetrate the upper valley of the River North Esk, was the Peebles Railway, which opened from Hardengreen Junction (on the Waverley Route) to Peebles on 4th July 1855. Like the other railways that followed this valley, the Peebles Railway was largely financed by local people and operated by the North British Railway. The next railway to open, was a branch from Esk Valley Junction to Polton, which opened on 15th April 1867. Five years later on the 2nd September, another branch was opened off the Peebles Railway, from Hawthornden Junction to Penicuik. This line was the closest to the actual river, crossing and recrossing it several times, before reaching its terminus at Penicuik. The final railway to follow the valley was the Edinburgh, Loanhead and Roslin Railway. This railway was opened from Millerhill Junction to Roslin on the 23rd July 1874. Three years later, on the 2nd July 1877, an extension was opened to Glencorse for passenger services. A further extension served the Penicuik Gas Works, three quarters of a mile from the terminus of the passenger services.

Generally the railways settled down to a long period of service, to the residents of the valley. Branches served the many mills and mines in what was once a thriving industrial area. The first withdrawal of services took place on the 1st May 1933, when passenger services were withdrawn on the Glencorse branch. The Polton and Penicuik branches lost their passenger service on the 10th September 1951, whilst the Glencorse branch was cut back to Roslin Colliery (23 chains west of Roslin Station) on the 1st July 1959. Three years later saw the withdrawal of passenger services on the Peebles Railway, which were cut back to Rosewell Station on the 5th February, and finally withdrawn on the 10th September. The goods service on the Peebles branch was withdrawn the same day as the passenger service, leaving only the Polton and Penicuik lines with a goods service, from Hardengreen Junction. The former service was withdrawn on the 18th May 1964, whilst the Penicuik goods was withdrawn three years later, on the 27th March.

*Mileages*

| | |
|---|---|
| MILLERHILL | 0 miles 00 chains |
| Gilmerton | 2 miles 24 chains |
| Loanhead | 4 miles 20 chains |
| Roslin | 5 miles 73 chains |
| Glencorse | 7 miles 51 chains |
| Penicuik Gas Works | 8 miles 29 chains |
| ESKBANK | 1 mile 57 chains |
| Hardengreen Junction | 2 miles 15 chains |
| Esk Valley Junction | 2 miles 53 chains |
| Broomieknowe | 3 miles 25 chains |
| Lasswade | 3 miles 59 chains |
| Polton | 4 miles 63 chains |
| BONNYRIGG | 3 miles 53 chains |
| ROSEWELL | 5 miles 37 chains |
| Rosslynlee | 6 miles 68 chains |
| Pomathorn | 9 miles 8 chains |
| ROSSLYN CASTLE | 6 miles 64 chains |
| AUCHENDINNY | 8 miles 17 chains |
| ESK BRIDGE | 9 miles 14 chains |
| PENICUIK | 9 miles 74 chains |

*Ordnance Survey 1:50,000 map number:– 66*

*Public Transport*
Dalkeith is well served by buses to Edinburgh and the neighbouring towns. There is a regular service from Edinburgh to Peebles, which follows closely the route of the Edinburgh, Loanhead and Roslin Railway and then the Peebles Railway from Leadburn, which is two miles to the south of Pomathorn. There are also buses from Edinburgh to Penicuik and Rosewell, which follow the route of the Peebles Railway. Because of the close proximity of these lines, the walker can in fact make several circular walks, covering all or part of the branches. One based on Bonnyrigg or Rosewell Stations, would follow the Peebles Railway to near Pomathorn Farm (on the B6372), returning along the Penicuik Railway, to the starting point.

## II/1a:   Rosewell to Rosslynlee Hospital

**Bonnyrigg Station** is reached by following the B704 towards Gorebridge, from its crossroads with the A6094 through the town. The station platforms have survived, albeit partially landscaped to provide a picnic site at the start of the official walkway to Penicuik. Nearby, the former station master's house is now used by a local turf accountant.

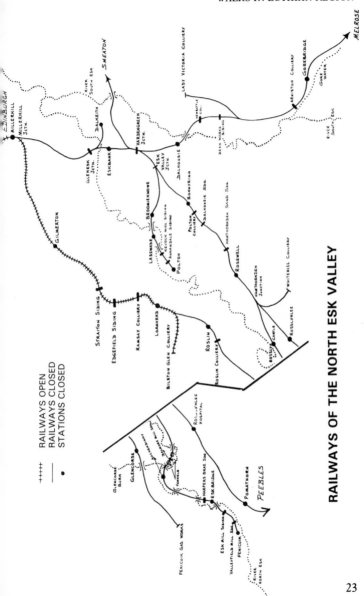

RAILWAYS OF THE NORTH ESK VALLEY

+++++ RAILWAYS OPEN
───── RAILWAYS CLOSED
• STATIONS CLOSED

Wasteland to the south of the station occupies the site of the exchange sidings for the nearby Polton Number Two Colliery, whilst traces can be found of the branch which once served a factory to the north of the railway. The first section of the trackbed is well covered with refuse from the nearby housing estates, several sections of the trackbed being fully carpeted. The walker passes the sites of two farm crossings, still marked by the concrete posts which once supported the crossing gates. Nearing Dalhousie Siding, one passes the skeletal remains of a LNER platelayers' hut, the concrete frame still supports the original roof, offering scant shelter in case of inclement weather.

**Dalhousie Siding** is marked by the remains of a heavy earth and timber built buffer stop, whilst a picnic site occupies ground where the crossing keeper's cottage once stood. The siding was presumably provided for the agricultural traffic to and from the nearby farms. Continuing on, one passes a watchman's shelter, again built in concrete, before reaching the site of the branch which once served the Dalhousie Sand quarry. Unfortunately a large dog kennel on the opposite side of the trackbed greets the walker with a raucous cacophony of barking. This precludes the possibility of exploring the area, the walker is forced to quickly pass underneath the A6094, to reach the level crossing to the east of **Rosewell Station**. A derelict cottage, which was once two cottages, stands alongside the crossing. The station platforms remain, albeit bereft of any buildings, although the base of a crane remains in the nearby goods yard. Again this station once had extensive siding accommodation, handling traffic for the nearby colliery and the lines to Peebles and Penicuik.

To the south of the station, stands a very unusual Roman Catholic church, more at home in a Mediterranean country than these northern climes!

Leaving the station, the line crossed the B7009, from Rosewell to Roslin. Traces of rails still survive in the road, guiding the walker to Hawthornden Junction. The walkway veers away to the right, on the alignment of the Penicuik branch, whilst on the left can be seen the branch which served Whitehill Colliery and Brickworks. The large bing pit heap, nearby is the spoil from the former colliery. The Peebles Railway continues on as a grass covered track, on top of the original stone ballast. One enters a waterlogged cutting, overgrown in places, ending at the fenced off site of **Roslynlee Station**. Luckily there is an easy detour through the fields on the western side, passing the stone and timber buildings of the former station. The owner appears to take an interest in old Rolls Royce cars; unfortunately the same care is not taken of the buildings and station site.

The trackbed beyond the station was used for one of the numerous pipelines, laid in the late seventies and early eighties. This has disturbed the former drainage of the railway, which though clear of undergrowth can be very boggy during periods of wet weather. The route passes to the north of the Roslynlee Hospital, which was provided with a halt a few years before closure of the Peebles branch. A mound at the end of a track to the hospital presumably marks the site of the halt, and the nearby Holme Mill siding. Beyond the hospital, the drainage appears to recover to a small extent, to reach the site of another level crossing at Firth Mains. Again the crossing keeper's cottage has survived, having been converted into a rather attractive private house. The walker wishing to return to Bonnyrigg, can leave the trackbed here, and follow the lanes to the B7026. By turning left along the minor road to Penicuik at Maybank, the walker will reach the trackbed of the Penicuik Railway, near the site of Esk Bridge Station.

## II/1b:   Penicuik to Rosewell

The minor road from Maybank to Penicuik crosses over the former railway on a considerable gradient, to the east of the site of **Esk Bridge Station**. An entrance to the walkway has been created, via the network of sidings on the western side of the railway. Traces can be found of a branch which heads away to the east of the trackbed, presumably to serve a nearby mill or quarry. The trackbed itself is used by lorries, which ply to and from the sewage works, beyond the next bridge over the River North Esk. Passing over this bridge, and the sewage works, the walker finds the railway continues to be a generally well drained path on the original ash ballast, much frequented by the local population. Woodland is passed on either side, before the trackbed crosses back to the south bank of the river, on a girder bridge. This is used by the local graffiti artists as a practice area for their literary skills.

The railway engineers must have had to alter the original route of the river in some places, as the line squeezes alongside its southern bank. A heavy brick built retaining wall prevents the river from eroding the trackbed, as it follows the river to **Auchendinny Station**. The single platform with small goods yard are passed, as the trackbed crosses the river on a Bow-String Girder bridge and enters a short cutting to emerge at the entrance to the Dalmore Mill. This mill is still operating, forcing one to follow a narrow path alongside the various buildings.

Having squeezed past the mill, the trackbed recovers its normal width as it runs high above the gorge of the North Esk. Looking down onto the turbulent river, one can see the remains of a footbridge, which once allowed pedestrian access to the lands on the south bank. After years of neglect, it is in a dangerous state, and it cannot be many years before it completely collapses into the river. On a nearby hillock between the river and railway, stands the remains of Old Woodhouselee Castle. This castle watches over the railway as it enters another tunnel, emerging at the impressive stone and brick viaduct which carried the Penicuik Railway over the River North Esk for the last time. The viaduct marks the end of the gorge section of the river, as the valley levels out to form rich agricultural land. The trackbed passes under two stone overbridges, and a further bridge carrying the pipeline from the Gladhouse Reservoir, which brings water to the population of the Edinburgh

*Tunnel near Old Wooodhouselee Castle*

district. Through this landscape the railway passes on a low sided embankment, forming the basis of a very attractive walk as it reaches the wooded cutting which marks the site of **Rosslyn Castle Station**.

The platform remains in situ, its surface having been repaired as part of the conversion of the trackbed into the official walkway. A minor road past Lea farm passes over the railway. At the base of this bridge can be found a concrete plinth, painted red, with white stones being used to form the former station's name. With the rich mixed woodland forming a dense backcloth for the site, few will be able to pass without pausing to rest in this sylvian setting. The trees hide the roar of modern society, replacing it by the melodic chorus of birdsong, soothing the most troubled of souls. Beyond the station, the trackbed climbs up to reach the Peebles Railway at **Hawthornden Junction**.

From Hawthornden Junction, the walker can follow the Peebles Railway to Rosewell, or Bonnyrigg, where there are several cafés and public houses, providing refreshment at the end of a very enjoyable day's walk.

# East Lothian Branchlines: The Macmerry & Gifford Branches

The first railway to penetrate the rich coalfields in the valley of the Tyne Water, was the Macmerry branch. This line left the East Coast Main Line at Monktonhall Junction, opening for goods services to Smeaton during December 1866. The goods service was extended to Ormiston on May 1st 1867. Passengers had to wait a further five years to travel by train to Macmerry, when a passenger service from Waverley was started on the 1st May. Clearly these lines were promoted for the mineral traffic from the many collieries along their course; passenger traffic was of secondary importance.

Towards the turn of the century, the railway promoters sought to open a branch from Ormiston to Gifford and Garvel. This line, which was to become the Gifford & Garvel Light Railway, opened to Gifford on the 14th April 1901. The populace of Garvel had to be content with a "coach" service to Gifford, for their connection with the railway network.

The lines were never great money spinners for passenger traffic, and with the competition from motor buses after the first world war, the LNER soon sought the withdrawal of the passenger service. The Macmerry Branch lost its passenger service from Ormiston on the 1st July 1925. Gifford lost its passenger service from Monktonhall on the 3rd April 1933, although Smeaton Station had been closed since the 22nd September 1930. The freight services remained whilst the pits remained in production, but with the closure of the pits, so the freight services were withdrawn. The goods service on the Gifford branch was cut back to Humbie on the 12th August 1948 after that section had been breached by flooding, and to Saltoun on the 2nd May 1960, the same day as the Macmerry branch lost its goods service from Ormiston. Five years later, the line was cut back to Smeaton, on the 3rd May 1965. The final section from Monktonhall Junction to Smeaton, survived to serve a Coal Preparation Plant, near Dalkeith, until 1980.

*Mileages*

| | | |
|---|---|---|
| GIFFORD | | 0 mile 00 chains |
| HUMBIE | | 3 miles 69 chains |
| Highlea | Siding | 4 miles 53 chains |
| SALTOUN | | 6 miles 01 chain |
| Lemplock Well | Siding | 6 miles 58 chains |
| PENCAITLAND | | 6 miles 61 chains |
| Branders | Siding | 7 miles 09 chains |
| Pencaitland | Colliery | 7 miles 38 chains |
| Meadow | Colliery | 8 miles 25 chains |

| ORMISTON | | 8 miles 35 chains |
| | ORMISTON | 0 miles 00 chains |
| | WINTON | 1 mile 18 chains |
| | Penston Colliery | 1 mile 66 chains |
| | MACMERRY | 2 miles 34 chains |
| Ormiston | Colliery | 8 miles 49 chains |
| Elphinstone | Colliery | 9 miles 24 chains |
| Limeylands | Colliery | 9 miles 29 chains |
| Coulsland | Siding | 10 miles 75 chains |
| Dalkeith | Colliery | 11 miles 16 chains |
| SMEATON | | 12 miles 55 chains |
| Carberry | Colliery | 13 miles 16 chains |
| Monktonhall | Junction | 14 miles 34 chains |

*Ordnance Survey 1:50,000 map number:– 66*

*Public Transport*

Pencaitland is served by a regular bus service from Edinburgh, some of which operate on to Haddington via East Saltoun. There is also a limited service from Haddington to Gifford, via East and West Saltoun. Smeaton is about two miles from Dalkeith, where there are frequent buses to Edinburgh. There is also a limited service from Westcraig (to the north of Smeaton) to Edinburgh. The frequency of these services are reduced, with some alteration to the routes on a Sunday.

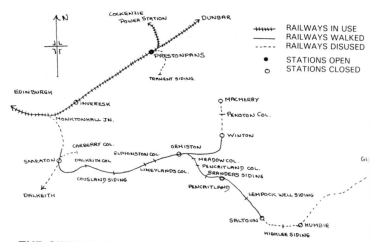

## THE GIFFORD AND MACMERRY BRANCHES

*Saltoun Station*

## II/2: Saltoun to Smeaton

The viaduct which carried the Gifford and Garvel Light Railway over the Humbie Water was demolished in 1986. Very little traces remain of the two arched bridge, apart from some fallen abutments and the traces of the pier in the river. A clear track guides the walker past fields of inquisitive cows, to the site of Saltoun Station.

Considering that **Saltoun Station** lost its passenger services in 1933, the survival of the small single storey timber built station building is remarkable. Although the interior has been destroyed, the external appearance remains largely the same as that seen by its passengers over thirty years. The building remains on a short length of platform looking out onto a grounded coach body and a stone built house that was presumably the accommodation for the station master or crossing keeper. It is worth following the lane to Duncrahill for a short distance, to discover a further coach body by the side of the house. The large station site is now used to graze cattle, causing the ground to be very muddy in wet weather. A warning attached to the former station buildings, warns of dire cattle diseases and the need to take a disinfected footbath: a sign of former times.

Leaving the station behind, the walker reaches the start of the Pencaitland Way, an official footpath that uses the former railway to Crossgatehall, a distance of approximately 6 miles. A signal post, probably resited as the Gifford Branch never would have had the luxury of the track-circulating that is indicated by the triangular white plate on the lattice signal post, marks the start of the walkway. A notice board on the opposite side of the trackbed, gives the walker some insight into the history of the lines and the sights along the way. There are similar notice boards along the way, although most of these have been mutilated by the local vandals.

Having crossed the Kinchie Burn by means of an impressively high earthen embankment, the walker passes the buildings of the Glenkinchie Distillery. An overbridge that is probably a replacement of an earlier bridge, takes a track over the railway to the nearby distillery.

A boggy cutting has to be negotiated, where the railway passes under the minor road from Lempock Wells to Templehall, before the site of **Lempock Wells Siding** is reached. The only trace of which is a widening of the trackbed, and a low grass covered mound. Nearby can be found the first of several concrete tombstones, marking the site of former collieries. The concrete has eroded making it very difficult to read the inscription, which records the site of the Huntlaw Pit, owned by Fletchers of Saltoun. This mine was apparently one of the oldest mines in the area, and was presumably served by the siding. The mine has disappeared, its only memorial is the tombstone by the side of the railway.

Nearing Wester Pencaitland, a replacement bridge allows the walker to cross over the minor road to Templehall, before the track curves round to reach the site of **Pencaitland Station**. The former station site has disappeared beneath a number of large grain silos that give out a cacophony of moans and groans as the grain is loaded. The former station master's house is now a well maintained private house, looking out on a gradient post marking the change from the climb of 1 in 50 up to the station site, to the level through the station. Surprisingly it is original, judging by photographs taken while the station was still in use for rail traffic.

The railway leaves the ugly silos behind, and follows alongside the A6093, to reach the site of Woodhall Colliery. Again a plaque records the history of the mine, which was first sunk in 1852. Woodhall was not fully exploited until 1904, and was abandoned in 1944. The colliery has largely disappeared in a forested plantation, although it is possible to trace some of the sidings alongside the trackbed. Further signal posts guide one past the infilling of the trackbed, which has improved the alignment of the nearby main road. Traces of the abutments of the former bridge, which carried the road over the railway, can still be found. A pleasant woodland cutting takes the walker to the bridge over the Tyne Water, which still proclaims it was bridge number one on the Gifford Branch.

It is worth scrambling down the embankment on the north end of the bridge, to view the stone and brick built three arched viaduct over the water. Presumably the missing bridge over the Humbie Water would have looked very similar to this bridge, although it would have been a taller, twin arched bridge. Returning to the trackbed, the walker passes a sewage works, whose access road crosses the railway south of the site of the short lived Meadow Colliery. This crossing still has rails buried in the tarmacadamed surface. Since this colliery was sunk before the opening of the G&GLR, it would appear that the colliery was rail served before the opening of the line to Gifford. No doubt the G&GLR used part of the colliery branch, as a start of its route, as the bridge numbering indicates that the first bridge it built was the viaduct over the Tyne Water.

A further underbridge allows one to cross a tributary of the Tyne Water, before reaching the site of Ormiston Junction. The Macmerry Branch joins in from the right, as a clear track used for access to a landscaped slag heap. This operation is soon to be undone, as the site is to be used for a car scrap yard. The Macmerry Branch can be followed past this yard, until it disappears in field reclamations, where it turned northwards towards Winton Station.

Heading towards Smeaton, the trackbed passes underneath the B6371, to reach the expanse of **Ormiston Station**. This is a watershed between the rural scenery of the walk so far, and the heavy industrial landscape of the remainder of the walk. This station was a major source of traffic to the railway, serving not only the nearby town but no less than 11 industrial concerns, listed in the Handbook of Railway Stations. One of these was a colliery at the station, traces of which can be seen beyond the remains of the passenger platform. Further signals, again probably resited from elsewhere, allow one to gain a higher viewpoint of the site. Leaving the station behind, the trackbed was followed on the south by a narrow gauge line that once served the Oxenfo(o)rd Collieries.

The trackbed runs alongside the Bellyford Burn, which is a tributary of the Tyne water, passing the sites of collieries on either side of the burn. Numerous tombstones record their names, and the walker may detour to view some of their remains. Perhaps the most impressive is the large brick built building of the Bellyford Colliery which is near the junction of a branch which served several collieries near Elphinstone and Tranent. The scenery is very different to the rural vistas south of Ormiston. It is now a landscape of numerous bings (pit heaps) and the tumbledown remains of mines which nature is slowly trying to reclaim. No doubt the landscapers will come along some day, and replace this mecca for the industrial archaeologist by a green desert of landscaped hills and valleys.

Having passed the plaque which records the Oxenford Colliery, owned by the Ormiston Coal Company, there is a subtle change in the scenery. Gone are the traces of the collieries, to be replaced by a hilly moorland, grazed by sheep and cattle. No doubt this section has once been industrial, but nature has covered the scars. A curious concrete and stone base is passed on the opposite bank of the stream, before the walker comes to the site of Couslands Limeworks. A quarry and stone preparation plant still occupies the site, although nowadays it is totally dependent upon road traffic. However, it is still possible to trace the siding which once served the limeworks.

The trackbed deteriorates beyond the limeworks, probably because of the landscaping operations alongside, blocking the original railway drains. Several sections are waterlogged, ending in the landscaped site of the sidings at Crossgatehall which served the Dalkeith and Old Ends Collieries. These sidings mark the end of the official walkway. The original cutting has now been infilled, although it is still possible to pass beneath the bridge which carries the A6124 over the railway. Beyond this bridge further reclamation has eradicated the trackbed and the branch to the Old End Colliery. Only where the lines crossed the minor road to Smeaton does the trackbed become a recognisable entity again. On the west side of the crossing, the trackbed is used by a private access road to a series of electricity sub-stations on the site of Dalkeith Colliery. The walker is advised to follow the minor road to reach the site of **Smeaton Station**.

Smeaton Station was an island platform, with wooden buildings which survived for many years after the withdrawal of its passenger services. The island platform separated the line to Macmerry and Gifford which turns away eastwards, and a line which continued on towards Thornybank and Dalkeith. This line was authorised at the same time as the Macmerry branch and continued through Dalkeith to Hardengreen Junction on the Waverley Route. The line closed as a through route before the Second World War, and it probably never had a regular passenger service. Traces of the island platform remain, and the walker is faced with a choice of continuing along the Macmerry Branch towards Whitecraig or heading south along the branch to Dalkeith. Perhaps the former choice wins, allowing the junction of the branch to Carberry Colliery to be viewed, before one reaches the sprawl of Whitecraig, where hopefully it will not be too long that the walker has to wait for a bus to Edinburgh or Dalkeith.

# The Gullane & Haddington Branches

The branch to Gullane came about as the result of Golf. A group of local land owners formed the Aberlady, Gullane and North Berwick Railway Company. The act for its construction was passed on 24th August 1893, the branch starting at Aberlady Junction, 1.5 miles east of Longniddry. The branch was opened to Gullane on 1st April 1898. However, the extension from Gullane to Williamston (where it would join the North Berwick branch) was never built. As part of the unrealised plan, the earlier North Berwick station (opened 17th June 1850) was replaced by a two road terminus with a unique scissors crossover on a curve. The local company was absorbed by the NBR in 1900. Gullane was one of the places served by a new service inaugurated in 1914 from Glasgow to the Lothian Resorts of Dunbar, North Berwick and Gullane. This service appears to have been the first named train in Britain to feature its name on a locomotive headboard – "The Lothian Coast Express". The Gullane branch was an early victim of the inter-war economic depression, with the closure of its passenger service on 12th September 1932. With the subsequent closure of the goods traffic in 1965, the Gullane branch ceased to feature on the railway map.

The Haddington branch was opened in 1846 and although the town became popular as a dormitory town for Edinburgh, the passenger service was withdrawn in 1949, whilst the goods service remained until 1968. After closure the railway was considered by the Scottish Railway Preservation Society for re-opening as a preserved railway. However, these plans came to nothing, although the trackbed was purchased by Lothian Regional Council. This was to allow the railway to be used by a projected light railway system to improve the public transport in the Edinburgh area. Currently these plans have not come to fruition and are unlikely to do so in the current economic climate.

*Mileages*

| | |
|---|---|
| GULLANE | 0.00 miles |
| ABERLADY | 2.75 miles |
| LONGNIDDRY | 5.25 miles |
| LONGNIDDRY | 0.00 miles |
| HADDINGTON | 4.75 miles |

*Ordnance Survey 1:50,000 map number:– 60*

*Public Transport*

Gullane is served by buses from Edinburgh to North Berwick, which pass near to Longniddry Station, which is served by local trains from Edinburgh to North Berwick and Dunbar. These operate on weekdays and on Sundays in summer. Haddington has a frequent bus service to Edinburgh.

## II/3a:   Gullane to Longniddry

Like many places once served by a railway, the site of **Gullane Station** is derelict and forlorn. The buildings have been demolished, leaving only a weedgrown platform standing above a sea of dereliction. Only a parked bus indicates any sign of activity amidst the general picture of decay. Leaving the station behind, conditions are poor initially, although a way can be picked through the undergrowth which is claiming the trackbed. Passing Saltcoats Farm, conditions improve as the trackbed is used as access to hides by the local bird shoots.

Nearing a small coppice the trackbed is littered with a plethora of spent cartridges. Emerging out of the wood, the trackbed crosses fields until it reaches a stone bridge carrying a minor road leading to West Fenton over the railway.

## GULLANE & HADDINGTON

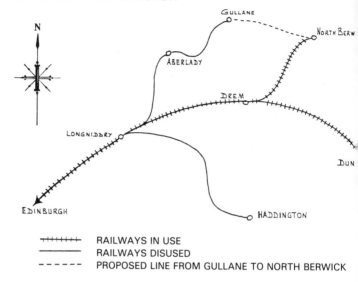

```
┼┼┼┼┼┼   RAILWAYS IN USE
─────    RAILWAYS DISUSED
- - - -  PROPOSED LINE FROM GULLANE TO NORTH BERWICK
```

Beyond this point the trackbed has been ploughed into the adjacent fields. This process has removed all traces of the railway until **Aberlady Station** is reached, apart from at the overbridge for the minor road to Luffness Mains and a short length of trackbed in the nearby woods. Again the platform buildings have been removed, leaving only the curving platform edge to follow the curve of the railway. Nearby is a whitewashed building, possibly part of the goods facilities. Continuing on, the trackbed disappears, emerging as a farm access road leading to Ballencrieff Mains farm.

Passing the farm the trackbed displays its final glory as it curves westwards on a gently rising embankment to reach **Aberlady Junction** where the branch joins the North British main line to Edinburgh. The junction is crossed by a footbridge that does not quite look right. Whilst the bridge is old, being built in Glasgow, it rests on modern masonry piers. It is not clear whether this is the original bridge raised in height, or a bridge built in this location having been reclaimed from another location.

## II/3b:  Longniddry to Haddington

Unlike the Gullane branch, the Haddington branch has received a more protected future since closure. Originally the line was considered by the

*Aberlady Station. View back to Gullane.*

SRPS as part of their plans for opening a preserved railway in Scotland. Although this idea fell through, the trackbed was spared by the Lothian Regional Council. As part of a scheme for improving public transport in the Edinburgh locality, the trackbed was retained for possible reopening as a light railway (on the lines of the Tyne & Wear Metro). Consequently the trackbed has remained relatively clear of obstructions and only two small bridges have been removed. Recently plans to strengthen the overbridge which takes the present (1930s) route of the A1 over the railway near Haddington, have caused questions to be asked about the retention of the trackbed.

Clearly the easiest way of strengthening the bridge would be to remove it by infilling the trackbed, but this would cause problems for the possible reopening of the line. At present the debate continues but it is unlikely to favour retention of the trackbed in the current economic climate. Since the combination of the Gullane & Haddington branches make for a good day's walk, it is assumed that the branch will be approached from the east, by means of the B1377 from Aberlady Junction.

The Haddington branch can then be gained by following the lane down to Setonhill Farm which having crossed the East Coast Main Line passes underneath the Haddington Branch. Although the bridge was removed, a replacement bridge was provided in 1987. It is a fairly easy climb up to either embankment. From this bridge, it is a short walk back towards Longniddry station, the trackbed being fenced off from the adjacent ECML for safety reasons. **Longniddry Station** although slightly modernised with resurfaced platforms, retained much of its period charm until 1986, when all surviving buildings were demolished, after being one of the few Edinburgh suburban stations to have survived the mass slaughter of the 1950s and 60s. Turning round for the walk to Haddington, a hare may rush past on the ECML before the trackbed curves away to the south east on a gently rising gradient.

On a clear day there are good views down the rich farmland leading onto the wide Firth of Forth and the hills of the Kingdom of Fife in the distance. After passing underneath a bridge carrying a lane from Setonhill over the track, the gradient slowly eases off. This bridge being built to double track width like many similar branches, although the line only occupied a single track. The overbridge across the minor road past Coates Farm has been dismantled. Whilst it is easy to descend the embankment down to the lane, the trackbed can only be regained on the east side of the southern abutment. The other side being separated from the adjacent fields by an impenetrable beech hedge.

Beyond this obstruction, the line gradually levels out as it heads due south east, reaching a summit level in a cutting after it passes underneath a minor road from the A1 to Huntington. Gradually the calm and tranquillity is replaced by the background grinding rumble of traffic passing along the A1. Over the summit the line curves to head downhill eastwards to Haddington. Halfway along it is crossed over by the A1 by means of the concrete skew bridge, dating to the construction of the A1 Haddington by-pass. Amazingly this bridge has also been built to a double track width, surely an over optimistic degree of planning about the future prospects of the branch.

On the other side of the A1, the trackbed passes into Haddington, although before the station is reached the trackbed is occupied by large buildings housing a local grain haulier and haulage contractors. At **Haddington Station**, the station building and platform remain in a very good state of preservation. Whilst the buildings may have lost a canopy, the platform has been re-faced and edged, the remainder being covered by a surface of red stone chippings. A newly built brickbuilt buffer stop being used to mark the end of the platform. It is a very unusual sight, there being very little indication why such renovation work has been carried out. Perhaps the railway may be re-opened, or has some person plans to re-use the station area as a museum or a recreation facility?

# III:
# WALKS IN FIFE REGION

## Railways of the Wemyss Coalfield

Coal has been mined on the Wemyss Estate for centuries without a break. David, the 2nd Earl was granted a charter by Charles II to build a harbour at Methil for the shipment of coal, most of which was destined for overseas. In 1854, the railway arrived, with the opening of the Leven Railway from Thornton Junction to Leven. In 1865 plans were drawn up for a branch from Cameron Bridge to the Muiredge Pit, near Buckhaven. This branch became part of the North British Railway empire in 1877, when the Leven & East Fife Railway, as it then was, was absorbed by the NBR. Two years later, the Earl of Wemyss built a railway from Buckhaven to Thornton Junction, through his estates. This was extended to the harbour at Methil in 1887.

During this period the estate's mineral rights were worked by the local firm of Bowman and Company, together with the larger Fife Coal Company, which had interests in other mines in the county. The improvements in the docks at Methil saw Bowman & Company develop the Rosie Colliery as well as the sinking of a new shaft at the docks, which became known as the Denbeath Mine. The Fife Coal Company started a new mine at Wellsgreen and constructed a private branch line from this mine to Wemyss Castle Station, where the traffic was forwarded to Methil docks. In 1889, the NBR bought the line from Thornton to Methil along with the docks at Methil and Leven. One clause being that the NBR maintain at Wemyss Castle station, a private waiting room for the use of the Wemyss family.

The Earl was soon busy with plans for more railways on the estate. In 1898, plans were drawn up for the building of the Wemyss Estate Private Railway and were submitted to the NBR for their approval. Arrangements were made concerning the handling of traffic, brought via the WPR to the dock sidings and the two bridges which would allow the railway to cross the Methil Branch. Having lost most of its former importance, the NBR gave permission for the lifting of the Muiredge Branch at the point where it was to be crossed by the Private Railway.

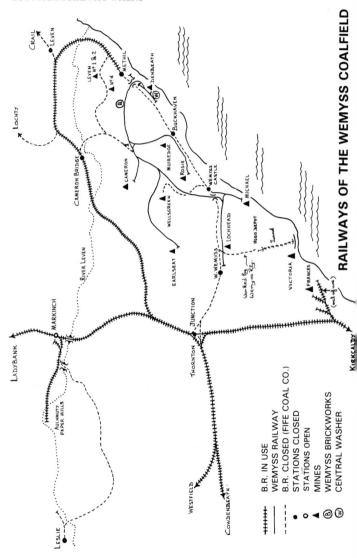

**RAILWAYS OF THE WEMYSS COALFIELD**

CRAIL
LEVEN
LOCHTY
LEVEN No 1 & 2
No 4
METHIL
DENBEATH
BUCKHAVEN
CAMERON
CAMERON BRIDGE
MUIREDGE
ROSIE
WELLSGREEN
WEMYSS CASTLE
MICHAEL
River Leven
EARLSEAT
W. WEMYSS
LOCHHEAD
HUGO DEPOT
Tunnel
Worked by Wemyss Rly.
VICTORIA
FRANCES
(not in use)
MARKINCH
LADYBANK
THORNTON JUNCTION
KIRKCALDY
AUCHMUTY PAPER MILLS
WESTFIELD
COWDENBEATH
LESLIE

B.R. IN USE
WEMYSS RAILWAY
B.R. CLOSED (FIFE COAL CO.)
STATIONS CLOSED
STATIONS OPEN
MINES
Ⓑ WEMYSS BRICKWORKS
Ⓦ CENTRAL WASHER

38

Having secured the NBR's co-operation, the Earl entered into a lease with the Wemyss Coal Company for the latter to construct and operate the railway.

The main reason behind the construction of the railway, was the need for an independent route to the docks, from the modernised colliery at Lochhead and the other mines of Earlseat and Michael (East Wemyss). Earlseat was the most northerly of the mines, and a passenger service was run to allow workmen to reach this colliery. When the Wemyss Collieries were nationalised, the railway remained an independent concern.

Gradually the system was reduced, owing to the closure of the mines, by 1967 the only production was at Lochhead and Michael Collieries. These ceased production by 1970 and the railway was closed, apart from traffic from Methil to the washery at Denbeath. This traffic consisted of coal from the modern Seafield Colliery to the west of Kirkcaldy, the Wemyss Railway usually provided one engine per week to haul this traffic from Methil West Yard to the washery. This traffic survived for a few years, but it too stopped and the railway was finally closed, its services no longer required. The earlier line, from Buckhaven to Thornton, built by the 2nd Earl lost its passenger services on 10th January 1955. The goods traffic continued to Methil until December 2nd 1963, when it was routed via Cameron Bridge and Leven.

*Mileages*

| | | |
|---|---|---|
| METHIL | | 0.00 miles |
| BUCKHAVEN | | 1.25 miles |
| WEMYSS CASTLE | | 2.50 miles |
| WEST WEMYSS | | 4.25 miles |
| THORNTON | Junction | 5.25 miles |

*Ordnance Survey 1:50,000 map number:– 59*

*Public Transport*
Leven is served by a frequent bus service from Kirkcaldy, which is well served by trains from Edinburgh and Dundee. The bus service from Kirkcaldy to Leven passes through the villages of East Wemyss, Coaltown of Wemyss, and West Wemyss. It follows most of the route of the earlier Wemyss Electric Tramway route.

## III/1a:   Cameron Bridge to Thornton Junction

The L-shape of the ex-NBR line, from Cameron Bridge to Thornton Junction, via Buckhaven, forms an interesting walk of about six to seven miles. **Cameron Bridge** station, can be reached by following the A915, from Windygates. Before reaching the bridge over the railway and the River Leven, a path through the grounds of the nearby distillery allows the walker to inspect the station site. The distillery is still rail connected and a fleet of private owner grain wagons are still used, probably for

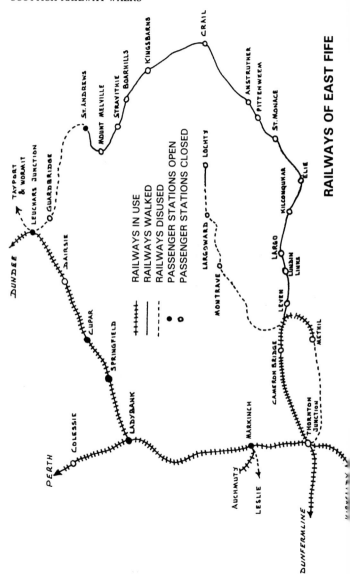

RAILWAYS OF EAST FIFE

RAILWAYS IN USE
RAILWAYS WALKED
RAILWAYS DISUSED
PASSENGER STATIONS OPEN
PASSENGER STATIONS CLOSED

CRAIL
KINGSBARNS
BOARHILLS
STRAVITHIE
MOUNT MELVILLE
ST. ANDREWS
GUARDBRIDGE
LEUCHARS JUNCTION
TAYPORT & WORMIT
DUNDEE
DAIRSIE
CUPAR
SPRINGFIELD
LADYBANK
COLESSIE
PERTH
ANSTRUTHER
PITTENWEEM
ST. MONACE
ELIE
KILCONQUHAR
LARGO
LUNDIN LINKS
LEVEN
LARGOWARD
LOCHTY
MONTRAVE
CAMERON BRIDGE
METHIL
THORNTON JUNCTION
MARKINCH
AUCHMUTY
LESLIE
DUNFERMLINE
KIRKCALDY

works internal traffic only. The island platform is devoid of buildings, but the covering cloak of grass is well trimmed, to provide an attractive reminder of the passenger service.

The NBR branch to Muiredge Colliery can be gained, by returning to the main road, and following a clear path on the east side of the bridge, once the River Leven has been crossed. This branch may have been double track at one time; sadly the only surviving section is currently under threat from the proposed Windygates By-Pass. If built, the road would use this line and part of the Lochty Railway in a route from Cameron Farm to Duniface Farm.

The trackbed remains intact for about a quarter of a mile, until landscaping has removed many traces of it as it passes through a large school. A path through the grounds gives access to where the branch crosses the main line of the Wemyss Private Railway. Although the NW curve, onto the WPR, has largely disappeared, traces can still be found of the 2 curves from the WPR southwards onto the Muiredge branch. The WPR line, from Methil to this junction, and the continuation of the branch, have both been converted into official footpaths and covered with a reddish gravel (known as blaze). An industrial estate has been built on the site of **Muiredge Colliery** forcing a detour through the nearby housing estate to reach the next major road to be crossed, the A955 from Methil to East Wemyss. Where this road was crossed by the Muiredge Branch, traces may still be discerned of the original level crossing.

After a short walk along this road towards East Wemyss, a lane, signposted as a public footpath to East Wemyss, heads south to gain the trackbed of the NB line from **Buckhaven Station** . Although the station site has been obliterated by another industrial estate, the trackbed towards East Wemyss is well used by local walkers. In fact the trackbed is actually a double trackbed, the southerly one being the NBR line, the northern one being a branch of the WPR which served Rosie Colliery. Initially the two trackbeds run parallel, but the WPR then starts to twist and turn, whilst gaining height, before turning northwards to gain the landscaped site of the Rosie Mine. Maybe the nearby landslip of the NBR is caused by the underground workings of the mine. However it is only a partial fall, resulting in the slip of the seawards half of the trackbed, down towards a watery encounter.

Beyond this point the NBR line heads away inland to cross the nearby A955. The original crossing (underbridge?) has suffered from random dumping as well as road improvements. Across the road, the line heads round the back of the Main Street, to reach the site of **Wemyss Castle Station**. Before the station is reached, the embankment which brought the main line of the WPR to this location approaches the NBR line from the north. Between the two lines, traces can be found of the line of the Fife Coal Company branch from Wellsgreen Colliery, which has run parallel to the WPR line through the nearby Wemyss Den. As the walker reaches the station, the initial thought is that the station buildings have been removed.

However, by walking round the large modern building, the stone built building which was the original passenger station, with the private waiting room for the Wemyss Family, can be inspected. Although many of its windows have been blocked up, it manages to convey some of its former grandeur. Beyond the station, the trackbed passes through the brick built abutments, which once formed an overbridge, which carried the WPR over the NBR line. Beyond this bridge, the trackbed passes a series of large single storey buildings, that originally were the main workshops of the Wemyss system. Since then the buildings have been used for agricultural purposes and have suffered at least one damaging fire. However, it is still possible to imagine the former bustle of the never-ending battle to maintain steam locomotives, which once took place in these now derelict buildings. Only rails and an occasional nut or bolt remain from the former railway occupants.

Once past the workshop's site, the two lines ran parallel towards Lochhead Colliery. Beyond the mine, a branch from the NBR line, headed across the WPR to reach **Hugo Depot**. Whilst the junction and initial section of this branch has disappeared, the continuation towards Coaltown of Wemyss can be walked. This line passes over an access lane to Lochhead Farm, before reaching the nearby village. At the back of the houses, the former reserved track of the Wemyss Electric Tramway is crossed, before one emerges once again onto the A955. The gates of the railway crossing still survive, in part, whilst several brick built buildings mark the site of the former depot. Nearby can be found the bricked up entrance of a tunnel, which heads down towards the Victoria Colliery, near East Wemyss, on the banks of the Firth of Forth. The other end of the tunnel is also bricked up, although a couple of air spaces allow a torch light to pick out the low roof of its interior.

Returning to the main line, the trackbed becomes very overgrown as it turns to head underneath the A915, to reach the derelict remains of **West Wemyss Station**. The remains of a house watches over a platform, which gradually gains height above the trackbed, to end in what may have been a loading platform. West Wemyss station lies at the edge of Moss Wood, and the trackbed is used as a forest access road from the station, to a minor road to Mackie's Mill. Across this road, the line crossed over the River Ore before reaching the complicated network of lines that once formed **Thornton Junction**. Sadly only the stone built piers of the bridge remain, although a large black pipeline crosses the river, producing ominous rumbling sounds to dissuade any attempts at pipe walking! Beyond the bridge, the line of the railway has been landscaped to form part of a golf course, which is another good reason for terminating further exploration of the railway. The access road may be used to reach the A92, from Kirkcaldy to Glenrothes, where there is a good bus service between the two towns.

# III/1b: Methil to Lochhead Colliery

The starting point for the exploration of the lines of the Wemyss Private Railway, and the Fife Coal Company is the ex-NBR station of **Methil**. Situated in the midst of a haulage yard, the single storeyed buildings miraculously survive, albeit having been converted into office accommodation. From this location it is a short walk to the still operating site of the Wemyss Brickworks, between Sea Road and Cowley Street. The trackbed can still be traced through the brickworks, but access is restricted, and the trackbed should be gained, off Stark Street, to the west of the brickworks.

Passing through playing fields, the trackbed crosses the A955 and heads for the junction with the ex-NBR branch to Muiredge Colliery. Beyond this crossing, the trackbed becomes a narrow field path before it reaches the level crossing with the B930. A couple of the large gate posts, which once supported the crossing gates, still mark the site of this level crossing. Beyond this point, a branch headed northwards to serve Cameron Colliery. The trackbed can still be traced by a series of field boundary fences, as it heads towards the former mine site, still marked by a couple of low industrial buildings. Continuing along the main line, the trackbed forms a well-used path, albeit in parts passing through reclaimed fields, with more gate posts marking another level crossing with a minor road to Wellsgreen Farm. The next junction, where the Earlseat branch left the main line, is difficult to detect, owing to a rubbish dump being located on the first part of the branch.

The dump can be detoured, by picking up the line of the Fife Coal Co. as it runs parallel to the Wemyss Line, to reach the **Wellsgreen Mine**. Nearing the derelict spoil heaps of this mine, the Wemyss Line can be regained to reach the level crossing with A915. The small brick built shell of the crossing box still remains, its window bricked up and roof long since removed. Over the road, the trackbed passes through reclaimed fields before emerging at the side of an attractive mixed woodland, full of large mature beech trees. Although the trackbed is very overgrown, the mature woodland provides a pleasant detour, as the walker gradually nears the site of **Earlseat Colliery**.

Having passed the first reclaimed mine area, the trackbed veers northwards to pass by the empty shells of the cottages which once provided limited accommodation for the miners, before it reaches the site of the main colliery workings. This desolate location, where notices warn of the still smoking spoil heaps, can still reveal railway relics to the walker. Near to the site of the crossing with the road to the cottages, there survive a few sections of narrow gauge track, heading into the nearby woods. (At this point the walker may go across country to gain the nearby NBR line from Thornton to Buckhaven. However, one has to return to the junction of the Earlseat branch and the main line, at the edge of the Wemyss Den, to return to the WPR.) Walking through the Den, there is a choice of the well-used trackbed of the WPR or the more overgrown line of the FCC. These two lines crossed on the level in the middle of the Den, from which both trackbeds are well used as they head towards the site of **Wemyss Castle** station.

The Wemyss line, forms the northern boundary of the station site, gradually climbing to cross the NBR to the west of the station. This bridge has been dismantled, although the solid brickbuilt abutments remain in situ. Beyond was originally a triangular junction, now part of a haulage contractor's yard, where a branch headed south to serve the **Michael Mine**. Although the mine has long since closed, its buildings and pithead gear still remain. The short branch has been reclaimed, although traces still survive of the level crossing over the A955. However, with the opportunity to view the derelict buildings, this branch makes for a most interesting detour from the steady walk along the main line.

Beyond the junction, the line pases the WPR workshops before passing through a wasteland which once formed Scotts Road Sidings. These sidings were once very important in the operation of the railway. The trackbed continues as a well used path to reach its westernmost extent, the now reclaimed site of the **Lochhead Colliery**, which is the end of the exploration of the lines of the Wemyss Private Railway.

# Railways of the East Neuk

St. Andrews, the home of golf, was first connected to the railway network with the opening of the line from Leuchars Junction by the St. Andrews Railway Company on 1st July 1852. The line was built by Thomas Bouch, who achieved notoriety with his Tay Bridge work, at a cost of £5,625 per mile. The station in St. Andrews became known as the Links Station, near to the present day Old Course Hotel. Although the St. ARCo was technically an independent concern, the line was operated by the Edinburgh, Perth and Dundee Railway. Two years later, on 3rd July 1854, the Leven Railway was opened from Thornton Junction to Leven. Again this line, which formed the first link in a chain destined to reach St. Andrews, was operated by the EP&DR.

On 8th July 1857, the line from Leven was extended to Kilconquhar, with the opening of the East Fife Railway. The East Fife and Leven Railways were amalgamated on 22nd July 1862 and the new company extended the line to Anstruther, opened on 1st September 1863. Meanwhile the EP&DR, which operated all of these "independent" lines, had been taken over by the North British Railway, on 29th July 1862. The St. ARCo and the L&EFR were both absorbed into the NBR on 17th December 1877. So the scene was set for the authorisation of the missing link from Anstruther to St. Andrews, which took place on 26th August 1880. The section from Anstruther to Boarhills was opened on 1st June 1887. The line was opened by the Anstruther and St. Andrews Railway at a cost of £9,000 per mile, which included the construction of a new station in St. Andrews and two major viaducts. The first viaduct was over the Kenly Burn at Boarhills, the second viaduct crossed the Kiness Burn at St. Andrews. Considering the average cost of new railway construction at the time was £35,000 per mile, the A&St.AR was constructed remarkably inexpensively with few major engineering features.

Although the coast route was complete, the new railway provided the filling in a somewhat indigestible sandwich. The new company was full of ideas, whilst the NBR suffered from an over provision of red tape. When the A&St.AR asked the NBR to extend the prestigious 5.30 pm Edinburgh Express from Anstruther to Crail, the NBR refused due to the lack of facilities to allow the engine to run round the train at Crail. A public fund was started in Crail to finance the construction of such a run-round loop, at an estimated cost of £1,100. In spite of an offer by the A&St.AR secretary to reduce his salary to help its financing, there was insufficient money available in Crail and the scheme lapsed. The A&St.AR surrendered its independence in 1897, when it was taken over by the NBR.

With the traumas of the openings overcome, the Fife Coast line settled down to a quiet operating period. There was a major fire at the new station in St. Andrews on 4th July 1901, which virtually destroyed the main buildings. Only the entrance, staircase and a bookstall were saved. The NBR became part of the LNER in 1923, seven years later the LNER withdrew the passenger services from the intermediate stations between Crail and St. Andrews, on the 22nd September 1930. The stations involved being Kingsbarns, Boarhills, Stravithie and Mount Melville, of which only Boarhills served any community, albeit small.

The LNER provided a limited service on the coast line, the majority of the services terminated at Crail. There were only three through workings a day between Crail and St. Andrews, usually operated as part of a through Edinburgh to Dundee stopping service. The prestige train was the Fife Coast Express, which ran as two trains from Edinburgh and Glasgow, both of which terminated at Crail. Pre-war summers brought a considerable amount of holiday traffic to the coast line. The stations were often piled up with holidaymakers' luggage. After the war the fortunes of the line entered a steady decline.

The freight service from St. Andrews to Crail was withdrawn on 5th October 1964. One year later the passenger service from Leven to St. Andrews was withdrawn, on the 6th September. The goods service from Crail to Leven lingered on for a while, it being withdrawn during 1966.

St. Andrews retained its rail connection with the outside world, via Leuchars Junction for a few more years. On 6th January 1969, this service was withdrawn, largely on account of the "poor state" of the viaduct at Guardbridge. When the time came to lift the branch, it was decided first of all to remove the junction at Leuchars. The locomotive and wagons being stabled on the St. Andrews side of the junction. Once the foul deed had been performed, the BR engineers were asked how they intended to move the train. A few red faces were visible, when it was learned that the planned route via Crail was no longer possible, due to the track having been removed a couple of years previously.

Finally, on 6th October 1969, the vestigial passenger service from Leven to Thornton Junction was withdrawn. Although Leven Station was closed, the line from Thornton Junction to Methil remains in use by a freight service to the distillery at Cameron Bridge and the docks and power station at Methil.

Coming off the Leven to Thornton line, at East Fife Central Junction near Cameron Bridge, was the Lochty Branch. The construction of the line by the East Fife Central Railway was authorised on 24th August 1893, and opened on 21st August 1898. The line ran parallel to the coast line, passing through the agricultural hinterland. Although it was intended to provide a passenger service and extend the line to Stravithie Station, neither took place and the line remained a goods-only line, operating unobstrusively until its closure on 1st August 1964. A short stretch at the eastern end was retained as the privately owned Lochty Railway, which became the unusual home for the ex-LNER A4 pacific number 60009, *Union of South Africa*.

*Mileages*

| | |
|---|---|
| LEVEN | 0.00 miles |
| LUNDIN LINKS | 2.00 miles |
| LARGO | 3.00 miles |
| KILCONQUHAR | 6.75 miles |
| ELIE | 8.25 miles |
| ST. MONANCE | 10.50 miles |
| PITTENWEEM | 12.00 miles |
| ANSTRUTHER | 13.00 miles |
| CRAIL | 17.25 miles |
| KINGSBARNS | 20.75 miles |
| BOARHILLS | 22.25 miles |
| STRAVITHIE | 24.50 miles |
| MOUNT MELVILLE | 27.00 miles |
| ST. ANDREWS | 28.25 miles |
| GUARDBRIDGE | 32.00 miles |
| LEUCHARS JUNCTION | 33.25 miles |
| | |
| LEVEN | 0.00 miles |
| EAST FIFE CENTRAL JUNCTION | 1.50 miles |
| KENNOWAY | 3.00 miles |
| MONTRAVE | 7.75 miles |
| LARGOWARD | 11.50 miles |
| LOCHTY | 16.00 miles |

*Ordnance Survey 1:50,000 map number:–* 59

*Public Transport*
Leven is served by frequent buses to Kirkcaldy, as well as an hourly service along the coast road to St. Andrews, which passes by many of the stations on the Coast Line. St. Andrews is also served by buses to Dundee and Leuchars, some of which connect with trains at Leuchars Junction. Cameron Bridge is served by buses to Markinch and Kirkcaldy. There is a limited service from Leven to St. Andrews which passes through Largoward on the Lochty Branch. Lochty is only served by a post bus from Crail, the nearest bus stops being the Peat Inn and the main road from Dunino. The frequency of these services is reduced on weekends.

## III/2a:  Leven to St. Andrews

The starting point of this walk, Leven, is well served by public transport. Fife Regional Council are considering a proposal to restore the passenger service from Thornton Junction, using the freight only line via Cameron Bridge. The bus disembarks its passengers at the new bus station in the lower reaches of the town. From here it is a deft meander through the shopping centre, pausing perhaps for an early cup of coffee or tea in a café, followed by the negotiation of a council housing estate. The walker eventually passes the forlorn, abandoned old bus station, to reach the safety of Station Road. Like an apparition out of the past, the pace of the walker increases, hurrying as passengers used to do to reach the station before the train departed. Sadly the haste comes to nothing as the station site is reached, revealing the grassy covered landscaped site. Only a white painted paling fence remains to mark the boundary of the railway land, now used to provide housing for the citizens of Leven. How much longer will the Station Inn and Station Road remain, with their melancholic names, acting as a guide to those in search of the abandoned courses of disused urban railways?

Heading east, the walker can make a reasonable approximation to the route of the railway, as a way is navigated past the housing development. Eventually the housing is left behind as a new use is found for the trackbed, which now forms part of a golf course. The remaining miles to Largo, passing the intermediate station of Lundin Links, see the trackbed pass through several golf courses.

As the end of one course marks the start of the next one, there are few obstacles (or bunkers) to trap the walker. Occasionally the trackbed is occupied by a tee but generally the trackbed is used as a means of access around the courses. In places the trackbed has been partially landscaped to improve the access gained from the trackbed. Nearing the site of **Lundin Links Station**, a small bridge over an abandoned lane has been removed. However it presents no great obstruction to the walker. Very little remains of the station, the site of which has been converted into a car park. The trackbed has been landscaped to blend in with the surrounding countryside, in case the cars worry at the site of a nasty railway.

Nearing Largo, the trackbed reappears as a sandy embankment, which can be followed to where it crossed the main road through the town. Across the road, the trackbed occupies a ledge between houses as it heads towards the three-arched viaduct over the Boghall Burn. This section is very overgrown, a dense growth of nettles, rose bay willow herb and saplings, all of which are intertwined by the voracious growth of brambles. The foolhardy, armour plated explorer having negotiated this obstacle in the hope of reaching the viaduct, finds the way is blocked by the high fence of a house which is built on the final section of the trackbed leading onto the viaduct. Consequently a detour through the town is required, pausing perhaps at the Railway Inn to admire the impressive viaduct and the statue of Alexander Selkirk, who inspired Defoe's tale of Robinson Crusoe.

By following the easternmost road out of Largo towards the A921, the trackbed can be regained by the car park which occupies the site of **Largo Station**. The conversion has removed many traces of the railway, only a stone built wall of a loading dock remains along with a carved stone depicting the station name supported by the British Railways "Lion and Wheel" emblem. Initially the trackbed out of Largo has been adopted as part of the Fife Coastal Footpath, signposted to Elie five miles distant. After the previous worries about being attacked by low flying golf balls, the trackbed from Largo to Kilconquhar comes as a welcome break. Although in places the original ballast remains in situ, it is fairly well rounded so as not to be too hard on the walker's feet.

The railway navigates a close approximation to the straight line towards Kilconquhar, passing through open duneland grazed by an assortment of sheep and cattle. On a clear day, there are good views to the south across the Firth of Forth to Edinburgh, with her backdrop of hills. Nearing the site of **Kilconquhar Station** the trackbed curves away from the previous course to avoid too close a contact with the village and nearby main road.

After a long period of quiet amidst the sand dunes, the sudden intrusion of the noise of traffic acts as a warning of the imminent arrival in civilisation. Of the station, only the single lengthy curving brick built platform, along with the grass covered area of the former goods facilities, exist to record its site. However, they form the most tangible station relics encountered so far on the walk. Beyond the station, the trackbed has been reclaimed for agricultural purposes. Although the bridge which carries the minor road to Earlsferry over the railway at St. Ford is still in situ, the trackbed only recovers its original form in the nearby forest.

The walker is effectively forced to walk along the nearby A917 to reach the site of **Elie Station**. Again the station site has been converted into a housing estate. A large brick built building occupies the position of the former station buildings. Only a weather worn palisade fence attached to a large timber gatepost remains as an unwanted relic of the station. Once past the housing estate, the trackbed is initially reclaimed for agricultural purposes, before it recovers its abandoned form heading towards St. Monans. This section of intact trackbed ends abruptly at the masonry bridge over the St. Monans Burn. One side is the railway, on the other, agricultural reclamation again regains its grasp of the trackbed. Very little can be seen of the site of **St. Monance Station**, now a large field making for a long haul towards Anstruther. Perhaps the walker may prefer to abandon the walk at Elie and make use of the regular coastal bus service, to reach Anstruther in the hope of regaining the trackbed.

**Anstruther Station** has largely disappeared, having been converted into a wasteland that purports to be a car park. Beyond the station the trackbed has been partially converted into a road, running between a Victorian school building and the local graveyard. This strange combination makes for an interesting interpretation of the saying "from the cradle to the grave". Having passed the school, the new road heads back towards Anstruther, whilst the trackbed resumes its course on towards Crail. The walker continues in the hope that all the nasty reclamation has been left behind, but the hope is short lived. It is possible to follow the railway to reach the overbridge which carries the minor road to Rennyhill over the railway. Here the landscape destroyers have again been at work, removing almost all traces of the route of the railway. Perhaps the relative lightweight construction of the line, following the undulations of the land with relatively minor earthworks, has allowed it to become an easy target for reclamation, in these fertile areas of the former Kingdom. Only the sighting of the occasional bridge guides one towards Crail, in the search for the vestigial remains of the railway that the land reclaimers could not reach.

Crail is an attractive fishing village, with several hotels and guest houses offering reasonably priced accommodation, for the walker seeking shelter for the night before resuming the walk on towards St. Andrews. It is also served by regular bus services to Leven and St. Andrews. Even if the walk is to end here, it is worth walking down from the railway to view the attractive harbour and its colourful array of buildings with their warm reddish-orange pantiled roofs.

**Crail Station** lies adjacent to the A918 on the northern outskirts of the village. The station buildings remain intact, albeit slightly modified, to form the basis of a garden centre. Unless the centre is open, the presence of a high security fence prevents a closer examination being made of the site. Leaving the station, the trackbed is affected by road realignments for a short while, until it emerges underneath the bridge which carries the B940 over the former alignment. The walker is rewarded with fine view across the Firth of Tay towards Arbroath and Carnoustie, whilst the trackbed turns northwards towards St. Andrews. It comes as a welcome relief to walk once again on an unadulterated trackbed. It is used mainly as a series of farm access roads for the next

*Crail*

few miles. The remains of a brick built lineside bothy are passed, whilst the feet make occasional contact with a concrete sleeper, left over from the demolition of the railway.

The walker passes the remarkably intact shell of a wooden lineside bothy, a typical construction of the NBR with its corrugated iron roof rusting slowly beneath the blue sky. Nearing the ruins of Crookston Farm, the railway crossed a small burn. Although the original girder bridge has been removed, a metal sleeper spans the gap between the masonry abutments, providing a short plank walk for the morning's amusement. The trackbed falls and rises with the undulations of the surrounding countryside as one arrives at the deserted grass covered site of **Kingsbarns Station**. Although this station was one of the first closures on the line, it stayed in use as a passing place until the closure of the line. Now the site is being overtaken by nature as a variety of flowers, bushes and grasses reclaim the trackbed and cover the brick built platform.

Leaving the dereliction of Kingsbarns behind, the next point of interest is the abandoned site of the former military base at Kilduncan. The standard design concrete barrack blocks watch over a small pond, where ducks glide about in stately fashion, only to go "bottoms-up" in search of a tasteful morsel in this peaceful haven. Where the access road to the camp crossed the railway, a faded notice still reminds the ghost of the long gone serviceman to "Stop, Look and Listen before crossing the line". The trackside fencing supports an abundant growth of brambles, providing a bountiful source of refreshment for the autumnal walker. Far away from modern roads and housing, there is very little human competition for this natural gift.

Nearing Boarhills one emerges from an overgrown section onto new ballast lying on top of a concrete underbridge. The brick abutments indicate this bridge may have been rebuilt at some stage. It is advisable to seek an exit at this point. Although it is possible to continue on towards the Boarhills Viaduct, it is fenced off and the exit down the embankment is dangerously steep and slippery. Boarhills Viaduct, crossing the Kenly Burn was reported to be unsafe when the line was closed. Although it is still standing, it is in a very poor state of repair. The lane from the earlier concrete underbridge allows one to make a detour via Boarhills Village to view the viaduct, or to head via Lower Kenly to regain the trackbed, beyond the site of **Boarhills Station**. Whilst the station platforms remain, the original buildings have been demolished and an attractive modern house built on the site. The platforms and intervening trackbed have been converted into a garden with well kept lawns.

Although it is possible to regain the trackbed beyond the station, following its exact course through the reclaimed fields is very difficult. It is only when the remains of the abutments of the bridge, which carried the railway over the minor road to Bonnytown, are spotted that one can navigate onto the correct course. Even past this relic, the trackbed is still

51

landscaped, although traceable through the fields when they are in stubble. Only when the route passes alongside a small wood to the north of Bonnytown does the trackbed reappear. Amidst the cast-off cartridges of the local marksmen, grow a profusion of brambles. It makes for a pleasurable location for a lunch time stop, far away from the bustle of modern traffic. The sound of birdsong in the nearby woods adds a musical aperitif to the tranquil scene. Beyond the woods the trackbed disappears again, but its course can be easily followed as the walker reaches the site of **Stravithie Station**. Shortly before the station, the trackbed re-emerges as a double track formation. This construction being part of the planned extension of the Lochty Branch, which was never completed. The station site is occupied by a couple of new houses, although part of the original platform remains. A lane which skirts the northern edge of the trackbed can be used as a means of detouring past these houses.

Across the A959, the route becomes a dark cutting which is now occupied by a dense variety of saplings. At the far end, the cutting has been filled in by its use as a rubbish dump. The walker should follow a lane past the buildings of Prior Muir, to cross the railway above the rubbish dump. Although the trackbed has been landscaped, leaving only the bridge under the minor road to Allanhill as a guide to its route, a green lane which leads to the access lane to Cangour Farm provides a reasonable detour. This lane, overgrown in places, is edged by mature deciduous trees, forming a colourful tunnel to guide the walker. When the detour returns to the trackbed, it is only to view another vista of landscaped fields. The crossing keeper's cottage, adjacent to the lane leading to North Lambieletham, gives an indication of the route of the railway. This isolated cottage can be reached via Scooniehill or across the fields when they are in stubble. Whilst the cottage has been modernised, the rails remain in situ across the lane as a reward for the walker's patience in reaching this location.

Once over the crossing the trackbed becomes a green lane used by local equestrians, following a tributary of the Kiness Burn by a series of small radii twists and turns. In a wider section of the trackbed, which may have been a quarry, stands a small wooden stable. Nearing the A915, this rural calm comes to an end, as road improvements have removed all traces of the railway including the site of **Mount Melville Station**. The bridge which carried the road to Lumbo over the railway is the only surviving artefact to mark where the railway turns towards St. Andrews. Its course is difficult to follow and the walker is advised to use the main road as a means of reaching the destination of the walk in St. Andrews.

Once in the most learned of Scottish cities, the final surviving section of the Fife Coast railway can be followed, signposted as the "Viaduct Walk". This walk crosses the other major viaduct of the former Anstruther and St. Andrews Railway, that over the Kiness Burn.

Beyond this viaduct, with its secure safety rails, the trackbed has been converted into a series of car parks, built on top of the filled-in cuttings of the railway. Only at the derelict site of **St. Andrews Station**, does the walker discover the true depth of the railway, as the walk drops down onto the empty void of the station's former island platform. The buildings have all been demolished, leaving only the scars of their foundations on the platforms. The trackbed has been filled in to the original platform height and the resultant flat land forms yet another car park. No longer are the original entrances flanked by their award winning gardens, with the station's name painted proudly on the stones. Now St. Andrews is trying to eradicate all traces of its railway. A ramp heads uphill from the dereliction of the station to allow the walker to reach the nearby bus station, where there are services to many major centres within central Scotland.

## III/2b:  Leuchars Junction to St. Andrews

**Leuchars Junction** is no longer a junction station, since the withdrawal of its final branch service to St. Andrews in 1969. However, its lengthy platforms give an indication of its former importance. The bay platform, which was used by the services to St. Andrews, has been filled in. Fortunately the attractive station buildings and footbridge have escaped major modernisation schemes. From the station, the A919 should be followed to Guardbridge. Having crossed over the Motray Water, one should turn right up a narrow lane, passing a church on the left hand side, to reach a playing field. The St. Andrews Railway ran along the edge of this field. The walker no doubt will want to walk back to view the remains of the bridge, which carried the railway over the Motray Water. The girders were removed soon after the closure of the line, leaving the circular stone pillars and some bracing, to mark its site. A nearby pipe bridge crosses the same water, albeit with notices warning that it has only to be crossed by "authorised persons".

On the far side of the water, a curving embankment climbs up to the site of **Milton (or Leuchars) Junction**. The intrepid walker, having reached this site, is rewarded by the remains of a gradient post, just before the former junction. Drivers of passing trains look on in amazement, as one carefully removes the undergrowth, to capture this relic on film. Returning to the playing field, a path runs along the former trackbed, as it passes behind the nearby houses. This can be followed, until some houses are reached, whose extended gardens stretch across the trackbed. The walker can make a detour into the nearby field, to regain the trackbed as it passes behind the car park for the nearby paper mill. This mill once had its own steam locomotive, which was housed in the still extant brick built engine shed. By the road, can be found a small weighbridge, with its tracks still remaining alongside.

The trackbed passes behind the former engine shed, passing a defunct lineside hut, before more gardens block the way forward. A further detour into the adjacent field, allows the walker to pass alongside the gardens and extensive pigeon crees, regaining the

*Remains of the viaduct over the River Eden*

trackbed at the entrance to Guardbridge Station. In one of the gardens stands a large building with several doors opening onto the trackbed. It is a strange building, looking very much like a station building, although it was not used for this purpose. **Guardbridge Station** has been extensively landscaped, leaving a large well kept lawn, to mark its site. Only the stone circular base of a crane has survived the eradication of the former railway buildings. The passenger platform was on a sharp curve, as the line turned to cross over the River Eden. The stone pillars of this bridge remain, alongside the former road bridge, which has become a pedestrian only crossing, after the constrution of the new road bridge.

Having passed a public house and several private houses, the walker can regain the trackbed as it emerges from its only overgrown section. The next part of the trackbed has been adapted to form an access route to the Eden Estuary nature reserve, allowing one to follow the route with very few problems. The official walkway ends where the lane to Coble Shore crosses the trackbed. Beyond this crossing, it is necessary to squeeze past a section used for storing straw bales, to reach a further section of walkable trackbed.

The walking is very pleasurable, passing through fertile farming country, with the rich birdlife on the mud flats of the Eden Estuary. Sadly, beyond this tranquil scene lies the sinister buildings of RAF Leuchars, from which comes the roar of modern jet aircraft, shattering the fragile tranquility of this sylvan setting. The walker soon reaches a ruined farm cottage, which somebody has begun to renovate. Beyond this building the trackbed has been landscaped, forcing the walker onto the nearby coastal footpath. This path runs along the foreshore and then turns up onto an embankment which protected the nearby low lying ground from unwanted waterings with salt water. The embankment is well used by local equestrians, although it can be very windswept at times. It guides the walker to the only surviving underbridge on the branch, which marks the recovery of the trackbed from its lengthy dose of landscaping.

The bridge carries the railway over a small burn, which drains the nearby fields. Leaving the bridge behind, the trackbed soon reaches the many golf courses, which make St. Andrews the mecca for golfing aficionados. Surprisingly the golf courses have not intruded onto the trackbed, which appears to have been kept as a means of service vehicles' access between the courses. This has resulted in it becoming a pleasant walk, forming a nature reserve alongside the well-tended greens and fairways. One will be rewarded by the sight of the remains of several gradient posts and mileposts, along the way. The only obstacles that have to be faced are occasionally miss-hit golf balls. Nearing the city, the railway reaches the Old Course, the holy of holies for the golfer.

Soon the route reaches the modern buildings of the Old Course Hotel, the last hotel built by the former railway-operated British Transport Hotels. The buildings were built on the site of the original **St. Andrews Station**, which became the goods station when the new station was opened, in conjunction with the opening of the railway from Crail. The modern hotel buildings have removed all traces of the railway, apart from the former Station Master's house, which has been adapted to form the Jiggle Inn. Perhaps the buildings have remained to provide an oasis of traditionality, amidst the modern buildings. The railway bridge over the A91, has also been removed, although the abutments remain, proudly proclaiming the builder's name and construction date. Beyond this, the trackbed reaches the desolate site of **St. Andrews (New) Station**. The buildings were unceremoniously ripped down, leaving only the scarred base of the former island platform, to form the basis of a car park.

The railway left the station via a deep cutting, although even this has been infilled, to provide a linear car park for the city. Only where the railway crosses the Kinness Burn, does the infilling cease, and the railway emerges from its heavy burden. The three arched stone viaduct is worth a detour, via the nearby Botanic Gardens, to allow it to be viewed from below, as it is very difficult for its beauty to be observed from the trackbed. This short detour brings to an end a very pleasant walk. St. Andrews is well served with catering establishments, which will replenish the walker for the return journey to Leuchars. There is a regular bus service to Leuchars Junction, which may be more attractive, if one suffers from an attack of over indulgence in the aforementioned catering establishments.

# Leuchars to Wormit (via Tayport)

The Kingdom of Fife is a bulging peninsula that splits the wide estuaries of the Forth and Tay. Its first modern railway took the form of a main line running SW to NE from Burntisland to Ferryport on Craig (later named Tayport). Communication onwards to Dundee was by means of a ferry from Tayport to Broughty Ferry. The line was opened from Cupar to Tayport by the Edinburgh, Perth and Dundee Railway on 17th May 1850. With the opening of the St. Andrews Railway in 1852, the EP&D moved its existing Leuchars Station down to the junction at Milton, to "promote the rapid exchange of traffic between the two railways". This proved over optimistic, inadequate siding space led to complaints about the delays at a station where there was no accommodation or comfort for passengers.

With the opening of the first Tay Bridge on 1st June 1878, the ferry at Tayport was abandoned. The Newport Railway built a line from Tayport through Newport to link up with the Tay Bridge at Wormit. This line was opened on 13th May 1879. With the building of the second Tay Bridge, the Tayport line became a rural byway. It was, however, one of the few Scottish branches which offered a Sunday service; indeed, it had to strengthen certain Sunday trains for churchgoers bound from Tayport and Newport to Dundee.

Apart from the closure of Leuchars Old in 1921, the line survived the Second World War. Leuchars Junction to Tayport was closed to passengers on 9th January 1956. The branch was cut back to Newport East on 18th September 1967 although special buses operated the service from 22nd May 1966 to permit the construction of the Tay Road Bridge. The final closure, from Newport to Wormit Junction took place on 5th May 1969.

*Mileages*

|  |  |  |
|---|---|---|
| LEUCHARS | Junction | 0.00 miles |
| LEUCHARS | Old | 0.75 miles |
| TAYPORT |  | 5.50 miles |
| NEWPORT on TAY EAST |  | 8.00 miles |
| WORMIT |  | 10.25 miles |

*Ordnance Survey 1:50,000 map numbers:– 54, 59*

*Public Transport*

Leuchars Junction is served by many of the trains that run between Edinburgh and Dundee. There are also bus services from Leuchars to St. Andrews, Dundee and Stirling. Newport on Tay is well served by buses to Dundee and most major towns in Fife, whilst there is no charge for pedestrians crossing the nearby Tay Road Bridge. Wormit is served by regular buses from Dundee. There is a campaign to re-open the station,

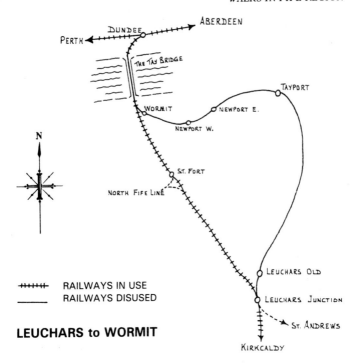

```
                                    ABERDEEN
             DUNDEE
PERTH

              THE TAY BRIDGE

        WORMIT        NEWPORT E.          TAYPORT
              NEWPORT W.

N

              ST. FORT

    NORTH FIFE LINE

                              LEUCHARS OLD
                              LEUCHARS JUNCTION
                                   ST. ANDREWS

                           KIRKCALDY
```

┼┼┼┼┼ RAILWAYS IN USE
_____ RAILWAYS DISUSED

## LEUCHARS to WORMIT

but as yet no definite agreement has been reached over the opening.

## III/3: Leuchars to Wormit

Sunday morning is a quiet time at **Leuchars Junction**. The tranquillity being broken by the arrival and departure of a train going to Dundee or Edinburgh. Although the station buildings remain, the bays used by trains going to St. Andrews or Tayport have been filled in. No snapping of the signal wire or thumping of a semaphore signal announces the arrival of a train, the signalbox being switched-out on a Sunday. The siding leading to the RAF base uses part of the trackbed of the Tayport Branch, but it heads off before a modern housing estate is reached, which is built across the trackbed.

The site of **Leuchars Old Station** has virtually disappeared, only traces of a boundary stone wall remains to mark the passage of the railway. On the north side of the main A919 level crossing, the trackbed emerges from its landscaped corpse as an untidy rubbish strewn weedy path. A hundred yards further on, the walker is greeted by an evil fence across

*Overbridge to Morton and Fetterdale at the start of the Tentsmuir Nature Reserve*

the trackbed. Not satisfied with using barbed wire in conjunction with the wooden fence, it has been laid in coils on the north side of the said fence. Using commando style techniques the obstacle is conquered, and the walker can look forward to an obstacle free 2–3 miles as the route makes a straight line towards Tayport. Being part of the original main line, the trackbed was originally double track although it was singled prior to closure.

On the east side the railway boundary is marked by a low stone wall, whilst on the other a large and deep drainage ditch marks the boundary. These two elements have contributed in the preservation of the trackbed, and prevented its reclamation, turning it into an unofficial nature reserve. At the northern edge of the wood the site of the level crossing on the minor road leading to Rhynd is reached. Parts of the crossing gates survive, albeit the white has turned into a greeny grey paintless colouration. A ''private land'' notice greets walkers approaching from the Newport direction.

Beyond the crossing the trackbed continues for about a mile with accompanying ditch before it has been ploughed into the adjacent field systems, south of Morton Farm. This forces a detour along the field boundaries before the safety of the trackbed is realised as it enters the Morton Links nature reserve. Duckboarded paths lead away from the trackbed to the various hides overlooking the Morton Lochs and surrounding marshy land.

A rather attractive stone built overbridge still carries a lane over the railway, allowing motorists access to a carpark which utilises part of the trackbed leaving the nature reserve, land reclamation has removed a short section of the trackbed, the resultant land being used for the dumping of dead foxes. Climbing over the barbed wire, the trackbed is regained by ascending the south face of the severed embankment, less than half a mile survives running alongside a mill, probably rail connected, before further land reclamation has removed all traces of the railway. A derelict timber yard occupies part of the harbour branch junction, with the remains of a narrow gauge system used to carry logs into a large cylindrical drying kiln.

Modern houses have been built on the site of the former **Tayport Station** although a plaque marking the visit of General Grant in 1877 to view the Tay Bridge, marks the existence of the railway. Although the route to Tayport was double track, the continuation to Wormit was largely single track. The trackbed has disappeared, initially landscaped and then by infilling of the cutting to nearly bridge parapet height. It looks strange to view this grassy mound with the surviving parapets standing like megalithic standing stones in the midst of a field of green.

Near the disused lighthouse the trackbed emerges from its emaciated form, and becomes part of a nature trail, the linear nature of the single track being carefully disguised by a path which twists and turns past strategically placed clumps of beech and birch saplings. Because of its official adoption, steps are provided at bridge abutments, left after the removal of the offending girders, and provide a welcome change to the usual scramble up and down embankment sides.

Nearing the B973 the nature trail ends, although the trackbed can be followed for a short stretch on the south side before it is severed by the rock cutting formed by the southern approach road to the new Tay Road Bridge. Beyond this obstruction the railway enjoys the brief solitude of a cutting before it suffers once again from urban renewal. Finally, it disappears into a modern housing estate. Amazingly at the entrance to this estate still stands the forlorn decaying buildings of **Newport on Tay (East) Station**. Presumably these buildings are the subject of a preservation order which has contributed to their survival. They certainly cannot be a welcome sight to the inhabitants of the estate.

After a few houses have occupied the trackbed by garden extensions, it can be regained as it forms yet another short nature trail until the bridge over a B road is reached. With a few missed heartbeats caused by the groaning sounds of the frail surviving girders, passage across the bridge can be made. The exhilaration of returning to an unkempt trackbed is short lived, for lurking in the midst of the wood is a dismantled viaduct.

Cutting the gentle sloping shores down to the River Tay is a steep corrie, which the railway crossed by means of a viaduct consisting of girders supported on masonry piers. This route being selected instead of a slightly more southern approach which would have avoided the needs for the viaduct completely. Fortunately the obstacle can be detoured and the trackbed regained at the entrance to **Newport on Tay (West) Station**.

Although very little remains of the station, one survival is a painted slab of rock still bearing the faint lettering of the station name. The encroaching lichens and mosses provide some protection against the twin onslaught of time and weather. Continuing on towards Wormit, after passing off as a derelict line, the railway becomes a nature trail which lasts until the suburbs of Wormit.

At **Wormit** the original tunnelled entrance to the station was replaced by a tunnel in conjunction with the second (and successful) opening of the Tay Bridge. The old tunnel is now blocked by a small industrial site, whilst the newer tunnel is now being blocked by infill at the Newport end. Access is still possible through the saplings at the station end. Parts of the platforms leading to Wormit Junction Signal Box remain, now devoid of most buildings. Fortunately the original buildings were preserved and are now re-erected at the Bo'ness Station of the SRPS Bo'ness & Kinneil Railway.

# A Branch Line in Central Fife

By 1850, the Edinburgh Perth and Dundee Railway was operating a regular service through Fife and plans were drawn up for a series of branch lines to serve other towns along with the rich Fife coalfield. One such scheme, having finally placated Lord Rothes, a local landowner, was for a branch line from Markinch to Leslie, which received its Parliamentary Act in 1857. The railway was to be built at a cost of £35,000, generating annual receipts of £4,319 from the industries of Leslie. Construction was delayed, and on 1st October 1860, agreement was reached with the EP&D for a working arrangement for the Markinch to Leslie railway, with a branch to serve the Auchmuty Paper Mills. The line was opened to passenger traffic in March 1861, the goods services starting one year later. Passenger fares were fixed between Markinch & Leslie at 1/- (5p) first, 8d (3.3p) second, 6d (2.5p) third and 4d (2p) parliamentary or fourth class.

The railway proved to be a benefit to the inhabitants of Leslie, excursions to Edinburgh and later Loch Lomond during the annual holidays were very popular. However, the rapid growth of bus services brought about the withdrawal of passenger services on 4th January 1932. The goods service on the main line was withdrawn on 9th October 1962, leaving only the branch line to the Auchmuty Paper Mills in use. Since closure, the trackbed of the Leslie branch has been converted into a walkway for most of its length and named the Boblingen Way, after the twin town of Glenrothes New Town, which has absorbed Leslie in its growth.

*Mileages*

| | | |
|---|---|---|
| MARKINCH | | 0.00 miles |
| AUCHMUTY | Junction | 0.50 miles |
| LESLIE | | 4.50 miles |

*Ordnance Survey 1:50,000 map number:– 59*

*Public Transport*

Markinch is served by many of the trains that use the line from Edinburgh to Dundee, via Kirkcaldy. Leslie is served by a frequent bus service to Markinch and Leven, the latter service allows the walker to combine an exploration of this line with the extensive network of lines between Leven and Kirkcaldy.

## III/4:  The Markinch to Leslie Branch

**Markinch** railway station provides a good starting point for the walk, with a regular service to Dundee, Edinburgh and the main centres of the former Kingdom of Fife. Leaving the station, a minor road can be followed alongside the western edge of the station. Passing as it does, the home of the A4 Pacific, "Union of South Africa", one may catch a nostalgic smell of a steam locomotive to raise the spirits at the start of the walk. After a quarter of a mile, having passed the distillery and several houses, a lane leads across the trackbed towards the new link road from Glenrothes to the A911.

Theoretically, this lane should be the way to gain the trackbed, beyond the first viaduct over the River Leven. However, a well trodden path runs parallel to the trackbed (in use at this point to serve the Auchmuty Mills), that allows the walker to reach the site of **Auchmuty Junction**. There was a signal box at this point, which closed 22nd January 1933. Leaving the junction, the height differential between the two lines rapidly increases, as the mills line drops as fast as the Leslie line climbs to the Leven Viaduct.

In spite of BR's efforts, in the interests of health and safety, to fence off the viaduct, the local population seem to be very determined to maintain access over the viaduct. This has resulted in the stout fencing being "modified", to permit access to pedestrian traffic. At the far end of the viaduct, still attached to the structure, stands a telegraph pole, perhaps the most outlandish relic of the walk. For those determined enough to obtain a photographic record of this feature, an accomplished variant of the high wire balancing act is required. Still it adds a touch of excitement to the walk.

Beyond the new road, the trackbed can be regained for a short stretch, before housing that forms the eastern limit of Glenrothes, occupies part of the trackbed. Eventually emerging out of this housing, albeit heavily landscaped, the trackbed can then be observed heading across a minor road and underneath the A92. Beyond the first road, stands the remains of an underbridge, which allowed some track to pass beneath the railway. Now the railway has gone, and its route is part of the Boblingen

Way.

Surprisingly it is a very pleasant walk, allowing one to reflect on the architectural gems (or lack of them) as progress is made through the New Town. Clad in walking gear, and armed with a camera and possibly a rucksack, this strange sight may cause panic amongst the local population. However, they seem to be fairly friendly, and to their credit, even refrain from dumping their rubbish on the trackbed. Although in places the official footpath and the trackbed part company, they generally remain in close approximation to each other. Only once, where houses have been constructed on part of the trackbed, does the footpath make a detour away from the line. Unfortunately there are very few relics of the railway that have survived the devastation caused by the conversion of the trackbed into an official walkway. Most of the bridges date from the rebuilding of the road network, to cope with the needs of the New Town. In the industrial area, where the trackbed reaches its southern limits, stands the remains of a stone built overbridge, still proclaiming its painted original bridge number.

Shortly afterwards the trackbed turns north, dropping down on a gradient, which has been exaggerated by the landscaping operations, to the second viaduct over the River Leven. This has now been adopted by the local authority, so no fences block the way across the bridge. Whilst the view from the bridge is very good, a deviation into the nearby fields allows the full majesty of the viaduct to be appreciated. Beyond the viaduct the trackbed turns westwards to reach the site of **Leslie Station**.

Where the trackbed turns, a branch trailed in (R) from the nearby paper mill. This remained in use until the withdrawal of the goods services from the main line to Leslie. Very little remains of its course, as a factory road has been built using part of the trackbed. The mill remains in use and permission should be obtained, if the walker wishes to explore further. Returning to the station site, the remnants of a brick-built platform remain at the junction of the branch from the paper mill. Beyond lies a wilderness that once was Leslie Station. Only part of the boundary wall and the vestige of a pair of stone pillars, stand as a memorial to the passage of the railway. One is left with only the images recorded by the photographers, to imagine what this site looked like in the happier days, when passenger trains still served Leslie. The main street is a short walk uphill, where perhaps a quick visit may be made to a pub or café before returning to Markinch, either by the trackbed, or by catching one of the frequent buses from the High Street.

# IV:
# WALKS IN TAYSIDE REGION

## The Dundee to Newtyle Railway

In the early 19th century, the citizens of Dundee sought to secure the trade which would assist in the town's flax industry. Authorised by Act of Parliament of 26th May 1826, the Dundee to Newtyle Railway opened to passengers on 6th December 1831. Three inclines at Dundee, Balbeuchly and Newtyle allowed this line to cross the Sidlaw Hills, which separates Strathmore from the Tay Valley. The line was built to a gauge of 4ft 6½ins and initially used horses for hauling trains on the level sections, these being replaced by locomotives in 1833. From Newtyle, the line was extended to Coupar Angus and Glamis. The former extension, built by the Newtyle and Coupar Angus Railway, was opened in February 1837. The latter, built by the Newtyle and Glamis Railway, opened to goods in 1837 and to pasengers on the 4th June 1838.

The D&NR soon discovered that the inclines were very expensive to operate, but the company could not afford to replace them. On 2nd December 1842 an attempt was made to lease the line. Although this was unsuccessful, a second attempt saw the Dundee and Perth Railway take over the ailing line in October 1846. The D&PR made several improvements, replacing the Balbeuchley Incline by a deviation via Dronley in November 1860. The next year saw the Law Incline at Dundee being replaced by a deviation through Lochee and Liff, to connect with the D&PR at Ninewells Junction. The Hatton Incline remained in operation until 1868, when the Caledonian Railway opened the Newtyle Deviation to passenger services, although goods were still handled at the original D&NR station in Newtyle.

Meanwhile north of Newtyle the N&GR closed the section from Eassie to Glamis during July 1846, and the section from Nethermill Junction to Eassie one year later. This year also saw the closure of the N&CAR. These routes were reopened (with the exception of the curve from Nethermill Junction to Ardler Junction) by the Scottish Midland Junction Railway on 2nd August 1848, in conjunction with the opening of the main line through Strathmore. Some of the intermediary stations were not reopened. The SMJR replaced the original route of the N&GR by a new line from Nethermill Junction to Ayth Junction, on 1st August 1861. The SMJR also opened that day, roughly on the alignment of the original N&CAR route, a link from Nethermill Junction to Ardler Junction. Twelve days later, the branch to Alyth was opened for passenger and goods services.

If the railway openings in the Newtyle area were complicated, the closures were piecemeal. Passenger services to Alyth were withdrawn on 2nd July 1951, the same year as services over the curve to Ardler Junction, which closed completely on 30th March 1952. Passenger services from Dundee to Newtyle and Alyth Junction were withdrawn three years later, on December 5th 1955. The section from Newtyle Junction to Auchterhouse closed completely on 5th May 1958, whilst goods facilities from Alyth Junction to Newtyle lasted until 7th September 1964. During 1965 Auchterhouse lost its goods service from Dundee on 25th January, whilst Alyth lost its goods service on 1st March. The main line through Strathmore lost its passenger service on 4th September 1967, although goods services were operated from Perth to Forfar for the region's agricultural traffic, until these too were withdrawn on 7th June 1982. No longer does Strathmore echo to the passing of a train, only to the roar of heavy lorries.

*Mileages (using final routes of the railways)*

|  |  |
|---|---|
| DUNDEE WEST | 0.00 miles |
| LIFF | 4.25 miles |
| LOCHEE | 6.00 miles |
| BALDOVAN (and Downfield) | 7.75 miles |
| BALDRAGON | 8.75 miles |
| DRONLEY | 11.00 miles |
| AUCHTERHOUSE | 12.50 miles |
| NEWTYLE | 16.75 miles |
| Newtyle | 0.00 miles |
| Ardler | 2.75 miles |
| ALYTH JUNCTION | 18.00 miles |
| ALYTH | 23.25 miles |

*Ordnance Survey 1:50,000 map numbers:– 53, 54*

*Public Transport*

Downfield is the terminus of a regular interval service operated by Dundee Corporation Transport. From Downfield, there is a limited mini-bus service to Auchterhouse. The main road from Auchterhouse to Alyth Junction is served by an hourly service from Dundee, some of which operate to Perth via Blairgowrie and others to Alyth. The frequency of the services is reduced on a Sunday, details of which can be found in the public transport timetables issued by Tayside Region.

# IV/1: The Dundee to Newtyle Railway

Dundee has grown rapidly in recent years, and this growth has removed many traces of the network of lines which once served the town. The walker trying to trace these urban routes is faced with a large amount of road walking and very little along recognisable trackbeds. Rather one is advised to join the route of the D&NR, at the terminus of the Downfield Bus service, which occupies the site of **Baldovan Station**. From this point a short walk along the minor road to Kirkton of Strathmartine, brings one past a series of modern houses built on the former route. Beyond these houses the trackbed resumes as a grassy embankment, with a well-used path guiding one up to its relative seclusion. The line soon crosses the minor road, and turns away from the road through a slightly boggy cutting.

The trackbed continues to be a well used path, forming a ledge, contouring around the northern slopes of Clatto Moor. The northern edge of the trackbed is supported by means of a stone wall, with heavy

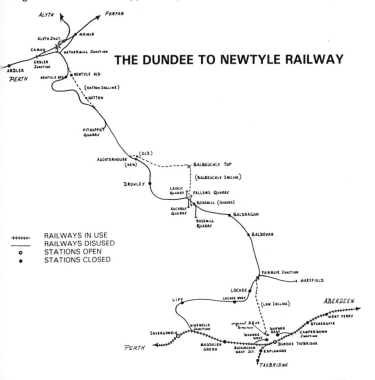

THE DUNDEE TO NEWTYLE RAILWAY

```
+++++   RAILWAYS IN USE
─────   RAILWAYS DISUSED
  o     STATIONS OPEN
  •     STATIONS CLOSED
```

65

buttressing to prevent the trackbed sliding down the hill into the valley of the Dighty Water. Labour was comparatively inexpensive when this railway was built, compared to the cost of land. Consequently the builders tried to occupy as little land as possible, to reduce the construction costs. The embankment ends at the site of **Baldragon Station** which is partially obscured by another housing estate. Traces of the platform survive, whilst the walker should head down to follow the estate road, to regain the trackbed to the west of the station site. The tarmac ends, and the trackbed resumes as a well used path alongside the minor road. Nearing Rosemill, the railway and road were separated by a narrow hedge. This has been removed and the trackbed covered in gravel to provide a pavement alongside the narrow road.

**Rosemill Station** was only a goods station, which served several quarries and a manure works. Before the station, the trackbed of a line may be observed, heading south away from the railway, to serve a quarry on the slopes of Clatto Moor. A loading dock and platform remain at the station site, beyond which the line crossed the minor road to North Auchray. The walker having crossed this road, is presented with a double width trackbed, with traces of branches on both sides along with numerous remains of brick built buildings. A line joins from the south, whilst another line heads north to serve a former quarry. The main line then crosses the Dighty Water alongside another quarry line to the south. Both lines cross the water by means of attractive stone built bridges, which provide the photographer with the opportunity to record both bridges without having to suffer the unpleasantness of wet feet.

Beyond this crossing, the new line continues as a well used path to Dronley and Auchterhouse Stations. However the walker in search of the original route, should turn north, into the site of Leoch quarry, which is being infilled with Dundee's refuse. The quarry removed many traces of the southern end of the incline, which rose with a slope of 1 in 25 for its length of nearly one mile. North of the quarry one can find the remains of the incline, as a tree lined cutting heading uphill to the west of Leoch Farm. Although the cutting supports a large number of trees, passage through them is still possible, to reach a grassy embankment as the trackbed reaches the minor road to South Fallaws. Over the road, the route continues as a tree lined green lane, past the buildings of Leoch Farm. A bridge over a line from the farm has been removed, leaving remains of the original stone abutments. Curious square shaped holes can be found in the northern abutment, suggesting that the bridge was either partially built in timber, or timber supports were used during the construction of the arch.

Continuing uphill, the walker reaches the minor road to Mid Leoch, where the trackbed is obscured by several mounds of stones. Behind the cottages of Mid Leoch, the incline was in another cutting. This again supports numerous trees, which have to be negotiated along with some boggy sections. A drier and easier solution is to follow the route in the field alongside. However, the cutting comes to an end, as the trackbed uses another grassy embankment to reach the summit of the line at **Balbeuchly Top**. When the incline was operating, a 20hp steam engine was used to haul both goods and passenger trains up and down the slope. A report of such operations indicates that no great difference of motion was felt descending the incline, the slope being so gradual as to occasion no disagreeable sensation. The remains of a stone built building, along with numerous mounds of stones, act as a memorial to the operation of the incline. From the summit, the railway turns sharply westwards towards the numerous buildings of Pitpointie Farm.

The trackbed is now a farm access road, in a shallow cutting with stone sided walls, again to reduce the amount of land used by the railway. The trackbed through the farm is obliterated by the many buildings, resuming beyond the main farmhouse as a tarmacadamed lane, to join the road to Kirkton Farm. On the opposite side of the road, the route is ploughed into the surrounding fields. A narrow strip may be left to permit one to follow the route, rather than detouring along the minor roads, to reach the bridge under the road to Eastfield.

Surprisingly, the bridge which carried the minor road from Eastfield to Knowhead over the original route of the D&NR still remains intact. It has found use as a log shed for one of the nearby cottages, where extended gardens merge onto the trackbed. The walker should follow the road to Eastfield, then take a lane to the north of the farm to reach the trackbed of the Dronley diversion. Although the map indicates this lane passed under the railway, it is difficult to see how this would have been achieved. More probably the lane crossed the railway on the level. The new route of the D&NR is a clear track, heading towards Auchterhouse, closing in to a tree covered embankment which was the original alignment of the railway. **Auchterhouse Station** was a large site serving several villages in the area. The twin platforms remain in situ, although all the original buildings have been demolished, leaving only a few foundations to betray their existence.

The well-used path which follows the trackbed from Baldovan, ends at Auchterhouse. The trackbed at the end of the station passes a large growth of rhododendron bushes, to pass underneath the minor road to Kirkton of Auchterhouse in a flooded cutting. The walker should head up to the road, and then use the embankment of the original route of the D&NR to regain the trackbed in a drier section. In passing this watery obstacle, one may find the base of a signal post, complete with a pulley, which would have controlled trains arriving at the station. Generally the trackbed is a lot more overgrown than the earlier section, but passage is still possible, albeit boggy in places. The route crosses Pitnappie Moss, a boggy saddle between West Mains Hill and Auchterhouse Hill, parts of which would appear to be a nature reserve. Nearing Wester Pitnappie, the trackbed becomes a flooded, overgrown cutting, as it starts its descent into the new Newtyle Station. To the west of the start of the cutting, may be found traces of a branch which served **Pitnappie**

**Quarry**. The most obvious relic is the bridge under the main A927, which is blocked at the western end, by the infilling of the nearby quarry.

Rather than revert to jungle techniques, one should head up to the main road, following it as far as the access lane to Millhole Farm. This access lane crosses the new route by means of an attractive three-arched stone bridge. The original route of the D&NR passed to the rear of the farm buildings, and can be seen as a clear track, contouring round the slopes of Auchterhouse Hill. Because the land is dropping down into Strathmore, this route appears to be climbing the hill, although it is in reality keeping a level before descending the Hatton Incline. Stone sleepers from the original railway, have been reused by the farmer for the construction of the base for the farm's fuel supply. The old route makes for a pleasant walk, a grassy level through open fields, well stocked with sheep. Nearing the site of **Hatton Station**, forestry descends the hill, to cover the trackbed, leaving only a narrow gap used by cattle. The station site was cleared in the late 1960s, about one hundred years after the closure of the station in October 1865. Very little has survived the afforestation; only a few low stone rubble walls possibly mark the original site.

The trackbed comes out of the forest and starts its descent of the Hatton Incline. This was originally operated by a 20hp winding engine, dropping trains on a slope of 1 in 13 into the original Newtyle terminus.

The incline is again a grassy track, covering the original ash ballast, on top of a loose stone base. Like the earlier sections, low stone walls supported the cutting sides as the incline descends past the remains of Hatton Castle. At the castle, the route passes through private gardens, forcing the walker to once again detour via the A927 to reach the original terminus of the D&NR. The original D&NR buildings of **Newtyle Station** are now used by an agricultural contractor, resulting in the main building surviving in a very good state of preservation. Unfortunately the ancillary buildings have had their roofs removed; local rumours claim this was the result of a failed attempt to demolish the listed buildings. Looking at the buildings, from the north, the walker can see the abrupt start of the Hatton Incline, at the end of the main building.

The line then crosses a minor road, alongside a well kept public convenience, to form a dirt track well used by some very young motor cyclists. To the west can be seen the tree-covered embankment of the new route, as it approaches the site of **Newtyle Junction**, where it joins the original route of the lines from Newtyle to Coupar Angus and Glamis. In the neck of the junction between the two alignments, lie the remains of a small turntable pit. Beyond the junction, there were two single tracks to **Nethermill Junction**, which marks the start of the complicated network of lines around Alyth Junction. At the junction, one can observe the separation of the final lines to Ardler and Alyth Junctions, the former gaining height on and separated from the latter, by means of a low stone sided embankment. Although the myriad of trees which form Belmont Woods obscure the site, it is still possible to see something of the layout.

Heading up the Alyth branch, by now a single track, the walker should look down to the east, to see the faint traces of the curving route of the N&GR route to Meigle Junction, which is marked by a curving line of trees. The Alyth line curves away westwards, below which was the original route of the N&CAR, but very little can be seen of this route. The trackbed reaches the A927, where the bridges which carried it have been removed. On the opposite side of the road, the trackbed of the Alyth Junction line, has been landscaped into the surrounding field, leaving only the abutments of the bridge over the Strathmore main line, as an indication of its route. The walker should then take a nearby farm track, which allows access to the line to Ardler Junction, again a single track, as it continues its gradual closing in to the main line. By the end of the woods, the trackbed joins up with the original alignment of the N&CAR, although as before, nothing can be seen of this earlier route.

The walker is faced with the removal of the bridge over the minor road, to Camno Level Crossing, which is not a very serious problem. **Ardler Junction** supports a good growth of trees, which all but obscure the remains of a brick-built bothy which once possibly provided comfort for the signalman in the nearby box. Having reached this location, one is advised to now join the Strathmore main line, and turn back towards Alyth Junction. This former main line is now slowly reverting back to nature. The double tracked width of ballast is still watched over by the line of telegraph poles marching on towards Forfar, complete with much of their wiring. A signal post is passed before reaching **Camno Level Crossing**.

The crossing keeper's cottage has been converted into a private house, the owner of which uses the original small cabin as a potting shed. In the final years of operation of the Forfar Branch, this crossing was one of those operated by the train crews, to reduce the operational costs of the line. Beyond the crossing, the ballast has been removed, making the trackbed an easier walk for tired feet. The walk passes the remains of the bridge, which carried the line from Nethermill Junction to Alyth Junction, over the main line. Alongside stands a tall signal post, which acted as a warning for the nearby level crossing. It is a short walk, back on the ballast, to reach the overgrown platforms of **Alyth Junction**. The twin main line platforms, and separate branch platforms have had all of their original buildings removed, apart from a small brick built building. Traces can be found of the bay platforms, between the branch and main line platforms, which terminated in the tall water tower.

The bridge which carried the main road over the branch line has been filled in. Only the lengthy stone approach walls remain, possibly confusing the walker into thinking that there were two bridges, until it becomes apparent what has happened. A scramble up to the bridge allows one to reach the main road, having possibly time for refreshment in the nearby hotel. There is an approximately hourly service back into Auchterhouse and Dundee. In the opposite direction, the buses alternate between Perth (via Blairgowrie) and Alyth.

# Railways to Crieff

At one time Crieff was served by railways in three directions, to Perth in the east, Gleneagles in the south and to Balquhidder in the west. The first link was formed by the opening on 16th March 1856 of the Crieff Junction Railway, from a station originally named Crieff Junction, later to be renamed as Gleneagles. The line from Perth was opened to Methven on 1st January 1858 and extended to Crieff on 21st May 1866. The situation remained unchanged for nearly thirty years, until the opening of the railway from Crieff to Comrie on 1st June 1893, that also saw the opening of a new station for Crieff. This line was extended to St. Fillans on 1st October 1901 and finally to Balquhidder, where it joined the Callander and Oban Railway on 1st July 1904.

The lines were or became part of the Caledonian Railway network. However passing largely through agricultural country they were not great money spinners to that company. During the first world war, the CR closed Highlandman Station (on the line to Gleneagles) on 1st January 1917 in the interests of economy. The station was reopened two years later on 1st February 1919. In the 1923 grouping the lines became part of the LMSR which closed the branch to Methven on 27th September 1937 to passenger services. After nationalisation, the line from Crieff to Perth was closed to passenger services and the line from Comrie to Balquhidder was closed entirely on 1st October 1951. In the interest of economy, a railbus was introduced in 1958 on the surviving service from Gleneagles to Comrie. Two "Halts" at Pittenzie and Strageath were opened to attract extra custom for these services, however, the railbus operation was not very reliable and the new service was not very successful.

Whilst the railbus was running, goods services were being withdrawn. Crieff to Comrie lost its goods services on 15th June 1964. Later that year on 2nd November the goods service was withdrawn from Crieff to Gleneagles. In the next year the Methven branch lost its goods service on 25th January. Two years later (1967) the final closures took place, the passenger service from Comrie to Gleneagles was closed to passengers on 6th July. Later that year, the goods service from Perth was withdrawn from Dewar's Siding (on the outskirts of Perth) to Crieff on 11th September. After that, the rich Perthshire countryside was left with many miles of unofficial nature reserves as the abandoned trackbeds were slowly reclaimed by nature.

*Ordnance Survey 1:50,000 map numbers:–* 51, 57, 58

*Mileages*

| | |
|---|---|
| CRIEFF | 0.00 miles |
| COMRIE | 6.00 miles |
| DALCHONZIE siding | 0.00 miles |
| ST. FILLANS | 11.75 miles |
| LOCHEARNHEAD | 19.75 miles |
| BALQUHIDDER | 21.75 miles |
| CRIEFF | 0.00 miles |
| INNERPEFFRAY | 2.00 miles |
| ABERCAIRNY | 4.25 miles |
| MADDERTY | 6.25 miles |
| BALGOWAN | 8.75 miles |
| METHVEN Junction | 11.00 miles |
| METHVEN Junction | 0.00 miles |
| METHVEN | 1.00 miles |
| TIBBERMUIR Crossing | 12.75 miles |
| ALMONDBANK | 13.75 miles |
| RUTHVEN ROAD Crossing | 14.75 miles |
| PERTH | 17.75 miles |
| | |
| CRIEFF | 0.00 miles |
| PITTENZIE HALT | 1.00 miles |
| HIGHLANDMAN | 2.50 miles |
| STRAGEATH HALT | 3.25 miles |
| MUTHILL | 4.00 miles |
| TULLIBARDINE | 6.50 miles |
| GLENEAGLES | 9.00 miles |

*Public Transport*

Crieff has a regular bus service to Perth and several buses a day to Stirling and Dunblane. There is a limited bus service to Comrie, some of which continue on to St. Fillans. There is no regular service from St. Fillans to Lochearnhead or Balquhidder. These latter two villages are served by an infrequent bus service that operates between Callander and Crianlarich. The service frequency is reduced on a Sunday.

## IV/2a: St. Fillans to Crieff

The easiest way to walk this line, using the limited public transport service in the area, is to catch the morning bus from Crieff to Comrie to walk the section from Comrie to St. Fillans. The early afternoon bus from St. Fillans is used to return to Comrie, allowing the afternoon to be spent walking from Comrie to Crieff. On arrival at Crieff, there are several buses back to Perth or Stirling if required.

**St. Fillans Station** is located on the hillside above the village at its

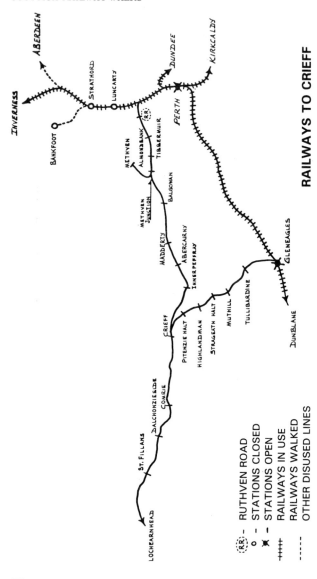

**RAILWAYS TO CRIEFF**

(R.R) – RUTHVEN ROAD
o – STATIONS CLOSED
✖ – STATIONS OPEN
┼┼┼┼ – RAILWAYS IN USE
▬▬▬ – RAILWAYS WALKED
------ – OTHER DISUSED LINES

eastern extremity. An access road at the end of the village leads up to the station site, which is now a caravan park. The station buildings now provide a shop and booking office for the caravaners. The main buildings occupy one platform, whilst a small waiting room and the signal box occupy the other (island) platform. All of the buildings are in a very good state of repair, even the pair of notice boards that adorned the side of the main building remain in situ. The only change from early photographs of the station which show these boards, is that the Caledonian Railway name that once headed the notices has been replaced by the pale blue enamel signs of British Railways. The signal box still retains a circular topping to each of its windows, to turn what otherwise would have been a simple window frame into an attractive ornamental frame. Beyond the station, the trackbed enters a waterlogged cutting, forcing a short detour through the nearby fields to reach the first overbridge, about half a mile from the station site. At this bridge, conditions rapidly improve to provide the walker with perhaps one of the most pleasurable railway walks in Scotland.

Shortly after, the trackbed passes beneath the A85, by means of a cavernous concrete overbridge. Between this bridge and the girder bridge over the nearby River Earn, the trackbed is joined by a forestry access road. This may have been the main reason for the retention of the bridge over the river. The two part company shortly afterwards as the trackbed heads away from the main part of the forest. Heading as a grassy farm track under the foothills of Mor Bheinn, the trackbed crosses over a couple of streams draining the forested slopes of their excess water, by means of a series of attractive bridges. The railway returns to the forest before it crosses over the Earn once again to reach the site of **Dalchonzie Siding**. This location was originally worked by trains from St. Fillans to Comrie, with a small wooden platform for passengers' use. Today the signal box and the adjacent accommodation have been converted into a single house. Well kept gardens now occupy the trackbed at this point, requiring a short detour to regain the trackbed on the siding side of the site.

In the undergrowth can be found the tops of several telegraph poles, many still with their white insulators of LMS origins. The trackbed is once again used as an access road round the edge of Drumlochlan Wood. Beyond, the trackbed dissolves in a couple of fields, before it emerges for the last time for a short section, ending in a dismantled bridge over the River Earn. Although this "gap" is detourable, a further bridge near to Comrie has also been removed which makes the short roadside walk into Comrie the easiest solution. Through the town, the route of the railway has been used in places for housing and in others as the usual ubiquitous car park. **Comrie Station** is now a caravan park and the only surviving trace of the station conversion is a small end section of a platform, underneath the main road bridge. In a nearby field stands a brick built building, with its original windows bricked up, which once may have been a railway building.

Leaving the bright lights of Comrie and the bemused looks of the inhabitants of the caravan park behind, the walker soon discovers that the spacious feeling of the St. Fillans section is replaced by the energetic growth of saplings as a way is made through this maze towards Crieff. Whilst admiring the girth of some of the specimens, one discovers another possible problem caused by the removal of a bridge over a drainage ditch near to the Carse of Lennoch farm. In, or after, wet periods, the easiest crossing of this watery obstacle is where the ditch first encounters the trackbed. Once the opposite side of the trackbed has been gained, there are remnants of several other bridges which have been removed, however these crossed over access lanes to nearby farms and consequently their absence presents no major problems. The trackbed is generally well ballasted with stone chippings, that can prove heavy going at times, not to mention the need to cast aside the omnipresent branches.

Nearing Thornhill Lodge the trackbed is once again used as an access road, the sighting of a strange four wheeled, petrol burning metal object hurtling along the trackbed may diminish one's relief to be out of the woods. Luckily this use of the trackbed has required the retention of two bridges over further drainage ditches before Thornhill Lodge is reached.

Beyond the lodge, the trackbed enters a cutting where it is used as a dumping ground for unwanted stone and brick masonry. Notices proclaim dire warnings to any person taking any of these "dumped" stones, truly an act of folly for the average railway walker. Having carefully avoided the "fallen" masonry, one can regain the trackbed before it enters a short tunnel underneath a lane leading to Laggan farm. The tunnel is open at both ends and is in generally good condition. Wooden planks form the side of the well ballasted trackbed, leaving a gap between the plank and the tunnel wall for drainage. These walls are a mixture of natural rock and short sections of brickwork, one small section of which has fallen from the roof of the tunnel. Emerging from the tunnel one enters a quiet, secret world, far away from the noise of the main road. Only the gentle bubbling of the River Earn and choruses of birdsong act to soothe the senses after the earlier onslaught of vegetation. In places the trackbed is overgrown and occasionally wet underfoot, however the only real obstacles are the occasional barbed wire fence and missing underbridge.

Gradually the trackbed approaches Crieff. The viaduct which crossed the Shaggie Burn has been removed, forcing a roadside detour before entering the town. On the other side of the river, there is a short walkable section ending where the trackbed passed beneath a minor road. Beyond this point housing developments occupy part of the trackbed before it disappears into yet another tunnel. Unfortunately both ends have been blocked up, although the cutting at the eastern end of the tunnel has recently been cleared of its former rich growth of vegetation. **Crieff Station** site is now occupied by a new Health Centre for the town. Traces of the original platforms and a goods shed still remain to remind the townsfolk of their town's railway history. Perhaps the most unusual relic is a small brick-built office, adjacent to the goods shed, which still proclaims the time when it was an outpost of the LMS empire. Nearby, lining the adjacent roadside, stand small brick-built buildings typical of the accommodation once used by local coal merchants on railway premises.

## IV/2b:   Crieff to Methven

The eastern exit from the site of **Crieff Station** has also been occupied by housing development. However, by careful circumnavigation, the walker can gain a path using the trackbed of the Perth branch to reach the site of **Pittenzie Halt** which was provided by British Railways on the Gleneagles branch. The two lines ran parallel to each other from Crieff to the lane leading up to Pittentian Farm. No connection was provided between the two lines, which were run as two separate single line sections. The "halt" was a very basic affair, consisting of a double row of paving slabs, resting on a base of small stones edged with wooden timbers. Only a few of these timbers remain to mark the site of an experiment in making the rail service more convenient for the population it was trying to serve. Unfortunately, there was very little housing near to the site chosen for the halt.

On the other side of the minor road stands the original crossing keeper's cottage and a small industrial works which uses the trackbed of the Gleneagles branch as its main access road. Between these works and the next lane, where the two routes parted company, both trackbeds have been ploughed into the adjacent field systems. However, there are generally sufficient fields in grass to allow one to reach the parting of the ways. The crossing keeper's accommodation at this location consisted of a large double storeyed house, nearer to the CJR than the later Perth line.

Beyond the lane, both trackbeds have been reclaimed to form a very large field. Heading towards where the Perth line passes underneath the link road between the A85 and B8062, one can observe the CJR route curving south for a close encounter of the caravan kind before it reaches the safety of the River Earn. Past the surviving link road overbridge, the trackbed recovers as a track heading towards the former station of **Innerpeffray**.

The station buildings of Innerpeffray have been converted into a house. Sadly many of the original windows have been replaced by large picture windows, marring an otherwise attractive restoration of the original stone-built station buildings. A detour through the fields to the south of the railway takes the walker past the station and the dismantled bridge over the nearby minor road. Shortly after the Pow Water is crossed by an attractive stone skew arched bridge. The trackbed is again used as a track heading towards the Long Plantation, complete with its high deer fences. Fortunately the prospect of a pole vault over the fence recedes as closer examination of the fence across the trackbed reveals a gate permitting access in and out of the plantation. The only problem one encounters is in the midst of the woods, where a bridge has been removed over the minor road from Tuchethill. Here extreme agility is required to get through a hole in the fence which blocks access back onto the trackbed from the road.

The next station of **Abercairny** has also been converted into a private house. A well trodden track using the original goods access, passes by the sole passenger platform amidst clumps of daffodils and beehives, regaining the trackbed beyond the station buildings. Heading towards Madderty, one is always apprehensive of the trackbed being reclaimed for agricultural operations. Surprisingly this has not occurred and one is provided with a pleasant country walk through the rich Perthshire countryside. Possibly the stone ballast used when the route was an operating railway may have prevented its reuse for farming purposes. Relics appear in many places, ranging from nuts and bolts to the white insulators from the telegraph system. Nearing Madderty conditions suddenly deteriorate, caused by the infilling of the cutting to the west of the station. In the boggy ground can be found a sleeper with Caledonian Railway chairs, but this is small reward for the unpleasant conditions. The easiest exit is to follow the cutting side and scramble up between the filled-in cutting and a nearby overbridge, to gain a lane leading to nearby Abbey Welltree. The field exits are generally prevented by awkward barbed wire fences, some of which are also electrified.

**Madderty Station** still retains its original station buildings, again a private house, along with its pair of platforms. On one platform may be discerned the brick built base of the signal box, at the eastern end of the station. A farm track passes via the large goods yard, to regain the trackbed as it heads alongside the Pow Water towards Balgowan Station. This watercourse has again been dredged, leaving mounds of silt on the land between the water and the railway. The trackbed supports an abundant wildlife: stoats, weasels, rabbits and hares may be observed hurrying for cover from the advancing footsteps of the walker. Flowers in great profusion including a variety of wild orchid, grow in this unofficial nature reserve.

In the adjacent fields can be seen cattle and sheep, heralding a return to a more mixed farming landscape from the predominantly arable farming previously encountered. Gulls may be seen following the plough in their never-relenting search for food. **Balgowan Station** was a wooden building, no trace of which remains, apart from some evidence of the presence of the single platform and the base of the buildings. Beyond the station site, the trackbed passes a semi-derelict sawmill, with its mounds of wood shavings on the trackbed. After the hard ballast surface, the softness of these shavings provides a welcome relief to the feet. The trackbed shortly afterwards enters Methven Moss, a strange world of silver birch and heather moss. The well ballasted line is slowly being reclaimed by the spongy moss and the silver birch, visited by very few human beings.

The moss is left behind as one emerges at a minor road leading up to Methven. Beyond this road the trackbed has been reclaimed for arable farming. By now footsore, the walker will probably leave the trackbed and head up this quiet country lane to the nearby village to fortify those parts of the body as necessary before catching a bus back to Perth or Crieff. The lane joins up with the end of the Methven branch. Albeit overgrown the trackbed is passable, ending in a new industrial warehouse built on the site of the original **Methven Station**. Traces of a stone built loading dock are the only remnants of the original railway equipment. However, the railway from Methven to Perth is another day's walk, and that, as they say, is another story.

# The Aberfeldy Branch

In conjunction with the early proposals for a railway from Perth to Inverness, a branch line was promoted to connect Aberfeldy with the then expanding railway network. Although these plans came to nothing, they were resurrected in an Act of Parliament of 22nd July 1861, authorising the construction of a railway from Dunkeld to Inverness, with a branch line from Ballinluig to Aberfeldy.

Construction of the branch was very slow, although the main line was opened to Pitlochry on 1st June 1863, the Aberfeldy branch was not opened until 3rd July 1865. The line was single track, with an intermediate station at Grandtully, where there was a small goods yard but no passing loop. Forty-one bridges were required, including two major viaducts over the Rivers Tay and Tummel near Ballinluig. Other civil engineering works involved the use of 800,000 cubic yards of earth in the construction of the embankments and excavation of cuttings.

The line had a non-eventful period of operation, providing a service for the local communities and for the tourist trade. The line was opened by the Inverness and Perth Junction Railway, which became part of the Highland Railway. The line became part of the London Midland and Scottish Railway (LMSR) after the 1923 grouping of the railways. On the 2nd December 1935 the LMSR opened a halt at Balnaguard, which provided passenger-only facilities for the nearby village. Like many other lines in Scotland, the Aberfeldy branch became a victim of Beeching's plans for the reshaping of British Railways. Goods facilities were withdrawn on 26th January 1965, the passenger service followed on 3rd May 1965. At the same time Ballinluig Station was closed, although its signal box remained to control the level crossing over the main line. The crossing loop was initially removed, but restored with the reinstatement of extra capability on the Highland Line.

Mileages

| | |
|---|---|
| Ballinluig | 0 miles 00 chains |
| Balnaguard | 2 miles 11 chains |
| Grantully | 4 miles 27 chains |
| Aberfeldy | 8 miles 59 chains |

Ordnance Survey 1 to 50,000 map number:– 52

Public Transport

Aberfeldy is served by buses from Perth and Pitlochry, which also serve Ballinluig and Grantully. Ballinluig is also served by some of the express coach services that operate from Perth to Inverness. Details of all of these services may be found in the public transport timetables, issued by the Highlands and Islands Development Board.

## IV/3:   The Aberfeldy Branch

Although it is possible to walk the route of the branch in both directions in one day, a more pleasurable walk is to traverse it in the one direction. The easiest way based on Ballinluig is to catch a late morning bus to Aberfeldy before walking back to Ballinluig. This also serves as a reassurance, that the bridge still remains in situ over the River Tay and warn of any obstacles between Grantully to Aberfeldy, provided the bus is not routed via Weem.

The site of **Aberfeldy Station** has been partially occupied by a housing estate, with a perimeter road on part of the trackbed. Few relics survive, mainly parts of the original fencing and the occasional sleeper. Leaving the estate behind, the trackbed forms a path through the fields, heading towards a nearby distillery. A detour around this establishment is required, due to the removal of a bridge over a burn at its edge and the landscaping of the trackbed through the grounds. Walking past the well-maintained buildings, allows one to obtain good views of the traditional copper stills that are an essential fitting in the making of the "water of life".

Beyond the distillery, the trackbed can be regained as it heads across fields, parallel to the main road. Many of the original telegraph poles, with their arms still supporting their ceramic insulators, remain to mark the southern boundary of the railway. Although the bridge over the access road to Duireaskin Farm has been removed, gentle paths take the walker down to the lane and back up to the trackbed. Shortly afterwards the trackbed has been landscaped into the surrounding fields, leaving only the telegraph poles to mark the former route. A detour along the nearby A827 is advised, in order to regain the trackbed where it crosses over the road. Road improvements have removed some of the embankment and most of the railway bridge. The trackbed can be regained as it enters a forest on the banks of the River Tay.

Whilst the main road is never far away, the walker enters a secret world where the quiet serenity of nature soothes the pressures of modern living. Passing through cuttings and over embankments, the

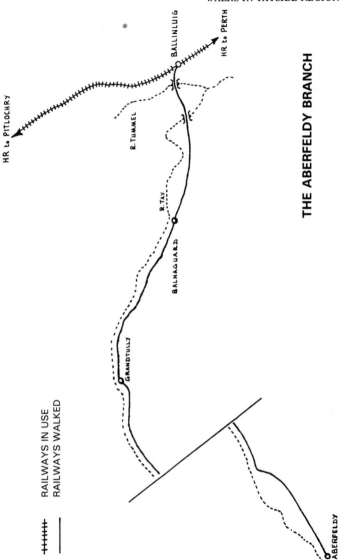

HR to PITLOCHRY

HR to PERTH

BALLINLUIG

R. TUMMEL

R. TAY

BALNAGUARD

GRANDTULLY

ABERFELDY

RAILWAYS IN USE
RAILWAYS WALKED

**THE ABERFELDY BRANCH**

trackbed provides a well used track through a mature mixed woodland. In autumn the assorted greens are replaced by a rich variety of autumnal tints, as nature marks the passing of another year in a blaze of colour. Nearby, the watery music of the River Tay is accompanied by a variety of birdsong or perhaps the rushing of a small brook, cascading downhill underneath the railway and into the river. Perhaps a roe deer will be sighted as it leaps away into the surrounding woodland, startled by the sudden strange footfall of the walker.

Nearing Grandtully, the tracked vehicles that have used the trackbed head away to the nearby road, whilst a well used path guides the walker through the broom, which has colonised the railway. **Grandtully Station** is now used as a car park and base for the Scottish Canoe Association. The single platform and nearby twin goods loading platforms, provide ample space for a well deserved picnic. A small house stands at the end of the site, which was presumably the Station Master's accommodation. Access to the station site is still controlled by a well maintained metal crossing gate.

Toilets are provided during the summer months, in winter the walker has to seek the warmth and comfort of a nearby public house. Beyond the station, the trackbed can be followed to a farm near the new bridge of the A827 over the River Tay, which replaced a severely weight restricted crossing at Grandtully. An exit round the rear of the farm buildings onto the B-road should be followed, to avoid a missing bridge over the road. The railway can be regained, by climbing the northern embankment adjacent to the remains of the bridge abutment. The walker enters a sanctuary for local bee (and game) keepers. Several

*Grandtully Station*

bee-hives are passed before the ash ballast becomes strewn with the golden grains of corn.

The ever-present trees sometimes bear the strange fruit of large plastic containers attached by string to a branch. Holes in the base of the containers allow the grain held in them to fall the short distance to earth, when the plastic is given a slight nudge. Occasionally a low shelter with a floor of straw is sighted, adding further puzzlement to the nature of the beasts or fowl for whom these strange offerings are intended. Suddenly the russet brown of a brace of pheasants will be seen, flying for safety from the nearby undergrowth. One can only assume that all this is used to rear game birds.

Nearing Sketewan, the trackbed enters a cutting which becomes increasingly waterlogged as the walker proceeds along it. The water gradually rises up the legs, past the shoe line, the boot line and well up on the wellington line, forcing a retreat to the safety of the cutting side. Beyond this obstacle, the trackbed has been landscaped into the surrounding fields, forcing a detour along the B898 to Balnaguard. In the village, a small stone building still sports an enamelled sign proclaiming "BALNAGUARD – LMS HALT PLATFORM" in black letters on a yellow background. A lane leads down to the trackbed, where a silage mountain has covered the site of the **Balnaguard Halt**. Avoiding this obstruction, the trackbed once again becomes a well used track as it heads towards Ballinluig. Fortunately it is largely built upon an embankment, as the surrounding land is easily flooded by the River Tay. An apple tree grows nearby, possibly the result of a core being thrown out of the window of some long departed branch train. Its abundant crop provides an unusual source of refreshment. Other trees provide shelter for a variety of birdlife, to the delight of the ornithologists.

The first major viaduct of the railway over the River Tay remains in use as a private road, although signs proclaim no liability is accepted for its use. The ironwork still advertises its final painting by the railway administration, sadly its present owners do not appear to have given the ironwork a preservative coat of paint. However, the bridge's presence does avoid the need for a lengthy detour for the nearest crossing of the River Tay. Over the bridge the trackbed disappears beneath the realigned A827 as it heads across the headland towards the River Tummel. When the railway was closed, the road was altered to use the stronger railway bridge over the river. This bridge, the other major railway viaduct, remained in use until a new road bridge was built in conjunction with the improvements of the A9, the main Perth to Inverness road. Very little remains of the earlier road and rail bridges, apart from their truncated abutments.

Across the river the trackbed emerges from beneath the embankment of the new road bridge, as it curves sharply towards the empty platforms of **Ballinluig Station**. Nowadays trains only stop for passing purposes, due to the line being single track from Perth to Pitlochry. The walker dependent upon public transport has to seek the nearby bus stop and await the arrival of a bus to regain the railway network at Perth, Dunkeld or Pitlochry. Luckily the village still supports a well run café, which provides a haven of warmth, comfort and refreshment whilst waiting for the bus and recalling a pleasurable day's walk along a very attractive disused railway line.

*The original D&NR station at Newtyle*

# V:
# WALKS IN
# GRAMPIAN REGION

# The Deeside Way

*Time*
The basic one way walk from Peterculter, shortened to Culter and pronounced Cooter, to the Duthie Park in Aberdeen should be completed in three to four hours. The return walk, of thirteen miles should be completed in seven to eight hours, including a lunch stop.

Being essentially a linear walk, the easiest way to effect a return is by using the frequent bus service that operates from Aberdeen (either from Union Street, or from the main bus station that is opposite the railway station) to Culter. This could be used to reach the starting point of the walk, or return from the finishing point.

*Start and Finish*
The starting point of the walk is the former station of Culter, which is to the south of the A93 as it passes through Peterculter. The finishing point is in Aberdeen, beside the main entrance to the Duthie Park at the end of Polmuir Road.

*OS Map:* 38 (Aberdeen)
The walk follows the valley of the River Dee, starting in the rich agricultural land around Peterculter. As the route nears Aberdeen, the scenery changes gradually, passing through the suburban sprawl of Cults and ending in the urban landscape of Aberdeen. However at all times it is a pleasant walk, a long finger of a tranquil countryside, right into the heart of the oil capital of Britain. The route of the old railway has been converted into a well used walkway that is much appreciated by local cyclists and horse riders.

## V/1: Culter to Aberdeen
Peterculter is a large village on the main road from Aberdeen to Royal Deeside (the A93) at the junction with the B979 from Stonehaven to the north of Aberdeen. It lies at the boundary between the urban growth of

RAILWAYS TO THE GRANITE CITY

o   STATIONS OPEN
•   STATIONS CLOSED
+++   RAILWAYS IN USE
—   RAILWAYS DISUSED

Aberdeen and the rich agricultural land of the upper Dee Valley. The village has car parking facilities as well as several pubs and cafés. To reach the starting point of the way, walk down Station Brae, which is a lane leading down to the river, from the main road through the village (with a pillar box near to the junction). The lane heads downhill and then turns left to reach a road heading to a modern housing estate. On the left hand side of the entrance to this estate can be found a stone faced platform with a blue painted sign indicating that this was once Culter Station. The original buildings have been replaced by a timber hut, whilst a profusion of wild roses cover the site in a carpet of green.

Facing the platform and hut, turn right to start walking down the line towards Aberdeen. The original stone chippings used as ballast by the railway, have been covered in a fine sand, to produce a firm dry footpath. On leaving the station, there are good views out across the gentle meanders of the River Dee, to the deep green swathe of Craigingles Wood.

Continue past bridge number 1032 (as painted in black numerals on a white background, on the left hand abutment of the bridge), beyond which the path leaves the railway, dropping down to cross over the lane leading to Camphill, before returning to the railway. A similar thing occurs at the next bridge, except this time the B979 is being crossed on the western side of the village of Milltimber. Again the path drops away from the railway and down to the road.

Having crossed the road (be careful as it is very busy), turn left to follow the road for a short distance. Where the road turns left, to head uphill to Milltimber, follow a road which heads straight on, past several modern houses, to reach the site of Milltimber Station (just over one mile from Culter). There is a limited amount of car parking space at the former station, where the original stone built buildings are being converted into a family house.

The way passes the station and returns to its rural peace, passing several small woods which support a rich variety of deciduous trees. Even in these parts the daubings of the lesser spotted graffiti writer can be observed as the path heads underneath several bridges, giving access to the main road for properties on the south side of the railway. Benches and seats are provided at regular intervals, to allow you to rest and take in the views across the bubbling waters of the Dee.

The next station of Murtle (two miles from Culter) is soon reached, where the original wooden buildings have been converted into a house. Beyond the station, the way crosses over a burn and two lanes (leading up to Murtle House) on a modern concrete bridge built on the stone piers of the original railway bridge. The A93 can be reached by taking a set of steps, conveniently provided at this location, emerging where there is a phone box and low bridge warning sign, referring to this bridge.

The agricultural scenery now changes as the outskirts of Cults are reached. By bridge number 1022, which proclaims that it was built by

James Abernethy and Company, of Aberdeen in 1891, steps lead to a path which gives access to the western end of Bieldside. Continuing on there is a further exit at bridge 1020, which leads into Golf Road, in the centre of Bieldside. Once under that bridge, the overgrown platforms of Bieldside Station (three miles from Culter) are passed, before the view opens out over the well kept greens of a nearby golf course. A seat is provided for anyone wishing to rest and watch the playing skills (or lack of) of the golfers.

A further half mile brings you past further overgrown platforms, this time the station was West Cults. The scenery is now definitely suburbia, the growth of wild flowers at the side of the railway is replaced by well kept municipal lawns. It is difficult at times to realise that this was a railway; only the multi-coloured graffiti on bridge abutments mars the otherwise attractive scene. Many large houses are passed. Originally they had their main entrances facing onto a path leading alongside the railway, today they have to use their rear entrances to let their cars out onto the busy A93.

The name Cults comes from the Gaelic word for wood. At one time this area was part of a royal hunting forest that was given to the city of Aberdeen by Robert the Bruce in 1319.

Cults is a large sprawl, alongside the main road, with several cafés and pubs along with parking spaces and toilets. Numerous accesses are provided on and off the nearby railway. Whilst walking the trackbed, look out for the remains of a nineteenth century chain suspension bridge that once crossed the River Dee. Known as the Shakkin Bridge, it was built in 1837 by a local minister, to allow his parishioners (on the north bank) to reach his kirk on the south bank, without having to use the river ferry. It was damaged by floods in 1920.

The former station buildings of Cults (three and three-quarter miles from Culter) have now become the premises of a local timber merchant. At the western end of the platform can be found a cast iron sign, indicating that a nearby footpath was for the use of pedestrians only. Dire punishments would be inflicted on any other user, by the owning railway company, the London and North Eastern Railway. Nowadays it acts as a memorial to an age which made sure its notices would last for a thousand years.

Continuing on for a short rural interlude before the urban growth of Aberdeen is reached. The next station is Pitfodels, four and a half miles from Culter. The buildings are now a private house, whilst steps give an exit onto a minor road from the A93 to Norwood. Once past the station, the way passes several large allotments before it runs alongside the Garthdee housing estate. The estate road, on the south side of the way, has a frequent bus service into Aberdeen.

Having passed under bridge 1007, an ornate arched girder bridge and the modern concrete bridge which takes South Anderson Road (Aberdeen's Western By-pass) over the railway, the remains of Ruthrieston Station are reached. By now housing is present on all sides, with some of the more unusual flowers being escapees from the tidyness of the domestic gardens. With the rapid growth of Aberdeen, the once spacious grounds of the nearby villas are now used to provide room for the modern flats and offices.

Shortly afterwards you will come to Holburn Street, where the bridge which carried the railway over this busy road has been removed. Steps take you down to this road, which has to be crossed with care. A further flight of steps allows you to rejoin the railway, on the overgrown platforms of Holburn Street Station (six miles from Culter). A further missing bridge has to be passed, by means of two flights of steps, before the final section of the walkway is reached. This passes the northern boundary of the Duthie Park, ending up by the park's main entrance in Polmuir Road.

Nearby there is a small car park, whilst the Park has large lawns, playgrounds, flower gardens, exotic plants and birds. There is a self-service licensed restaurant and toilets in the grounds along with an aquarium and Winter Gardens. If you want to walk into Aberdeen, having come down into the car park, turn away from the park into Polmuir Road, and pass between the abutments of the bridge which once took the railway over the road. At the end of Polmuir Road, turning left into Fonthill Road and right into Holborn Street, will bring you out at the top end of Union Street. By turning right into Ferryhill Place and left into South Crown Street, you will emerge in the middle of Union Street, near to the main railway and bus stations.

# Railways of the Moray Coast

The Banff, Portsoy and Strathisla was authorised by an Act of Parliament of 27th July 1857, to construct a railway from Grange to Banff, along with a branch from Tillynaught to Portsoy. The line had a maximum gradient of 1 in 70, apart from the short branch to Portsoy Harbour which descended for half a mile at 1 in 30 to the harbour. The line was opened on 30th July 1859. However, owing to a derailment only one train actually operated that day and the full opening took place 3 days later. The Portsoy harbour line was subject to special operating conditions. The safety points used to derail runaway wagons, were linked to the level crossing gates at the base of the incline. The coming of the railway saw a rapid decline in the fortunes of the harbour and the branch was abandoned circa 1890 and lifted in 1910. A similar fate befell the branch which served the harbour at Banff from the town station.

The BP&SR obtained permission to extend the railway to Port Gordon, but these plans were abandoned in 1867. They were revived in 1882 when a line from Portsoy to a junction with the Lossiemouth branch near Elgin, was authorised on July 1st. The first four miles, from Portsoy to Tochieneal was opened on 1st April 1884. The direct curve to

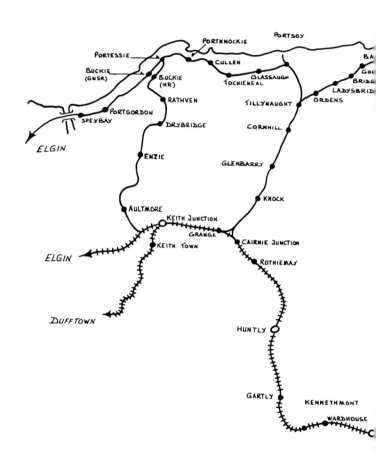

**RAILWAYS OF MORAYSHIRE & BANFFSHIRE**

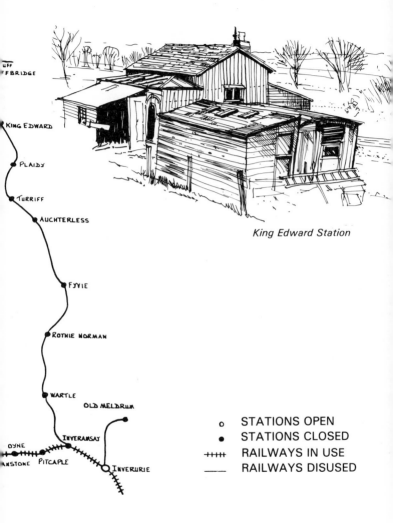

*King Edward Station*

UFF
FFBRIDGE

KING EDWARD

PLAIDY

TURRIFF

AUCHTERLESS

FYVIE

ROTHIE NORMAN

WARTLE

OLD MELDRUM

INVERAMSAY

OYNE

INSTONE   PITCAPLE

INVERURIE

o    STATIONS OPEN
●    STATIONS CLOSED
++++ RAILWAYS IN USE
___  RAILWAYS DISUSED

Cairnie Junction was opened on 1st May 1886, although it was authorised by an Act of Parliament on the 19th September 1887. By now these lines had formed part of the network of the Great North of Scotland Railway.

On the opposite bank of the River Deveron, shortly after the publication of the first prospectus of the GNofSR in 1845, plans were drawn up for a railway from Macduff to Turriff and Old Meldrum. These fell by the wayside due to the lack of support, however ten years later a railway was authorised from Inveramsay to Turriff. The GNofSR agreed to work the line, which adopted the new route due to the easier gradients at the expense of bypassing Old Meldrum. The maximum gradient being 1 in 80, at the summit of the line between Rothie Norman and Fyvie. On 5th September 1857, the first train ran into the station at Turriff. Meanwhile the Banff, Macduff and Turiff Extension railway was authorised to extend the iron way to the coast, on the 27th of July of the same year. The line avoided extensive engineering works, at the expense of a gradient of 1 in 66 to reach a terminus to the south of Macduff, a quarter of a mile south of the later Banff Bridge station.

Both of these lines were subsiduaries of the GNofSR, which absorbed them in 1860. After a few abortive attempts, the extension was on the hillside, overlooking the town, rather than at the harbour as was originally intended. With the opening of the extension and the intermediate station of Banff Bridge, the original terminus was closed and the buildings demolished. Although both routes survived the Second World War, the widespread closures of the fifties and sixties took their toll on both lines. The first casualty was the withdrawal of the passenger service from Inveramsay to Macduff, which closed on 1st October 1951.

The freight service was cut back, from Macduff to Turriff on 1st August 1961. The final goods service from Inveramsay to Turriff was withdrawn during January 1966. Meanwhile the passenger service from Tillynaught to Banff was withdrawn on 6th July 1964. The goods service was withdrawn the same day as the total closure of the coastal line from Elgin to Cairnie Junction via Buckie, on 6th May 1968.

However in 1984, after many years when only the ghosts of the railways were heard on the Banffshire Coast, the sight of a working railway returned to Banff. The route of the railway was used in part for the construction of a narrow gauge (15 inch) tourist railway, running from Banff to Swordanes for a distance of one and a quarter miles. Lack of publicity and customers, saw this line cease to operate at the end of the 1985 season.

*Mileages*

| | | |
|---|---|---:|
| CAIRNIE | Junction | 0.00 miles |
| GRANGE | North Junct | 0.50 miles |
| | GRANGE North Junct | 0.00 miles |
| | GRANGE Station | 0.75 miles |
| KNOCK | | 3.25 miles |
| GLENBARRY | | 4.50 miles |
| CORNHILL | | 7.50 miles |
| TILLYNAUGHT | | 10.00 miles |
| | TILLYNAUGHT | 0.00 miles |
| | ORDENS | 1.50 miles |
| | LADYSBRIDGE | 3.50 miles |
| | GOLF CLUB HOUSE | 5.25 miles |
| | BANFF | 6.00 miles |
| PORTSOY | Station | 12.75 miles |
| | PORTSOY Station | 0.00 miles |
| | PORTSOY Harbour | 0.50 miles |
| GLASSHAUGH | | 14.75 miles |
| TOCHIENEAL | | 17.00 miles |
| CULLEN | | 18.25 miles |
| PORTKNOCKIE | | 20.25 miles |
| FINDOCHTY | | 21.50 miles |
| PORTESSIE | | 23.00 miles |
| BUCKIE | | 24.25 miles |
| BUCKPOOL | | 25.25 miles |
| PORTGORDON | | 26.75 miles |
| SPEY BAY | | 29.00 miles |
| GARMOUTH | | 30.25 miles |
| URQUHART | | 33.50 miles |
| COLCOTS | | 36.00 miles |
| LOSSIE | Junction | 38.00 miles |
| ELGIN | | 39.00 miles |
| | | |
| MACDUFF | | 0.00 miles |
| BANFF BRIDGE | | 0.25 miles |
| KING EDWARD | | 5.00 miles |
| PLAIDY | | 7.25 miles |
| TURRIFF | | 11.75 miles |
| AUCHTERLESS | | 15.75 miles |
| FYVIE | | 19.00 miles |
| ROTHIE NORMAN | | 22.25 miles |
| WARTLE | | 26.00 miles |
| INVERAMSAY | | 29.75 miles |

*Ordnance Survey 1:50,000 map number:– 29*

*Public Transport*

Banff and Macduff are served by a regular bus service that operates between Aberdeen and Elgin, passing near to many of the stations from Turriff to Macduff and Banff to Buckie. Inveramsay is served by a limited bus service to Aberdeen. The frequency of all these services is severely reduced on a Sunday or local public holiday.

## V/2a: Banff to Portgordon

**Banff station**, with its fine example of a GNofSR overall roof, was demolished in the early 1980s. Today only a single platform remains to remind one of its location. Beyond the platform, stands a small wooden hut, which forms the Banff terminal of the West Buchan Railway. Opened in 1984, this 15 inch gauge line uses part of the trackbed of the original Banff, Portsay and Strathisla Company's route from Banff to Grange. The track originally was used at Fleetwood, moving north to Port Erroll (near Peterhead) before ending up at Banff. This line had to replace a couple of small underbridges in the section from Banff to Banff Springs, where it veers away from the original alignment to adopt a lower level route to the terminus at Swordanes.

Near to Banff Springs station, where there is a passing loop on the narrow gauge line, can be found the remains of the stone abutments of an underbridge of the original route. Beyond this bridge, the trackbed heads through the fields as a low grassy embankment. Before reaching the site of **Bridgefoot Station**, the walker passes a distillery that once had a small siding and loading platform for railborne traffic. The trackbed crosses a rather attractive small stone viaduct of the Burn of Boyndie before the dismantled bridge over the B-road to Whitehills forces the first detour of the day. The trackbed can be followed as it heads towards the A98, although in places the gorse makes for painful progress, especially to the brave souls attempting the walk clad in shorts. The bridge over the main road has been removed and road realignment works have taken in part of the trackbed, forcing a roadside detour to the B-road to Tipperty, where the railway can be regained.

Where the railway crosses the B-road, is the site of **Ladysbridge** station. The wooden-sided passenger and goods platforms stand complete with the remains of several lamp standards, that once illuminated the station for late night travellers. Nearby can be found the remains of milepost 61½ amidst the painful profusion of gorse, broom and brambles. Heading towards Tillynaught, the trackbed is crossed by the access road to the Mill of Blairshinnoch farm, where rails may be found in the roadway, still watched over by the pillars which once supported the original crossing gates. Beyond the crossing, the trackbed widens to provide space for a siding for traffic to or from the nearby farms, before it continues its straight course parallel to the Burn of Boyndie.

Although progress at times is hampered by the ever-present gorse and broom, generally it is a very pleasant walk rewarded by the sighting of several more mileposts. With the burn separating the railway from the road, it has become a haven of peace and safety for the local wildlife. Roe deer may be sighted running ahead of the walker, whilst the chorus of birdsong soothes the ear savaged by the roar of passing traffic. Wild flowers also grow in abundance on the trackbed, including many clumps of wild pansy, adding a touch of purple to the dominant greens and yellows. Eventually the burn and the railway part company as the latter heads towards the next station of Ordens. A bridge has been removed over an access lane before the station, but its absence is not too great a problem.

**Ordens** was one of the original halts of the railway, and its open wooden shelter still remains in situ on its small platform. Inside the shelter may be found traces of the faded paintwork depicting the halt's name to any traveller wanting to use its facilities. The trackbed near the halt is very overgrown and a detour via the nearby fields may be required to allow progress to be made. Although the overbridge which took the A98 over the railway by Ordens remains in situ, the next bridge under the B9025 has been removed. Beyond this the undergrowth becomes very dense – a horrendous tangle of gorse forces detours which cumulate with the missing bridge over the Burn of Boyne. From its forlorn abutments, one can view the remains of Tillynaught Junction, before following the burn's eastern bank to reach the nearby road bridge over the burn.

**Tillynaught Junction** was typical of the many railway junctions in the middle of nowhere. Although the station had road access, the railway had to provide considerable accommodation for the workers. A large block of flats, now abandoned, was provided for the ordinary workers. The station master had accommodation befitting his rank, provided on the station platform. The original buildings have been demolished, leaving only their floor plans on the overgrown platform. The main line heading south may be observed, before the walker heads north to follow the route towards Portsoy. The trackbed is used as an access road, providing good walking conditions after the earlier trial by gorse. A crossing keeper's house, now empty, stands beside the crossing of the access lane to Baley Farm. This farm has apparently abandoned the traditional agricultural crops and grows instead an intensive crop of coniferous trees.

Before entering Roughilly Wood, the walker passes beneath an overbridge carrying the minor road from Smiddyboyne over the railway. The bridge, still carrying its original number of 890, is unusual in having wooden palisade sides to the roadway, instead of the more usual stone parapets. The section through the woods is a tranquil path passing through an assortment of larch, spruce and scots pine. Partridges may be observed, whilst the glimpses of Portsoy church act as a beacon indicating the end of the day's walk. Coming out of the woods, the line passes beneath the B9022 amidst banks of primulas and daffodils in the right season. There is a clear path to the outskirts of Portsoy, although the bridge taking the railway over the Burn of Durn, near to the station, has been removed.

The absence of the bridge is not too great a problem, although one's companions may be worried to see one regaining the trackbed via the entrance path to the town's Roman Catholic kirk. A gate leads one away from the buildings into the nearby park, which was once the site of **Portsoy Station**. The original station buildings remain at the eastern edge of the park, a typical GN of SR station, with its timber overall roof. The station now is used as a grain warehouse, whilst the outbuildings are used by a wholesale food firm. The nearby goods buildings are used by a haulage firm. When the railway was extended towards Buckie, a new wooden station building was provided for the town. The new station was converted in the 1970s to provide accommodation for the local scouts. The buildings have been tastefully converted, although several windows have had their lower sections filled in to increase the security of the building.

Heading down past the eastern edge of the original station, can be found the trackbed of the harbour branch. This line, which closed before the turn of the century, has been converted into an official walkway, which still gives an impression of its rapid descent towards the harbour. The first overbridge still has a faded British Transport Commission notice that proclaims dire warnings to any person found dumping rubbish on the railway. The footpath is well used by the local population, who may cast back a puzzled glance at the antics of the railway photographer taking pictures of the former railway. The branch passes under two more bridges before it levels out near to a former warehouse which has been converted into flats. Beyond this, road alterations have removed any traces of the railway, if it indeed ever went any further to the now empty harbour.

Portsoy has several cafés and pubs which provide the walker with refreshment before either catching a bus back to Banff or looking for accommodation in the town for the night.

The landscaping of the site of **Portsoy (New) Station** to provide an attractive park and lake, continues in an easterly direction, until it reaches the town's bowling green. The adjacent club house has been built on the trackbed, blocking access through the bridge which carried the road to Durn House, over the railway. Fortunately the detour is relatively easy, passing through the entrance gate for the bowling green and then taking the path through a field growing a rich crop of horse jumps, regaining the trackbed beyond a gorse and bramble infested cutting. The intrepid explorer soon negotiates a missing underbridge, before reaching a small forest which once was adjacent to the railway. Unfortunately this forest is rapidly seeding itself onto the trackbed, which passed alongside on an embankment. One is forced to walk along the sloping side of the embankment, navigating round trees and brambles, until sanity returns as the line passes underneath the two bridges carrying the minor roads to Fordyce over the railway.

Nearing Glasshaugh Station, another bridge has been removed, this time over the Burn of Fordyce. Fortunately the airborne skills of the walker should allow the gap to be jumped, albeit with the ever present fear of an early watery landing. Very little remains of **Glasshaugh Station**, apart from the grass covered platform.

The trackbed maintains a very straight course, passing through very marginal agricultural land, most scrub with the occasional cultivated fields. The railway has become a haven for wild flowers and grasses, with a few clumps of gorse the only obstruction. Unfortunately the heavy pollen laden atmosphere may cause problems for the sufferers from hay fever. Walking through this forgotten nature reserve, with only the faint tracks of other walkers and marksmen as a guide, one can fall into a trance, broken only by the realisation that the trackbed has suddenly become much wider, marking the grass covered site of **Tochineal Station**. The platform remains, being slowly buried in a large compost/refuse heap, alongside the grass covered expanse of the former goods yard. An adjacent house may have once been the palatial accommodation for the station master.

Landscaping and road alterations have eradicated almost all traces of the railway, beyond the station site. A detour via a track, presumably the original access to the station's goods yard, brings the walker out at the realigned A98. This can be followed for a short distance in the direction of Cullen, until a pair of gates are reached, giving access to the original route of the A98, west of the bridge which carried it over the railway. The stone parapets of this bridge still retain their black and white markings, warning phantom motorists along the abandoned road about the presence of the equally abandoned railway below.

The nearby woods allow access back onto the trackbed, permitting the bridge to be viewed from the leaf covered trackbed. The girders proclaim that they were the product of the James Abernethy Engineering Works, in Aberdeen. The trackbed now heads away from public roads, through several rock-sided cuttings, on the slopes of Crannoch Hill. The way comes to an abrupt end in a waterlogged overgrown cutting, that passes Seafield Farm. One is forced to make a detour through the adjacent fields, to reach the safety of the access lane from the farm to Logie House.

**Cullen Station** has been eradicated by landscaping, and the site is now a housing estate, leaving virtually no trace of the former station. Fortunately the viaducts and embankments, which carried the railway above the town, remain intact, though the viaducts are mostly fenced off. Perhaps some day the route will be reopened for pedestrian traffic, allowing walkers to pass above the infernal roar and fumes of the internal combustion engine in the narrow roads below. The walker can follow the road to the Cullen Bay Hotel, or scramble up the steep embankment, at the end of the easternmost viaduct, alongside the municipal car park. The trackbed is overgrown, with a dense growth of brambles and gorse, interspersed with nettle and rose bay willow herb. However, a path can be found through this overgrowth, as the trackbed passes above the greens of the Cullen Golf Course. Passing the Cullen Bay Hotel, the route becomes an official footpath, that stretches through to the eastern outskirts of Portknockie.

Continuing on, the remains of **Portknockie Station** are reached. The grass-covered remains of the twin platforms are still watched over by the loading gauge and the base of the water column. Passing underneath A942, the trackbed continues as a good path for a short distance, until it reaches a farm alongside the cemetery at Tronach Head.

The walker is faced with an impenetrable bank of gorse, forcing a detour onto the adjacent coastal path or to the main road, to reach the village of Findochty (pronounced Finecktea). The landscape improvement artists have had a field day with **Findochty Station**, leaving only the former station fencing and a converted station house, to mark its former site. Everything else has been landscaped away, and the site used for a small brick building, that is possibly either a water pumping station or a TV reception station for a communal aerial system.

Across the A942, the trackbed has been merged into an unwanted wasteland, which soon becomes impenetrable, where the main road turns away towards the coastline. The road should then be followed, regaining the trackbed where it passes over the access road to Findochty Castle, although the bridge which carried the railway over the access lane has been removed. Alternatively, one can continue along the main road, turning up the minor road to the Moor of Scotstown, regaining the trackbed east of the site of **Portessie Station**. This station was originally a junction, for the Highland Railway line to Buckie and Keith, which closed during the First World War, although there was a freight service to Buckie for some years. This line was built to tap the fish traffic from the Banffshire ports, a dream which never became a reality. The station had an island platform that served the HR and one of the two GNofSR tracks, whilst a separate platform was provided for the other GNofSR track. These platforms remain, alongside the stone base of a water tower, marking the actual junction of the two lines. The intervening trackbed though very waterlogged, is a haven for wildlife including the spotted orchid.

Beyond the station site, the road to Rathven is carried over the two lines, by a girder bridge over the GNofSR line and a stone bridge over the HR line. The two lines then gradually part company, the HR soon merging into the modern buildings of the Buckie Industrial Estate. However the GNofSR line has suffered a better fate, for it has been turned into an official walkway, complete with lamps, ending at the landscaped and built-over site of **Buckie Station**. Factory buildings and landscaping have cleared all traces of the station, leaving an ugly scar in its place. Only the steps down to the station, from the High Street, have

*Half a footbridge near Buckpool*

survived the attention of the planners. Walking along the harbour road is quite a pleasurable experience, the port still has a large fishing fleet, and maintains a traditional fishy aroma.

Passing through the town, very little of the trackbed is walkable, due either to lack of access, or an over abundance of vegetation. One unofficial section that can be walked, is the viaduct section over the Burn of Buckie. Beyond this, a further road walk, brings one to a short walkable section, ending up at the site of **Buckpool Station**. Again, this has been converted into a housing estate, although the western ends of the former platforms emerge from the rubble-strewn edges of the housing development.

A good path then uses the trackbed, becoming an official walkway when the trackbed crosses over a small burn, midway to Portgordon. A turf-roofed house is passed on the outskirts of Portgordon, which is a very elongated village, sprawling along the tarmacadamed expanse of the A990. The site of **Portgordon Station** has been converted into a park and bowling green, leaving little trace of the former station. Portgordon is the last point served by the regular bus service from Elgin to Aberdeen, along the coast. It has two pubs as well as bed and breakfast establishments. The village sees very few tourists, and the walker is sure of a friendly reception in the village's drinking establishments.

Musing over a drink in a village which they say has more than its share of village characters, one's thoughts go back to the forgotten railway from Portsoy. Possibly the planned eventual conversion of it into a long distance footpath, will bring some benefit to these quiet fishing ports, or perhaps the influx would spoil the tranquility and friendliness.

## V/2b:  Macduff to Turriff

Unlike nearby Banff, **Macduff** station has retained its original GNofSR stone built buildings, complete with the timber overall roof. Now forming part of an industrial firm's premises, the station buildings and nearby locomotive shed are externally in a very good state of preservation. The trackbed beyond the station site, towards Banff Bridge, is relatively clear of any obstacles apart from the occasional gorse bush. **Banff Bridge Station** now is a private house, externally in a good state of preservation. A detour around the station is needed, accompanied by a chorus of barking dogs, to regain the trackbed to the south of the station. The trackbed can be followed for about half a mile, passing the site of the original terminus of the line, to where an underbridge once stood, leaving only a narrow (water?) pipe spanning the gap between the abutments.

Although the trackbed can be followed in places, houses and other obstacles require several roadside detours. A short stretch from the outskirts of the town, to the B9026 can be walked, possibly accompanied by the horses which are grazed on the trackbed. Beyond this bridge, the trackbed passes through a caravan site and several landscaped fields. A further roadside detour is required, until the minor road from Doune Park to Whitestones is reached. From this overbridge, to the Wood of Balchers, the trackbed runs parallel to the nearby road. Fortunately this has not yet been "found" by the dreaded highway planners in their relentless search for disused lines that can be converted into roads. The trackbed is reasonably walkable, the long grass supporting a variety of wildlife which runs for cover having felt the shock waves from the oncoming walker. Weasels, rabbits, partridges and pheasants are some of the creatures that may be observed.

Nearing Balchers the grass growing on the trackbed is cropped by the local farmer, leaving a lush lawn for the walker. Passing the southern edge of the nearby wood, the trackbed enters a cutting as it curves away from the road. Unfortunately the cutting is filled in and a detour via the nearby road is necessary, to observe the remains of the wooden buildings of **King Edward Station**.

The original buildings remain in situ, supporting a barnacle growth of sundry lean-to sheds. Land reclamation beyond the station has removed many traces of the trackbed, enforcing a detour via Croft of Danshillock to regain the railway near the empty buildings of Bridgend. The main reason for following the lane, which at times looks more like a river than a lane, is to view the single-span stone bridge over the Burn of Fishrie. Unfortunately the detour is not over, as one has to head past the buildings to cross over the burn, then follow its overgrown southern banks to regain the trackbed to the south of the bridge. However, the bridge is very impressive, spanning the burn in a single majestic sweep from two high embankments. The trackbed should be left where it crosses over the minor road from Strocherie (bridge removed) for beyond this point it is decidedly unpleasant with the horrible combination of waterlogged cuttings and missing bridges.

**Plaidy Station** is now occupied by a small plantation of fir trees, although some cottages remain nearby. Presumably the buildings were built by the railway company to accommodate the station staff. Beyond the station, the trackbed passes beneath the main road, to become a very good path as it heads past the Bogs of Plaidy. Having endured the trials and tribulations of the section from Macduff, the well-used track comes as a thankful reward. An inquisitive horse will follow the walker, acting as a guide through these open spaces, or perhaps as an escort off the premises. Only where the railway passed over the minor road from Luncarty, is there any real growth of gorse and broom on the otherwise clear trackbed. The bridge abutments provide shelter for a welcome stop, before embarking on the final miles towards Turriff.

The trackbed makes a gentle curve to head south past Tillyfar, running on the eastern slopes of the valley of the River Deveron. Good views over the valley are obtained, before the railway crosses a high earthen embankment at Knockiemill. The railway emerges at the B9025 on the outskirts of Turriff, where the town's sewerage works are located. Road alterations in this vicinity are gradually removing many traces of the railway, although it can be followed to the dismantled viaduct over the Idoch Water. The piers remain upstanding, pointing skywards in the hope that their girders will fall back out of the sky. On the opposite side of the water, the railway passes through a golf course, where sections of its embankment have been removed to extend and improve the course.

**Turriff** station now forms the municipal camping and caravan site. The remains of a goods platform and nearby house/office remain as a reminder of the former busy station. A crane base waits silently for the day when it is reused to load agricultural goods into waiting railway wagons. Beyond the platform stands the large warehouse once used by the Banff & Buchan Millers, with traces of a loading platform on its railway side. Sadly the building no longer handles grain traffic, it now forms the base for another haulage contractor. Turriff town beckons the walker to explore it in the hope of finding a café or pub to reminisce on the day's walk, before heading homewards.

# The Speyside Way

*Time*

Two versions of this walk are included, the first section to Aberlour should be completed in three hours, the longer section will take seven hours to complete, including a lunch stop.

Being essentially a linear walk, the easiest way to effect a return is by using the bus service that operates from Aberlour to Dufftown (moderately frequent except on Sundays) or to Grantown (a few buses per day with no Sunday service).

### Start and Finish
The former station at Dufftown lies ¾ml to the north of the town, beyond the entrance to the Glenfiddich distillery. Aberlour station is in the Alice Littler park, with an entrance off the town's square. Ballindalloch lies at the end of the B9137, approximately one mile from the Dalnashaugh Inn.

### OS Map: 28 (Elgin)
The walk follows the valleys of the Rivers Fiddich and Spey, forming an interesting walk through mixed agricultural land, interspersed by many distilleries to help raise any flagging spirits. The former railway line has been converted into an official footpath, generally providing firm and dry conditions underfoot.

## V/3:   Dufftown to Ballindalloch
Dufftown is located at the junction of roads from the towns of the Morayshire plain as well as two roads over the Grampian mountains to Tomintoul and Rhynie. The town has several cafés and hotels, toilets and ample car parking facilities. The walk starts beyond the former station site, now a Community Projects Agency workshop. There is a small car park and picnic place at the start of the walk, as well as an information board depicting the route. Leave the car park and head north towards the buildings of the Convalmore Distillery. The track is a sanded path on the ballast chippings of the original railway.

Having passed the modern and more traditional buildings of the distillery behind, the walk enters a mixed woodland that runs along the banks of the Fiddich. Shortly after entering the wood, a set of steps lead down from the trackbed, to allow the inspection of a culvert passing underneath the railway. Gradually the woods are left behind, as the trackbed crosses over the River Fiddich on a curving bridge resting on a series of stone pillars. The sand covering on top of the original stone ballast stops for about a mile, leaving the original ballast in situ, which needs to be walked with care to prevent accidental damage to one's feet and ankles.

The route passes through a series of rock cuttings, as it follows the course of the Fiddich to reach the derelict buildings at Birchdean. The remains are worthy of an inspection, revealing a derelict water wheel in what appears to be traditional distillery buildings. Beyond Birchdean the route crosses the Fiddich, to reach the site of Craigellachie station.

The former station (four miles from Dufftown) has been converted into an attractive park, with ample parking and toilet facilities. Benches and tables are provided for those wishing to have a picnic, whilst the nearby village has a café and hotel. The route passes an imitation signal

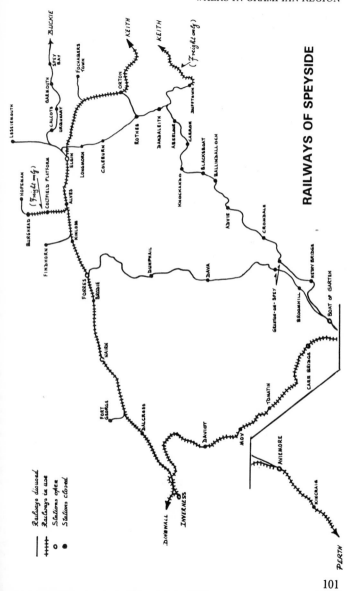

RAILWAYS OF SPEYSIDE

box, built out of logs in the former turntable pit, curving gradually westwards to pass underneath the leftmost of a pair of bridges, to follow the Spey valley towards Aberlour. It is now a firm earthen track, which is generally dry underfoot. Once past the typically Victorian buildings of the Craigellachie Hotel, head underneath the new road from Craigellachie to Aberlour, by means of a corrugated iron subway. Emerging from its curvaceous interior, one can look back along the line of the road to view the original bridge over the Spey built by Thomas Telford.

The railway is regained where it enters a short tunnel, emerging onto a shelf above the Spey, where a large brick-built retaining wall separates the track from the road above. Wooden benches are provided at regular intervals along the way, allowing one to rest and admire the view. By the junction of the A95 with a minor road signposted to the Bluehill Quarry, an access point with limited parking space has been provided. A mile further on lies the small town of Aberlour (two and a quarter miles from Craigellachie), where the path passes by the side of the former goods yard with its mountains of coal, to emerge in the well kept lawns of the Alice Littler Park. The former station buildings have been converted into a tea room run by the local community association. Aberlour (originally known as Charlestown) was built in 1812 by Charles Grant of Wester Elchies as a planned town for the estate workers.

Those wishing to end their walk at Aberlour, may walk into the nearby town where the bus service back to Dufftown departs from the Square, opposite the Lour Hotel. Alternatively, one could return back to Dufftown along the railway, making for a round trip of some 13 miles (allow about 5–6 hours). The town has several hotels, cafés and shops. Toilet facilities are provided at the rear of the station building, whilst there are ample car parking facilities.

To continue to Ballindalloch, go under the bridge at the end of the station and pass the nearby car park. Cross the Burn of Aberlour by means of a modern timber suspension bridge, built on the abutments of the original bridge. Walking towards Carron, you will pass several mileposts and a faded "Stop, Look and Listen" notice that are artefacts of the railway age. The route is generally a grassy track, occasionally wet underfoot. Nearing the minor road from Carron to the A95, the trackbed is used as an access road for a nearby works. Where the track turns to head for the nearby road, continue straight on past the overgrown platform and the white painted sign of Dailuaine platform. A short distance further on, a branch which served a nearby distillery passes underneath the minor road and joins the railway.

Nearing Carron (three and a quarter miles from Aberlour), leave the railway and join the minor road, in order to cross over the River Spey. This single-arched span once carried both the road and the railway, but one soon realises why the path uses the road and not the railway side. Once over the river, a "Speyside Way" signpost directs you back onto the railway, in a wandering path through the grounds of the Imperia

102

Distillery.

However, if you miss the signpost there is no real problem as the walk can be rejoined by turning left into the road leading to the distillery, opposite the village public house. There are limited parking facilities in the village, along with a pub and telephone kiosk. The small single storeyed stone building, to the left of the entrance to the distillery, was once Carron station. Turning right by this entrance, the path is a grassy embankment passing between the distillery and a nearby lane leading to Dalmunach. At the edge of the well kept grounds, continue straight on through a gate (with low stile) onto a grassy track that is again signposted as the Speyside Way.

Passing Dalmunach, there are traces of a wooden platform on the northern side of the trackbed. A short distance further on, another bridge is crossed, over the Ballintomb burn that was reconstructed by the army (as indicated in the concrete capping of the bridge ends). The walk is very pleasant, a mixture of woodland and pasture, with a great profusion of wild flowers that support an assortment of butterflies and small mammals.

The next access point is at the former station of Knockando (two and a half miles from Carron), that has been converted into a visitor centre for the nearby Tamdhu Distillery. The station has been renamed "Tamdhu" and retains its original wooden buildings and signal box. There is car parking nearby and toilet facilities when the distillery is open to visitors. The distillery is reached by means of a minor road from the B9102, which follows the northern bank of the River Spey. Once past the station, continue along the entrance road to the distillery and its various

*Milepost 71, in the undergrowth*

*Blacksboat Station*

buildings (by means of a dirt track used by lorries to reach a nearby loading apparatus) to rejoin the grassy track of the railway.

The Allt Arder is crossed on wooden duck boards, laid on top of the original stone built railway bridge. A small platform in the middle of the bridge allows one to rest and take in the view. The route then passes alongside a lengthy wood emerging at the site of Blacksboat Station (two and a quarter miles from Knockando). There is a limited amount of car parking at the station which is reached by turning off the B9138, which links the A95 and B9102.

Having perhaps paused to view the well restored station building and the nearby goods shed, you embark on the final section of just over two miles to Ballindalloch. Many mileposts are passed as the grassy track heads over another suspension bridge, this time over the Allt Gheallaidh. Once you have passed the lonely cottage of Dalnapot, you will obtain a first sighting of the lattice girder bridge, that crosses the Spey. This bridge still proclaims it was built in Dundee by the firm of C. McFarlane.

Across the bridge, the track curves gently westwards to the single storeyed stone-built building, passing alongside the once extensive sidings for goods and cattle. The station buildings are now an outdoor pursuits centre and mark the end of the walk. There is a limited amount of car parking space nearby, whilst those requiring public transport should walk up the B9137 (turning left at the roadside by the station, passing the many derelict cattle pens on the right hand side) to reach the A95 after approx half a mile. At the A95 turn left to reach the Bridge of Avon (where there is a well stocked shop) or Dalnashaugh Inn which is a quarter of a mile further on.

104

# VI:
# WALKS IN
# HIGHLAND REGION

## Forres to Boat-of-Garten

In 1845, the Scottish Midland Junction Railway, which became part of the Caledonian Railway, promoted a branch north from Perth to Dunkeld. By mutual consent with other interested bodies, the proposal was altered to a direct line from Perth to Inverness. With the failure of this scheme, the SMJR reinstated its original bill. Although it was passed, construction never started and the scheme lapsed. On July 10th 1854, an independent company, the Perth & Dunkeld Railway, obtained an act for a line 8.25 miles long from Stanley Junction to Birnam near Dunkeld, which was opened on April 7th 1856.

By 1860, agitation was renewed for a railway from Inverness to the south. A route was proposed leaving the Inverness & Aberdeen Junction Railway at Forres. It headed south, rising steeply to cross the hills separating the Findhorn and Spey Valleys, reaching a summit of 1,052 feet on the bleak Dava Moor. The line then followed the River Spey to reach Kingussie, where another steep climb took the line over the Grampian Mountains at the head of the Druimuachdar Pass, 1,484 feet above sea level. The railway then descended to Blair Atholl and the Pass of Killiecrankie. Having crossed the River Tay near Dalguise, the line reached Dunkeld where it made an end on junction with the P&DR.

The act was passed on July 22nd 1861, despite determined opposition. Under the act, the company adopted the title of the Inverness & Perth Junction Railway, amalgamating with the Perth & Dunkeld Railway on 28th February 1864. On 17th October 1861 the first sod was cut, progress being so rapid that the 13 miles from Dunkeld to Pitlochry opened on 1st June 1863. By August 3rd, the 36 miles from Forres to Aviemore were opened, with the final section over the Grampians being completed on September 9th. Although the construction was rapid, not all the stations were ready by the opening date. Accommodation was not provided at Dava until 1864, Killiecrankie and Dalnaspidal following in 1865.

On July 27th 1857, an independent company obtained an act for a railway from Keith to Dufftown, the Great North of Scotland Railway contributing to its costs and arranged to work the railway, which opened on 12th February 1862. The line was extended to Nethy Bridge (opened on 5th July 1865) and joined with the I&PJR at Boat-of-Garten on August 1st 1866. By now the I&PJR was part of the Highland Railway, amalgamating with other railways based on Inverness on 29th June 1865. Although the route from Inverness to the south was established, the Highland Railway was forced to open a shortened route from Inverness to Aviemore.

Leaving Inverness, the route was a severe climb, with several miles at 1 in 60, reaching a summit of 1,315 feet at Slochd Crossing, 22 miles south of Inverness. From this point the railway descended on equally severe gradients, to rejoin the original route at Aviemore. With the opening of the new route, which reduced the mileage from Perth to Inverness from 144 miles to 118 miles, on November 1st 1898, the original route became a secondary main line. Although most services were routed via the 1898 line, some trains continued to serve the original route.

The railway system in the area remained fairly intact until after the nationalisation of the railways in 1948. Passenger services were withdrawn on the GNSR line to Boat-of-Garten on 18th October 1965 although the line remained open to freight until 1968. Shortly after its centenary, the line from Forres to Aviemore was closed to all services on 18th October 1965. The section from Boat-of-Garten to Aviemore remained in use for the freight services to the GNSR until their subsequent withdrawal 3 years later. Out of the ashes, a preservation scheme was formed with the aim of reopening the line from Grantown-on-Spey to Aviemore. Currently services are provided from Aviemore to Boat-of-Garten, operated by a variety of industrial and ex-BR steam locomotives. Hopefully some day these will be extended along the Spey valley to Grantown, the cry of the Osprey being echoed by the whistle of a steam locomotive.

*Mileages*

| | |
|---|---|
| FORRES | 0.00 miles |
| RAFFORD | 1.75 miles |
| DUNPHAIL | 8.50 miles |
| DAVA | 14.75 miles |
| DAVA Summit | 17.75 miles |
| GRANTOWN on SPEY | 23.25 miles |
| BROOMHILL | 26.75 miles |
| BOAT-of-GARTEN | 30.75 miles |
| AVIEMORE | 36.00 miles |

*Ordnance Survey 1:50,000 map numbers:– 27, 36*

*Public Transport*

Forres is served by both rail and bus services to Inverness and Aberdeen. Apart from the occasional bus to Rafford and Dunphail, and post-bus to Dava, there is very little public transport between Forres and Grantown on Spey. Grantown is served by several buses a day to Aviemore on Mondays to Saturdays, although there is no Sunday service. Boat-of-Garten has also a Sundays-excepted bus service to Aviemore, as well as the summer only rail service operated by the Strathspey Railway Company. Details of most of the available services within this area are given in the public transport timetable issued by the Highlands and Islands Development Board.

## VI/1: Forres to Boat-of-Garten

With the opening of the I&PJR, a new station was required at Forres. A double junction was provided with the existing line from Inverness to Keith, so that trains could be run in each direction without reversing. To the south of the original station, a new triangular shaped station was provided to give trains in each direction platform accommodation with a new line being provided for the trains from Inverness to Keith, the original route became an auxiliary loop for goods and light engines, whilst the old station building became the station master's residence.

Since the closure of the Dava route and the rundown of the freight traffic, the layout at **Forres** has been greatly simplified. The station buildings were rebuilt in the 1950s, and stand beside the sole rail-served platform, on the north side of the triangle. A passing loop is provided where this line regains the original line, to the east of the station. The signal box which controls access to the goods lines rests on the site of the original station.

A walker detraining at Forres is greeted by a very faded ordnance survey one inch map which still depicts the Dava Route, and a notice proclaiming not all services shown on the map still operate. A glance westwards immediately confirms this, the trackbed that formed the west side of the triangle having been converted into a dense jungle of gorse. Whilst the platforms remain they are slowly being reclaimed by the verdant growth of gorse. On the eastern side of the triangle the situation is even worse, only the battered white gates of a level crossing betray the former passage of the railway. Nearby stands a stone suite of buildings that were probably a goods shed and possibly a horse driven "gingan". Walking southwards along the western side platform, a path leads the intrepid explorer onto the main Inverness to Aberdeen road.

Across the busy highway, the trackbed disappears into several modern housing developments. By following various estate roads, the Forres to Grantown A940 road is crossed, and the safety of the minor road leading to the Manachy Distillery is reached. After a short time, the hallowed ballast of the abandoned railway is reached, by a bridge which takes the lane leading to Sanquhar House over the railway. Once onto the trackbed, the dedicated walker can head back towards Forres to ensure as much of the trackbed is walked as possible. With housing nearby, the sad accumulation of domestic rubbish on this section of the trackbed is an unfortunate fact of railway walking.

Heading south, the trackbed, which initially is double tracked width, skirts the final houses of Forres, before it enters the first wooded section. To the south the hills which act as a watershed between the Findhorn and Spey valleys are clearly defined on the horizon. Their undulating slopes being covered in a dark green carpet of coniferous woodland, to a far greater extent than depicted on the relevant OS maps. The trackbed, since it once formed a main line, still retains most of its stone ballast. The stones form an unyielding surface and the crunching sound will accompany the walker as each stride towards Boat-of-Garten is made.

By now onto single track, the first landmarks that are passed are the well kept whitewashed buildings and lush green lawns that form the Manachy Distillery. In this vicinity once was located the Dallas Dhu Siding, which presumably served for railborne traffic to and from the distillery. Sadly very little trace remains of the siding; not even an unwanted piece of point rodding has survived the careful dismantling of the railway. By now the walker will have little faith in the cartographic abilities of the OS as the promise of open country turns out to be even more uncharted coniferous forest. On a hot summer's day, the lack of wind and the pleasures of the highland midge are a great cause for a considerable degree of soul searching.

Continuing on, the railway crosses over the river that passes through Forres before emerging into Findhorn Bay. Although it looks impressive on the map, it is very difficult to spot it in reality. Only where the trackbed opens out at Rafford Station does the rambler give up in disgust this piece of river spotting. The I&PJR provided a complete station where the minor road from the village of Rafford passed underneath the railway. However, the traffic did not come up to expectations and the Highland Railway closed **Rafford Station** to all traffic on May 31st 1865.

The station site provides a welcome opening in the forest; it is now used as a base for the timber extraction operations. Continuing on towards Dava, the trackbed curves gently south westwards on an embankment to reach the Newtyle Woods. The trackbed is used by the occasional wheeled vehicle which prevents its being reclaimed by the encroaching woodland. Two miles on into the woodland, the railway passes underneath a very ornate underbridge. The bridge carries an access road to Altyre House over the railway and the infamous Forres River, being built in the Victorian "mock castle" style. It is complete with battlements and semi-circular towers; the arrow slits being provided to allow the laird to ambush the passing trains.

Continuing southwards, the next major obstacle is a missing bridge over the Forres River in the darkest depths of the Altyre Woods.

However, careful penetration of the nearby forest reveals a safe crossing point upstream of the bridge abutments. Across the river, the trackbed has recently been cleared for use as a forestry access road, all the way to where the minor road to Tomnarnoon once passed beneath the railway. Unfortunately road alignments have not only removed the original bridge but also large sections of the surrounding embankments. Standing amidst all this dereliction are the remains of one of the stone abutments of the bridge; a monolith recording man's "technological development". Leaving this scene behind, the peace and tranquillity of the forest returns, for the final leg of the walk towards **Dunphail Station**.

The provision of accommodation at this location comes as a surprise, since only a few scattered houses and a nearby stately home comprise the settlement. Whilst the station buildings have been converted into a private residence, the long platforms have been reclaimed by a profusion of broom and willow. A detour around the station is required, before the walker gains the first sighting of the seven-span masonry viaduct over the river Divie. The bridge is 477 feet long and 105 feet high, and carried a single track over the river which eventually flows into the River Findhorn. High sided walls would have protected trains crossing the viaduct from the dangers of any strong crosswinds. In the middle of the walls, two commemorative stones record the construction of the I&PJR and the benefactions of the local landowners.

Beyond the viaduct the forests start to thin out, as the road and railway part company for the climb up to Dava. Only the steady crunching of the ballast betrays the presence of the walker in these empty moorlands. Ahead, sheep grazing near the trackbed are startled by the sudden noise and scamper up the gradient, warning their fellow sheep of the imminent danger. The procession is watched over by a bird of prey, hoping that its next meal is about to be unearthed by the sudden commotion. It is a peaceful location, no sound of mankind can be heard when the walker pauses to take in the view. Slowly the ears tune in to the rich natural symphony played by a babbling burn accompanied by an orchestra of animal and bird sounds. To the modern urban dweller this quietness is at first overpowering until the system adjusts and starts to appreciate the beauty of this natural calm.

These bleak moorlands were a constant source of trouble to the railway operators in the winter period. On more than one occasion trains were completely buried, after being abandoned in the snow drifts. On December 17th 1880, a train had become snowbound south of Dava Station, and had to be abandoned. Whilst the passengers managed to reach the shelter of the station, the train became completely buried. When it was finally located, the snow had accumulated to a height of 60 feet above the coaches. An up train carrying passengers and five cattle trucks, shared a similar fate on the other side of the station. Whilst the passengers made their escape to safety, the cattle refused to leave the safety of their trucks, and perished

*Station Master's House, Dava Station*

by suffocation in the deepening snow drifts.

In climbing the steady gradient towards Dava, the walker is constantly reminded of the climatic operational difficulties. For example, there is the slow increase in the relic count; the remains of bolts, spikes and porcelain telegraph insulators found on or near the trackbed. Then there are the Scots pines planted in rows on the crest of cuttings, for protection against snow; now slowly but surely reclaiming the cutting sides and even the trackbed. The remnants of snow fences still protect a faded concrete milepost, recording the once measurable rail distance from Perth. Linesmen's huts, built from a variety of material, provide accommodation for shepherds and their flock on these moors.

The tranquil calm of the moors is left behind as the main road returns to follow the railway to the scattered buildings of Dava. Approaching **Dava Station** from the south, the walker first passes the site of the goods facilities. Relics can still be found in the grass covered site, chairs of LMSR and occasionally Highland Railway origin being of the greatest interest to the enthusiast. Sadly their weight precludes them from being carried home as a souvenir of the walk! Beyond the goods yard, and its stone built loading platform, the remains of a signal post heralds arrival at the station site. The platforms remain in good condition, with the buildings being used as a private house and community centre. What is perhaps the biggest shock, is the length of the platforms which would accommodate a 15 coach train and still have space to spare. Presumably this length was provided for operational reasons rather than for the potential demand from this desolate location. Beyond the station, the trackbed straightens out for the final assault on Dava Summit.

Fortunately large sections have no ballast chippings, so the feet can relax on the gentle but firm trackbed. Again, rows of Scots pines watch over cuttings, whilst sheep herald the approach of the walker. The summit is a bit of a non event, the line actually making a double summit before it starts on its long downhill descent to the Spey Valley. It is only on the downhill section that one realises that **Dava Summit** has been successfully conquered. The other problem that soon faces the walker is the large amount of woodland that encircles Grantown-on-Spey. Soon after the walker has passed the summit, the forest is entered. Amidst the fragrance of the pine, lives that most antisocial of Scottish creatures, the highland midge.

Normally a resident of the west coast of Scotland, the midge has discovered a superb breeding ground in these forests. An unsuspecting human, pausing in these woods, soon becomes a target for these airborne blood suckers. Landing on any exposed human flesh, generally in large numbers, they announce their presence by a sharp nip which then turns into an irritating blemish. Consequently the walker has to keep moving and sweating, admiring on the way the rather attractive scenery that the railway is passing through. Although there are various chemical concoctions sold by chemists which claim to repel midges, not all are effective.

The railway scythes through a green sided cutting, formed by the mature woodland. Where the railway actually runs on a ledge above the valley bottom, the walled cutting is formed by large stone blocks. Having passed underneath the minor road to Lower Derraid, the next bridge is another "castellated" structure which carries an access road to Castle Grant over the railway. By now the first sighting of Grantown-on-Spey will be made, whilst the feet perk up at the thought of reaching civilisation once again and more relaxing surfaces to tread upon.

Surprisingly the bridge which carries the trackbed over the A939 near the outskirts of the town remains intact. Another mock castellated structure, it blends in well with the nearby main entrance to Castle Grant. This may have made the bridge a listed structure, as an example of the demands placed upon the railway engineers by the local landowners, and ensured its survival into a trainless age. Over the main road, the railway enters a brief agrarian section as it turns to parallel the main road, heading southwards to Grantown-on-Spey. After many miles of open moorland and dense forest, it comes as a pleasant relief to be back among fields once again. It also means the reappearance of fences across the trackbed, a feature that is noticeably absent on the long section over Dava Moor. Nearing the town, in proper railway tradition, the trackbed enters a cutting hewn out of the local rock, curving away from the houses. Forming a large radius quarter circle, the railway re-enters the forest, and having passed the local caravan site the walker reaches the desolate site of **Grantown-on-Spey West Station**.

Although the station buildings remained intact for many years after closure, they were finally demolished in the early 1980s in conjunction with the construction of an industrial estate on the extensive station site. The empty platforms are being slowly reclaimed back by nature, whilst an occasional rose bush clings onto life, a defiant remnant of the prize-winning station gardens. Only the well maintained station master's house has survived, amidst the scene of destruction and modern industrial building.

Grantown is over 24 miles away from Forres, so it is assumed that the walker will be ready to call it a day and head for either transport home or overnight accommodation. In either case, the town is reached by following the original access road to the station, turning left where it reaches the road which now serves the industrial estate. There is a fairly frequent bus service to Aviemore, with a very limited service to Inverness and Forres. However there are no buses on a Sunday. Walking into the town, there is a wide variety of accommodation, from homely bed and breakfast to a three/four star hotel. All should be able to offer a hot bath or shower, to relax those parts sorely affected by the trials and tribulations of the long day's walk.

Returning to the site of Grantown-on-Spey West, the next stage of the walk completes the journey along the Highland Railway to Boat-of-Garten. The trackbed about to be walked is owned by the Strathspey Railway Association, who hope one day to reopen the line from Boat-of-Garten to Grantown for passenger services. Unfortunately this involves the reconstruction of three major bridges, rebuilding a length of embankment and finding a new route through the industrial estate to reach the site of the former station at Grantown. Initially the railway leaves Grantown in a rubbish strewn cutting, before it emerges into open farmland which is typical of the route towards the Boat. In contrast to the miles of enclosed forest and bleak moorland, the agrarian scene comes as a welcome relief.

Passing Upper Craggan Farm, the trackbed has disappeared beneath road improvements of the A95. The road has been realigned, removing a considerable section of embankment, leaving the trackbed terminating abruptly at a small stone built underbridge, which takes a small lane underneath the railway. Across the main road, the trackbed enters a near impenetrable cutting, necessitating a short road walk before the railway can be regained at Gaich Farm. Looking along the trackbed, the remains of the bridge over the River Dulnain can be discerned. As the walker approaches the crossing, hopes rise that the rumours are false and the bridge still survives. However, after a pleasant walk through the fertile fields that form the Spey Valley, interspersed with the sighting of an occasional relic, including a couple of stone mileposts, the bridge is reached and the absence of girders becomes horribly apparent.

It is a Hobson's choice facing the walker, a plodge through the chilling waters with boots draped around the neck or a long detour to cross the river by the distant road bridge. If the latter option is adopted, the walker is liable to be "escorted" out of the adjacent fields by a herd of inquisitive bullocks. Beyond the village of Dulnain Bridge, a path leads down to the River Spey, near the sports field, allowing the trackbed to be regained with dry feet after a tortuous detour.

If the watery alternative is adopted, the same herd of cows look on in amazement at the antics of so called superior beings, wondering why they dismantle their feet before they cross the river. Continuing on, **Broomhill Station** is reached after a further mile or so on the unyielding ballast that still remains on the trackbed. The station master's house still watches out onto the lengthy platform, now overgrown with weeds. Further on, the trackbed widens out, grass now grows where once sidings stood. Nearby, the goods shed serves as storage for a local farmer. Beyond the station, the trackbed adopts a more westerly course for the "junction" with the GNofSR Speyside Branch. Although the railways converged at this point, three miles out from Boat-of-Garten, there was no physical connection between the two lines. Rather the lines ran as two independent single lines, making an eventual junction at Boat-of-Garten.

The footweary rambler can choose between remaining on the heavily ballasted Highland Railway route or the more gentle cinder ballast that remains on most of the GNofSR route. Before making the choice, a view can be obtained of the curving embankment of the Speyside Line, heading via two small dismantled underbridges to the remains of the Spey Viaduct. Heading towards Boat-of-Garten, the remains of a lineside bothy are passed before the trackbed passes underneath a bridge carrying the access road to Tullochgorm Farm over the railway. Beyond this bridge, on the northern side of the trackbed, can be found a mound of soil and large boulders which forms the remains of a chambered cairn, dating back to prehistoric times. It serves as a reminder of mankind's long occupation of this fertile valley.

On the opposite side of the track, although barely visible, can be found a group of standing stones of similar antiquity. By now the first sightings of Boat-of-Garten are made. A final obstacle of impenetrable jungle growing in a sheltered cutting near Lynchurn has to be overcome before the welcome sighting of the remains of the twin distant-signal posts herald the walker's imminent arrival at his or her destination.

The trackbed widens out, where once stood the GNofSR engine shed, to become a grassy field used as pasture for a couple of friendly horses. They wander up behind the walker, trying to secure a sugar lump or similar titbit from this unexpected source of entertainment. Attached to a fence hangs a notice indicating someone has plans to develop some of this land for private housing. Fortunately it only affects the shed site: the main line trackbed being kept for the possible extension of the preserved railway to Grantown.

Between this field and **Boat-of-Garten Station**, lies the Strathspey Railway Preservation Society's first major obstacle, the dismantled bridge over the minor road which heads down towards the River Spey.

When this road was improved, the local council agreed to replace the rail bridge when work starts on the extension. So a final banking is descended and a pavement walked on, before the footweary wanderer arrives at the station. A welcoming drink in the adjacent hotel, refreshes those other parts that won't be refreshed by a short steam-hauled journey to the "big city" of Aviemore.

Walking into the well restored buildings is like stepping back into a happier age for the railways. Whilst purchasing a ticket, genuine Edmondson variety, the eyes catch glimpses of LMSR and Highland Railway vehicles, whilst a sudden wisp of steam heralds the arrival of the train from Aviemore. The railway operates a regular service during the summer months. Outwith these times there is a bus service to Aviemore, although there is no regular Sunday service. Before boarding the train, the walker's mind goes back over the many miles which have passed since leaving Forres, and hopes that one day the sound and smell of a steam locomotive will linger over the line to Grantown.

# Invergarry & Fort Augustus Railway

The I&FAR is a classic example of a railway that should never have been built. It was born out of the bitter rivalry between the North British Railway and the Highland Railway, both of whom planned to construct a railway from Fort William to Inverness, through the Great Glen of Scotland. During the 1890s both companies sought an Act of Parliament for such a line and only after considerable expense did they agree to the mutual withdrawal of their proposed Acts along with a moratorium, for at least ten years, on similar plans.

In 1896, this uneasy truce was shattered with the announcement of a locally backed scheme to construct a line from Spean Bridge (where apart from a bridge there were several houses) to Fort Augustus, which boasted a pier on the Caledonian Canal, a Benedictine Monastery and a few houses. The intervening countryside was devoid of industry and supported only a few hundred people. Both the HR and NBR fought this scheme and it was perhaps due to the sheer determination of its main instigator, Lord Burton, that the I&FAR received its Act of Parliament on 14th August 1896, to construct the railway. So much money had been spent in obtaining this Act and in the construction of the line, that the company could not afford to operate the line when it was completed in 1901!

The line was officially opened on 21st July 1903 and was operated by the Highland Railway. On 1st July 1904, a platform was opened at Invergloy, whilst two years later on 30th September, the extension of the line from Fort Augustus to the pier was closed to all traffic. This section included an ornate, castellated viaduct over the River Oich and a

**RAILWAYS OF LOCHABER**

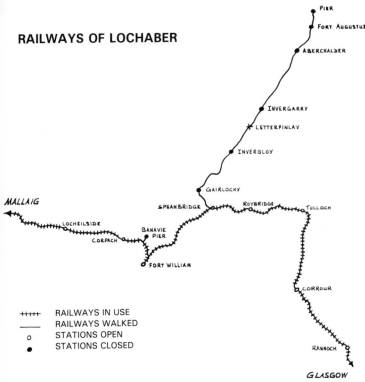

```
+++++   RAILWAYS IN USE
 ____   RAILWAYS WALKED
   o    STATIONS OPEN
   ●    STATIONS CLOSED
```

swing bridge over the Caledonian Canal. However, it generated only a modicum of income for the I&FAR whilst it was in operation.

Burdened with heavy operating costs and minimal income, the company was told by the HR, that the latter would cease to operate the line from 30th April 1907. The company approached the NBR to seek their agreement to operate the line. On 4th May 1907 the first NBR train ran on the I&FAR, a service which continued to operate until 31st October 1911. A day earlier, the station at Invergloy was closed to passenger traffic. Whilst the local population fought hard to retain their railway, the I&FAR board were forced to put out tenders for the scrap value of the line. The locals then sought an injunction to prevent the sale and in granting it, the Lord President of the Court of Session observed:–

"once a railway has been established, it is to a certain extent an asset of the public as well as an asset of the particular company."

After many long negotiations between the I&FAR, the NBR and the

115

Inverness-shire County Council, the NBR took over the I&FAR on 28th August 1914. During this period the council had learned that the cost of road repairs in the Spean Bridge and Fort Augustus area had risen by £600: an increase directly attributed to the withdrawal of the rail service.

In 1923 the NBR became part of the London & North Eastern Railway, who continued to operate the passenger service until 30th November 1933, when the final passenger train left Fort Augustus at 12.05 pm. In the last year of operation the railway carried 1,911 passengers which produced an income of £179. A weekly coal train continued to operate to Fort Augustus until 31st December 1946, when the line was finally closed. The track was lifted shortly afterwards, except for a short spur at Spean Bridge onto the nearby viaduct, which was used for shunting purposes until the early 1970s.

*Mileages*

| | |
|---|---|
| SPEAN BRIDGE | 0 miles 0 chains |
| GAIRLOCHY | 2 miles 52 chains |
| INVERGLOY | 8 miles 15 chains |
| INVERGARRY | 15 miles 6 chains |
| ABERCHALDER | 19 miles 27 chains |
| FORT AUGUSTUS Town | 23 miles 9 chains |
| FORT AUGUSTUS Pier | 24 miles 6 chains |

*Ordnance Survey 1:50,000 map number:–* 34

*Public Transport*

Spean Bridge is served by trains from Fort William to Glasgow. There is a bus service between Fort William and Inverness via Spean Bridge which follows the railway from Fort Augustus to Gairlochy road end. The frequency of these services is reduced, if not non-existent, on a Sunday. Details of these services may be found in the public transport timetable issued by the Highlands and Islands Development Board.

# VI/2   Spean Bridge to Fort Augustus

**Spean Bridge** station still maintains its atmosphere of a traditional railway station, with a passing loop although the semaphore signalling was removed when radio controlled train operation was introduced on the West Highland Railway. However, the Fort Augustus branch and bay platform now bear only the usual growth of trees that mark the route of many disused railways. As the viaduct over the River Spean has been removed, the walker should follow the main road to the Commando Memorial, to reach the trackbed by heading across the fields (boggy in places) from the monument. Having reached the railway, rucksacks may be left behind, before heading back to view the concrete piers of the viaduct. From the northern abutment, a path heads down to the river to obtain a better view of the piers. The original bridge consisted of a 50ft, a 120ft and two 60ft spans supported on piers rising 76ft above the river level.

Returning to collect one's accoutrements, a couple of waterlogged cuttings have to be negotiated in the early stages towards Fort Augustus. A fallen brick chimney stack, of some long abandoned railway worker's bothy, remains as a memorial to the passing of the railway. The line passes through forest, on a multitude of bridges over small burns, which contributed towards the expense of the construction of the railway. The trees part company at times to provide views of the Spean Gorge, no longer seen by travellers. The remains of a stone bridge spanning the gorge are passed, its abutments now supporting a girder bridge to maintain a crossing that is not marked on the map.

The first section of the line, as it passes along the Spean Gorge, is generally clear of any obstacle, apart from the occasional waterlogged cutting. Nearing Gairlochy, the railway is used as a forest access road, with the heavy equipment of a sand quarry being visible on the opposite side of the gorge. **Gairlochy Station** has now been converted into a caravan site. The original station had several sidings and a loading dock for the anticipated cattle traffic. The lengthy remains of the dock still stand, along with the curious abutment of an overbridge, it would have been the first since the Spean Viaduct. However, it is difficult to see why such a bridge was required in this location. Beyond the station, the B-road to Gairlochy, after road improvement works, no longer passes beneath the railway.

The original bridge over the B-road remains in situ and forms the start of a good track which uses the railway as it heads towards the lengthy waters of Loch Lochy. Still away from the bustle and noise of the main road, the railway reveals the occasional bolt buried in the earth or a piece of rail which once supported either a mile or a gradient post. The railway enters a forest as it turns inland to follow the valley of the Uisge Dubh for a crossing over the River Gloy. The track is less well used, long grass hides a profusion of wild flowers, growing in the peace of the trackbed, watched over by a rich assortment of deciduous and coniferous trees. The walker emerges at the entrance to Glenfintaig, where the bridge over the drive has been removed. Considering the number of bridges crossed since Spean Bridge, it is remarkable that this is the first bridge that has been removed. Because many of the others are of a reinforced concrete construction, possibly this has reduced the temptation to scavenge them for their steel content.

The dire warnings predicting a death by canine teeth fail to materialise as the walker heads on through a series of fields. The railway becomes a track again, passing by the abutments of another dismantled overbridge. This bridge, from nowhere to nowhere was presumably provided to allow cattle and sheep to pass over the railway. otherwise there is very little need for its provision. The girders were removed in the early 1980s, long after the final train had passed underneath them. Having reached the main road, for the first time since Spean Bridge, a detour up Glen Gloy is required to get to the trackbed beyond the dismantled Gloy Viaduct. This viaduct spanned the Gloy on two 50ft and a 100ft spans. A minor road signposted to Glen Gloy can be followed, turning onto the route of General Wade's Military Road (from Fort William to Inverness), where the minor road turns east into the glen.

For many years the section of the railway from the viaduct to Invergarry was impassable due to the dense growth of rhododendrons. However, the electricity board have cleared some of this growth to permit access to a power line which uses the trackbed. Where progress is prevented by a high bank of rhododendrons, a way should be made down to the nearby main road. The trackbed can be regained where a kissing gate opens onto a set of steps heading up to the railway, opposite a large white house on the loch-side of the road. This may have been the access to **Invergloy Platform** but the dense growth of vegetation prevents examination for any remains.

Fortunately a path weaves through further clumps of rhododendrons, as the railway heads northeastwards along the banks of Loch Lochy. The peace of the trackbed has been recently disturbed by the laying of a double pipeline by British Telecom, in the interests of improving telephonic communications in the area. The pipes are marked at regular intervals by posts carrying a plastic sign denoting ownership in blue on a yellow background. Still, it makes a change from the hosts of golden daffodils and is presumably more lasting. Again, many bridges are crossed including a large three-arched concrete viaduct with high sides to protect passing trains, near to the site of the passing loop of **Letterfinlay**.

It is difficult to see any traces of this location, the summit of the line (370ft), where the signal box was never staffed. It is worth pausing to admire the view, with mist swirling round the lofty summits on the opposite side of the loch, whilst the sun turns the waters into a shimmering silver carpet, broken by the occasional motor cruiser navigating its lengthy reaches. Maybe a large dragonfly is spotted, basking on the trackbed, its body a series of bright yellow and black hoops. It is the sort of creature at home in a horror movie, but it seems to tolerate the presence of walkers, fortunately. Heading on, the trackbed enters the South Laggan Forest near to the Corriegour Lodge, which is now a hotel and public bar. The railway becomes a well used forest track, bordered by tall foxgloves as it passes the final miles of Loch Lochy. In one burn, which passes beneath the railway, can be found several sections of rails, probably dumped there when the railway was lifted. The only obstacle is a high deer fence in the middle of the forest, which requires a climb over a many barred fence if the gate is padlocked.

Before Invergarry station is reached, a track heads into the hamlet of Laggan. Here can be found a café, bed & breakfast and a very

*Wade's Road and the railway on the southern flank of Loch Lochy*

comfortable youth hostel, where one can relax for the night before heading on towards Fort Augustus. Laggan is also served by bus services to Fort William and Inverness. Returning to the trackbed, the forest track continues to the site of **Invergarry Station**. Although the station buildings have long since gone, the large island platform and subway still remain. Trees now grow on the platform whilst part of the site has been converted into a depot and workshops for the regional roads department. The station also had a private waiting room, for the inhabitants of the nearby Invergarry House, in case they fancied a train ride. A water column was also provided at the station.

Beyond the station the track becomes less well used as the route enters a more mixed forest. Rhododendrons start to reappear although they don't block progress yet! By now the railway is following the banks of Loch Oich, on the opposite bank to the main road. There are fewer bridges over streams as steady progress is made towards Fort Augustus. Where the forest ends, the walker is faced by a high bank of rhododendrons, and the only way out is to drop down to the nearby Wade's Road, running alongside the shore of the loch. Wade's road, built to improve communications after the 1715 and 1745 rebellions, which ended in the bloodbath of Culloden, can be used to detour the foliage problem. Having passed a castellated three-arched viaduct, the trackbed may be regained by the small cottage at Leitirfearn.

The path dodges through the trees and rhododendrons to reach the Loch Oich tunnel. The ground here is very waterlogged, although with suitable footwear the tunnel can be walked through, to view both of the mock castellated entrances. A drier solution, which avoids the tunnel and several watery cuttings beyond the tunnel, is to return to Wade's Road and follow it to the viaduct over the Calder Burn. This low viaduct has been used as a farm access road, although this use appears to have stopped, perhaps because the bridge is unsafe.

The banks of Loch Oich are now left behind as the trackbed heads across the fields, to the missing bridge over the main A82. Having negotiated this obstacle, the walker reaches the site of **Aberchalder Station**. The railway provided a passing point at this location, although there was never a signal box. If necessary, the points could be operated by the token for the section. The station is marked by the remains of a concrete edged platform, which supports a luxuriant growth of scrap motor cars. Beyond the station site, the trackbed disappears into further forestry plantations.

Although parts of the trackbed can be walked where it emerges out of the forest, there are many obstacles, natural or otherwise, which would force many roadside detours. The best way to reach Fort Augustus is to head across country to the nearby Caledonian Canal. The towpath, on the northern bank of the canal, provides a tranquil walk, passing two locks before reaching Fort Augustus at the top of the triple staircase, that drops the canal down into the waters of Loch Ness. Landscaping operations have removed most, if not all, traces of the station of **Fort Augustus**. Originally there were two terminal platforms and a through platform, for traffic to the pier as well as a turntable.

Of the pier extension, traces of the swing bridge may be discerned at the top of the staircase locks. Beyond which a very overgrown embankment heads to the castellated piers which form the remains of the expensive bridge over the River Oich. The trackbed beyond the bridge may be walked, although it is easier to gain access to the trackbed at the remains of the bridge which took it over the main road out of Fort Augustus. The route of the extension can then be walked to reach the site of the **Fort Augustus Pier** station, which is a private house (or houses) and should only be viewed from the entrance gateway, to respect the privacy of the occupants. Fort Augustus is now a tourist centre, with many cafés and pubs which provide refreshment at the end of the walk.

# The Ballachulish Branch

The history books record that the Ballachulish Railway was opened on the 24th August 1903 for passenger traffic and that the final passenger train ran on the 26th March 1966. Many people therefore were witness to both the first and last passenger trains. The railway started at Conel Ferry and ran for a distance of nearly 28 miles to Ballachulish, at the entrance to Glencoe. Perhaps the line's only claim to fame was that it was one of the last branch lines built in Britain. Consequently concrete played a major part in the various civil engineering structures, indirectly ensuring the survival of many of them after the closure of the branch. The freight service initially included slate traffic from the Ballachulish Quarries. Towards the end the main source of freight was materials connected with the construction of the Aluminium Works at Kinloch-leven, transported by road from Ballachulish. One year before the closure of the line, this traffic was re-routed via the West Highland Railway to Fort William, possibly to help in justifying the closure.

*Mileages*

| | |
|---|---|
| CONNEL FERRY | 0.00 miles |
| NORTH CONNEL | 0.50 miles |
| BENDERLOCH | 2.75 miles |
| CREAGAN | 10.00 miles |
| APPIN | 13.25 miles |
| DUROR | 18.75 miles |
| KENTALLEN | 22.50 miles |
| BALLACHULISH Ferry | 25.50 miles |
| BALLACHULISH Town | 27.50 miles |

*Ordnance Survey 1:50,000 map numbers:–* 41, 49, 50

*Public Transport*
Connel Ferry is served by trains and buses from Glasgow to Oban. There is a limited bus service from Oban to Fort William that runs parallel to the railway from Connel Ferry to Ballachulish. Express coach services from Glasgow and Edinburgh to Fort William and the Isle of Skye also call at Ballachulish. Details of all these services may be found in the public transport timetable issued by the Highlands and Islands Development Board.

## VI/3:  Connel Ferry to Ballachulish

**Connel Ferry Station** has become an unstaffed halt on the Oban Line, served by three trains daily in each direction. Only one platform remains in use, although the original buildings have been replaced by the dreaded bus shelter. A ground frame is used to permit access to an oil terminal on the Eastern side of the station. To the west of the station, the Ballachulish branch curves away north, entering a wooded rock cutting before emerging into a desolate wasteland by Connel Bridge. Originally it was planned to provide a triangular junction at Connel and a concrete bridge on the unbuilt side of the triangle stands over a nearby minor road leading to Loch Nell.

These smaller bridges, although built of concrete, were designed to give the appearance of being built of the more traditional stone. An attractive casting used for the edges gives an illusion of stone blocks,

121

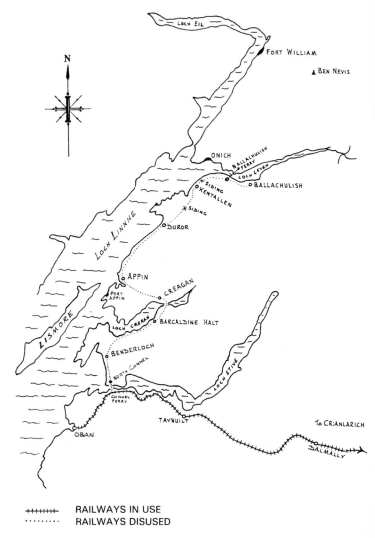

**THE BALLACHULISH BRANCH**

which only reveals the bridge's true identity on a closer examination.

When built, the Connel Bridge allowed for the passage of both rail and road traffic. Toll Booths and traffic lights allowed the bridge to be used as a single track roadway, when it was not being used by rail traffic. Now only road traffic uses the bridge, the toll having being removed, though traffic lights still maintain the single file traffic. At the south end of the bridge the tollbooth and original traffic lights survive although road improvements have removed parts of the trackbed at each end of the bridge. Over the bridge, a short section of trackbed to the south of the A828 marks the site of **North Connel Halt**, but the only surviving item of the station furnishings is part of the approach fencing. The next few miles towards Benderloch provide a very pleasant walk, passing the Connel International Airport before the coastline is joined for the first time.

Road improvements near Ledaig are using more of the trackbed, until the road heads inland and the trackbed once again appears for a short section towards the site of **Benderloch Station**. The platforms remain in situ, although the buildings have been demolished. To provide access to a caravan site on the opposite side of the railway to the main road, girders have been laid across the platforms. The village supports a couple of shops which sell ice-cream and soft drinks, a useful source of refreshment in hot weather.

Beyond the village the coastline is followed for a short length, until the railway heads inland and the trackbed disappears into a jungly undergrowth, as a short headland is traversed before the coastline is regained at Loch Creran. The warmth of the Gulf Stream, which washes these shores, has assisted the rapid growth of vegetation as it reclaims the trackbed. Alongside Loch Creran, some parts of the trackbed have been used to provide laybys for the adjacent main road, allowing motorists to take in the view and have a welcome rest.

Nearing the site of **Barcaldine Platform** the trackbed clears and is edged by a profusion of rhododendron bushes. These make for a colourful vista in the right season. The actual station site is now an industrial works which has eradicated all traces of the halt and the trackbed. A detour along the shoreline is required before the trackbed can be regained at a girder bridge over the Abhainn Teithil. Shortly afterwards road improvements have removed the bridge which carried the branch over the main road and the continuation of the trackbed northwards.

It is possible to regain the trackbed in the forest for a very overgrown stretch that finally clears at the Creagan Viaduct. Fortunately most of the growth consists of young silver birch and beech saplings, so it is still possible to walk "through" the trees. This practice is not advised for the occasional gorse bush, which here bear a greater affinity to trees than bushes. It is a strange feeling to be walking through trees, with no visibility in any direction, hoping that the trackbed remains intact underneath one's feet. Thankfully, normality is restored as the trackbed

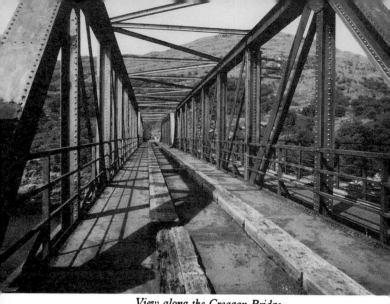

*View along the Creagan Bridge*

curves onto the **Creagan Viaduct**.

Planning indecision about the future of the viaduct as a possible road bridge has allowed it to remain in situ. The view from the bridge, either down or up the loch, boosts morale sapped by the previous labours. Leaving the viaduct, the line gently curves round to the west, crossing once more over the main road (bridge missing). Beyond this minor obstacle and through a rock cutting, a path leads temptingly downward to the Creaggan Inn, a useful source of liquid refreshment. Nearby is the site of **Creagan Station**. Although part of the station area has been used as a caravan site, the island platform and station buildings remain. Creagan Station appears to have been the odd station on the branch, the buildings being of single storey construction on an island platform, rather than the double storey "houselike" style using side platforms.

Having passed the Creagan Jungle Training Course, the next part of the line through Strath Appin comes as a welcome relief. Only a few obstructions impair progress towards Appin Station, which spawned the small hamlet of Portnacroish. Nearing the station a path leads down towards a wooden bridge built to commemorate Queen Victoria's Diamond Jubilee in 1897 and used to improve pedestrian communication with the village of Port Appin. Until this bridge was built, villagers had to cross the mudflats at low tide by means of following a set of marker poles which claim to denote the "safe path". By now the walker is thinking about finding a bed for the night. Having discovered no suitable resting places in Portnacroish, it may be necessary to make a short detour by means of the bridge and a quiet country lane to reach Port Appin.

Regaining the trackbed at **Appin Station**, the walker passes the silent platforms shorn of all their buildings. The surface has been compacted by the continued passage of motorised vehicles, as the trackbed is used to provide access to a boating clubhouse.

Past the boathouse, the trackbed slowly reverts to its overgrown state as it hugs the coastline, heading northwards on a stone shelf built adjacent to the pebbly beach. This is the last stretch of the trackbed that can be followed, in Strathclyde region. Road improvements have erased most of the trackbed until it is beyond the Salachan Glen, which marks the boundary between Strathclyde and Highland Regions. In this area near neighbours can have their seats of local government as far away as Glasgow and Inverness.

Nearing **Duror Station** the trackbed can once again be regained. Although the station buildings have been converted into a private house, passage can be made by following the seaward side of the station site. Apart from the buildings and platforms, there are some remains of the goods yard and a cattle dock. Leaving the station and past the graveyard, it is advisable to seek an exit from the line as conditions slowly deteriorate until impregnability is reached at the bridge carrying a small lane leading to Keil House over the railway. Normality returns 100 yards further on until a filled-in bridge carries the main road over the railway again obstructing progress.

Beyond this bridge is perhaps the nicest part of the line, as the trackbed becomes a grass covered lane heading inland for a couple of miles until it regains the coast at Kentallen. A short distance inland, a minor road used to pass over the railway by means of an overbridge. Although the bridge remains, the road has abandoned it in favour of a more level crossing over the railway. The road has one advantage however, being that it leads to the Duror Inn. Continuing on past the site of a siding halfway along the glen and a missing farm bridge, the trackbed emerges on the shores of Loch Leven.

Once again road improvements have removed parts of an embankment, but the trackbed can once again be recovered heading towards **Kentallen Station**. The station site is growing a fine crop of holiday homes and even a large glassy restaurant built over the platforms. The station buildings survive, albeit modified, as a bed and breakfast establishment. Past the adjacent car park, a clear path using the trackbed can then be followed towards Ballachulish. When the path leaves the railway, it does so for a good reason, usually because of a missing bridge over a stream. It is a very pleasant walk along the shore of Loch Leven, sufficiently distant from the road to be relatively immune to the noise of the adjacent traffic.

Nearing the Ballachulish Bridge, originally planned as a northerly extension of the railway to Fort William, the trackbed dives underneath the main road and heads inland towards **Ballachulish Ferry Station**.

Again conditions deteriorate steadily towards becoming an urban sewer, thanks to a rich deposit of rubbish thrown into the cutting, blocking the drainage system. A detour using the adjacent lanes is advised to reach the site of the Ferry Station. In spite of the major road changes in the area due to the construction of the bridge, its single platform survives albeit without any of its original furnishings.

From the end of the platform, very little of the trackbed towards Ballachulish Town has survived the road changes. only short stretches remain until nearing the outskirts of the town, the route can be once again regained; where the goods yard is being used by the contractors' plant involved in the construction of the Ballachulish by-pass. Although the platforms have been infilled, the wooden buildings of **Ballachulish Town Station** stand defiant to the modern age. Sadly they are now being used as a showroom for the veteran cars which started the cancerous decay in the life of the Ballachulish Branch.

*Underbridge near Invergloy Platform,*
*Spean Bridge to Fort Augustus*

# VII:
# WALKS IN
# CENTRAL REGION

## The Callander and Oban Railway

The rail link from Stirling to Crianlarich and Oban was completed in three stages. Initially it was the Scottish Central Railway which formed the main line from Stirling to Perth, opening to passengers in 1848. From a junction with that line at the cathedral town of Dunblane a branch was promoted to serve the towns of Doune and Callander. This concern opened to passenger services on 1st July 1858. Further progress westwards required the railway engineers conquering Glen Ogle. The glen was a forbidding place with rocky, boulder-strewn hillsides, towering crags and on occasions, wild weather. It was not an easy task to build a railway halfway up the hillside through the ''Khyber Pass'' of Scotland. In 1868, over a hundred years after General Wade built a military road through the glen, work started on the construction of the railway. On the 1st June 1870 the first steam hauled passenger train climbed through the glen to reach Glenoglehead Station. Three years later the line was extended to Tyndrum, opening on 1st August. The cost of construction had seriously affected the Callender & Oban's finances. It took until 1880

*'Pipetrack' Bridge, north of Balfron*

and a further injection of finance, for the railway to reach Oban.

On April 1st 1886 the C&O opened a short branch to serve the village of Killin and the nearby Loch Tay. It was planned to extend this branch along the banks of Loch Tay to reach Aberfeldy, but the plans came to nought. The C&O's summer excursions became very popular with Victorian travellers, but contending with the winter weather was a different affair. On Friday March 4th 1881, the night mail due to arrive in Oban at 4.35 am became buried in huge snowdrifts at the head of Glen Ogle. The first rescue party from Killin failed to reach the train. Later that day a party of eighty men reached the stricken train and brought the passengers down to safety in Killin. The train finally reached its destination on the following Tuesday morning.

Foot travellers exploring the course of the river Earn westwards from Crieff found the country became more rugged and spectacular the further west they travelled. After six miles the township of Comrie was passed, and a further seven miles brought the explorers to St. Fillans nestling at the east end of Loch Earn. The loch ran as a narrow ribbon loch for seven miles before the village of Lochearnhead was reached. The first advance of the railway into this exciting landscape took place on 1st June 1893 when the railway was opened between Crieff and Comrie. The Comrie, St. Fillans and Lochearnhead Railway was promoted to fill the gap between Comrie and the Lochearnhead station of the C&O. This station was two miles from the village and was re-named Balquhidder when the new station was opened near the village.

Although the C.St.F.&L.R. was unopposed in both Houses of Parliament, it was passed to a select committee to consider its environmental impact. The committee gave the railway a clean bill of health and the Royal Assent was received on 4th August 1897. Nevertheless, the company went to great trouble to ensure the railway did not intrude on the landscape. It is a pity that modern planners do not follow the example set by the company. At Tynereach near St. Fillans the railway was laid for some distance along the foot of a rocky slope with the road running alongside. The company at its own expense moved the road back 22 yards and in the strip of land between the railway and the new road laid down a small plantation to hide the railway from the roadside view. The railway was opened to St. Fillans on 1st October 1901. The seven miles along the hillside above Loch Earn took a further three years to build. It was on the 1st May 1905 that the railway was opened to Balquhidder.

The first casualty was the extension of the Killin branch to Loch Tay, which was closed to passenger services on September 11th 1939. It was a token closure as the rails remained in situ for access to the locomotive shed for the branch. After the war, the goods and pasenger service from Comrie to Balquhidder was withdrawn on 1st October 1951, an unhappy 50th anniversary for the C.St.F&L.R. Only in the cleft in the mountain-side above Lochearnhead was there still evidence of a living railway.

In closing, the C&O acted out a final defiance to the machinations of the axeman from England. The line was due to be closed on 5th November 1965, from Dunblane to Crianlarich including the Killin branch. Rock falls had been a constant hazard and a system of trip wires was devised to operate the signalling system should rocks fall onto the track. In the early hours of the morning of 27th September a rock fall blocked the line in Glen Ogle. Services were diverted via the West Highland and a few days later it was announced that since repairs would cost £30,000, the railway between Callander and Crianlarich would be closed immediately. The service from Dunblane to Callander remained operational until 5th November 1965. Although on the face of it, there was only a slight spillage of rock over one rail, the BR engineer claimed that further thousands of tons were poised to crash down onto the railway. The locals, fighting to keep the railway open, were presented with a fait accompli.

To date the rocks have not crashed down onto the empty trackbed or the unsuspecting walker, although the deserted trackbed in Glen Ogle is overhung by menacing rocks and the slopes are littered with boulders that have broken loose and crashed into the valley. No longer does the Glen echo to the sharp exhaust of a Highland Castle or Clan, or a Black Five fighting its way up the twisting gradients with a long holiday train.

*Mileages*

| | | |
|---|---|---|
| CRIANLARICH Lower | 0.00 miles | |
| LUIB | 6.25 miles | |
| KILLIN Junction | 8.00 miles | |
| KILLIN Junction | | 0.00 miles |
| KILLIN | | 4.00 miles |
| LOCH TAY | | 5.00 miles |
| GLENOGLEHEAD Crossing | 11.00 miles | |
| BALQUHIDDER | 17.25 miles | |
| BALQUHIDDER | | 0.00 miles |
| LOCHEARNHEAD | | 2.00 miles |
| ST. FILLANS | | 9.25 miles |
| KINGSHOUSE | 18.25 miles | |
| STRATHYRE | 20.50 miles | |
| CALLANDER | 29.00 miles | |
| DOUNE | 36.25 miles | |
| DUNBLANE | 40.25 miles | |

*Ordnance Survey 1:50,000 map numbers:–* 50, 51, 57

*Public Transport*

Crianlarich (Upper) is served by trains from Glasgow to Oban and Fort William. There is a limited bus service from Callander to Crianlarich via Killin, that increases in frequency between Killin and Crianlarich. St.

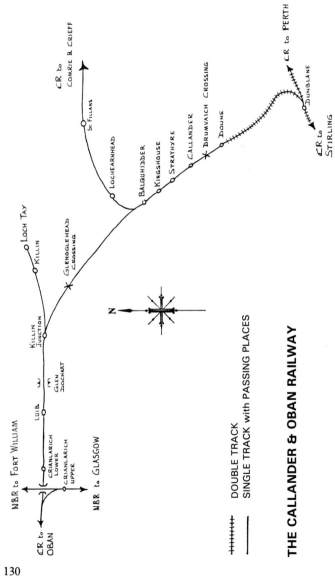

DOUBLE TRACK
++++++ SINGLE TRACK with PASSING PLACES

**THE CALLANDER & OBAN RAILWAY**

Fillans is served by a limited bus service to Comrie and Crieff, but there is no bus service between St. Fillans and Lochearnhead.

Callander is served by a regular bus service via Doune to Dunblane and Stirling, where there are frequent train services to Glasgow, Edinburgh, Perth and England.

## VII/1a: Dunblane to Callander

**Dunblane Station**, the starting point for this walk, is worthy of a closer inspection. Although its island platform has only a bus-shelter for the comfort of the passengers, the main station buildings date back in places to the Scottish Central Railway, which opened the station in 1848. Looking northwards, the signalbox still watches over the junction of the Callander and Oban branch. Nowadays the C&O is a short siding used either as a headshunt or for the stabling of unwanted stock. The trackbed of the C&O can be gained by following the Old Doune Road to the west of the station, turning left down a minor road adjacent to the Schiehallion Hotel. Initially the trackbed is very overgrown, with beech saplings rising out of a dense undergrowth of domestic refuse. Further on conditions improve, although a short detour via nearby fields is needed to bypass a section of the trackbed which has been converted into gardens.

Eventually the continually growing housing sprawl of Dunblane is left behind and the walker becomes part of the serene seclusion of the disused trackbed. It is not a solitary walk as the quiet is liable to be suddenly broken by pheasants breaking from cover as the walker approaches. Having negotiated a minor break near Auchinteck Farm, the first major obstacle is encountered. Sadly, although the piers which carried the railway over the Ardoch Burn remain, the important girders have been removed. Fortunately nearby farm lanes and minor roads provide a drier alternative to any attempted water walk. Continuing on past fertile farmland, another short break has to be negotiated before the safety of the Doune Trail is reached.

The final mile into Doune has been converted by the local authority into a nature trail. Perhaps this may not sound unusual, until it is realised that the trackbed has been converted with blind people in mind. An elevated wooden rail (a few inches off the ground) runs continuously along the side of the trackbed, allowing blind and partially sighted people to safely walk along the trackbed and benefit from the tranquillity of the scene. The walk is very attractive, heading through a rich and varied mixed woodland towards the small town of Doune. Here can be found public conveniences and several hostelries to refresh those parts not reached by the railway walking.

**Doune Station** is now used by a haulage contractor. Some of the platforms and the goods shed survive alongside the shell of the signal box at the Callander end of the station. Although the railway was double track from Dunblane to Doune, from Doune onwards it reverted into a single track line with passing places. Leaving Doune Station it passed underneath the main Callander Road (the A84). Road improvements have eradicated the need for the bridge, only fragments of the abutment of the bridge remain to indicate to the intrepid explorer that it once existed. The trackbed then parts company from the road as it heads in a straight line towards Kirkton Farm. Midway, the bridge over a burn flowing into the River Teith has been removed, leaving only a water pipe spanning the empty chasm between the two abutments. The burn can be jumped in places, forded by means of precarious stepping stones or by wearing wellingtons to avoid a detour to the nearest safe crossing place.

Half a mile further on, the dismantled viaduct over the Annet Burn provides the final major obstacle before Callander. A scramble down the embankment side leads to a path heading up to the nearby road. The break provides an opportunity to take a rest and fuel the body for the final stage to Callander. Fortified, a short road walk is used to regain the trackbed which is now on the northern side of the main road. The railway viaduct over the Annet Burn and bridge over the main road have both been removed. Farmland is left behind as moorland country is entered, fields in crop or cattle being replaced by green tracts of coniferous forest. Fortunately the forest has meant that the railway has been used as a "forest road", allowing for a fairly obstacle free walk into Callander.

Midway the crossing loop at **Drumvaich** is reached. Track clips and bolts can be found in the trackbed, whilst the neglected tall signal box and adjoining railway cottages survive, largely hidden from the nearby main road. Continuing on, brown patches may be observed in the distance crossing the trackbed. At first it is thought that they must be piles of autumn leaves, then the patches move. A herd of cows? Suddenly a realisation, the patches consist of flocks of pheasants enjoying the solitude and safety of the trackbed! The trackbed continues past quiet woodland and shows signs of it being used by local walkers and horse riders. The Keltie Water is crossed by means of an impressive stone viaduct with its western bank showing the first signs of the urban sprawl of Callander. Graually the trackbed is squeezed by this urban growth, until half a mile from the station, its main artery is severed by a housing estate built across the trackbed.

So a final roadside walk is required to reach the forlorn site of **Callander Station**. The site has been eradicated to provide a landscaped car park with the usual conveniences. It is a melancholic place; only a girder bridge to the east of the station gives an indication that a railway once passed through these parts. No more is there an Oban bogie waiting to welcome one; only a blue Midland Scottish bus to return the walker back to Stirling or occasionally to Crianlarich and Dunblane.

## VII/1b: Crianlarich to Callander

Alighting from the relative warmth of a steam-heated carriage into a swirling mist and a snowstorm at **Crianlarich Upper Station** requires a

*Drumvaich Crossing Signal Box*

great deal of soul searching. However, after a warm cup of tea in the nearby privately owned refreshment rooms, the prospect of a few days' walk amidst spectacular scenery spurs one on the way. Leaving the former NBR Upper Station, it is a short walk to the site of the ex-Caledonian Lower Station. Originally, the two routes were independent of each other; only wartime caused the present curve from the Upper Station onto the Oban line to be built. Eventually the CR route to Crianlarich was closed and the passenger service to Oban routed via this curve. The tracks leading into the Lower Station being retained as sidings for the timber traffic to the ill-fated pulp mill at Fort William but more recently to Wales.

The tracks past **Crianlarich Lower** now stand empty and rust encrusted. Of the station, only the platform on the south side remains. Passing on towards Luib, a few wagons mark the end of the rails and the start of the abandoned trackbed. Passing along the shores of Loch Dochart, a castle may be seen on one of the small islands in the loch. This secret view through the trees is hidden to the traffic which can be heard hurrying along the nearby main road. The safety of the trackbed is broken shortly afterwards by road improvements that have removed the rail overbridge near Pernellan Farm. Over the road, the railway continues at a higher level and soon enters a pleasant wooded cutting.

Continuing on, the trackbed shows some traces of ballast removal and two missing bridges have to be negotiated before the site of **Luib Station** is reached. Now a caravan site, the platforms have been filled in and virtually all their buildings removed. Only a stone base of a building (water tower?) remains at the west end of one platform, having been converted and extended into a toilet block. Between Luib and Killin Junction, the only major obstacle is the missing bridge over the Luib Burn. Attempting to ford the burn may be possible after a rare spell of hot and dry weather. Otherwise, walk down the burn to cross it at the nearest road bridge, then walk back alongside the burn to regain the trackbed. Whilst this involves a detour of about one mile, it does allow for the walker to make a safe and dry crossing of the fast flowing burn.

Shortly after this obstacle, the trackbed crossed the Ledcharne Burn on the Glen Dochart viaduct, the first of the major viaducts of the Callander and Oban Railway to be met on this walk. Because of its remote location, the Glen Dochart viaduct is not as well known as the more famous examples in Glen Ogle.

Nearing **Killin Junction** the trackbed has been cleared and the ballast removed, perhaps for a possible extension of the Glen Ogle trail. Isolated amidst a dark coniferous forest, the station platforms remain alongside the derelict station cottages. The station buildings have been replaced by an open timber-built shed which is used to house a sawmill for the forest workers. Leaving the junction, the main line turns south and continues its steady climb to reach a summit near Glenoglehead Crossing. For part of its way, the trackbed passes through further dark coniferous forest which occasionally breaks to give a view down towards Loch Tay and the village of Killin.

The Killin branch continues straight on, dropping down on a gradient of about 1 in 50. The short branch has to descend nearly 400 feet before it reaches Killin. The only minor obstacle to progress along the branch is the missing bridge over the A85 at Lix Toll. The abutments have been landscaped to provide easy ramps down and back up from the road.

Past this point, the trackbed becomes a very pleasant walk. Trees growing on each side of the grassy trackbed meet up above the walker's head, to give an illusion of walking through a green sided tunnel. Near Acharn Farm come the concrete sleepers which remain underfoot virtually all the way down to Killin. Beyond the farm buildings are the remains of the point rodding and lever frame used to control access to a private siding built to serve the farm. Near Killin a missing bridge over a minor road that goes round the south side of Loch Tay, necessitates a scramble down the embankment side to reach the road. A private road leading to Kinnell House can then be used to regain the trackbed near to the viaduct over the River Dochart. Having crossed this viaduct with its good view of the nearby Falls of Dochart, the site of **Killin Station** is reached. The construction of a small industrial estate on this site has removed any trace of the existence of the railway station.

The trackbed of the branch remains walkable to the site of **Loch Tay Station**, although access to the station is prevented. The wooden station buildings (closed 1939 although the track remained for access to the adjacent engine shed) have been renovated and converted into an attractive private house. Walking back along the trackbed, Killin is soon reached where there is a wide range of accommodation at the end of a pleasurable day's walk. There is also a limited bus service to Stirling and a Saturdays only service to Crianlarich.

Retracing our tracks up the Killin Branch and then following an indistinct path past Middle Lix Farm, the picnic site of **Glenoglehead Crossing** on the main line, can be reached. Nearby, several cottages remain on one of the two low-sided platforms that served as the original Killin Station until the opening of the branch in 1886. Although the cottages are still occupied, it is possible to walk quietly along the trackbed as it starts its descent of Glen Ogle. For a while the trackbed remains in close contact with the main road, but before it finally parts company it becomes a very waterlogged cutting, regaining the trackbed before it crosses to the opposite side of the glen.

Emerging from this cutting, the railway becomes part of the Glen Ogle Trail, as it crosses a small burn for the west side of the glen. The trail has wound its way up the glen from Lochearnhead, by means of a military road that predates both the railway and the modern tarmac road. The descent of Glen Ogle is probably the most spectacular section of this walk. Hugging the hillsides, at times it is built out on a concrete and stone shelf, spanning the many side valleys by means of stone and concrete viaducts. Fortunately the sinuous nature of the line permits the walker to catch glimpses of the many man-made structures which had to be built before the railway could be opened. Even today it is still possible to stand in awe at the toil and hardship that must have been present during the construction of this section of the railway. In the end it was all in vain, when at a stroke of the proverbial pen in far distant London, it was all officially abandoned. Luckily the lack of metal in the construction of the civil engineering structures has probably contri- buted to the survival of this route as an intact entity. On the opposite side of the glen, the drone of the traffic climbing up the main road, mars the tranquil solitude. Down below the grassy remains of the former military road can still be seen, making its own way up the glen.

Above Glenoglehead farm the landslide which caused the premature closure of the railway is passed. It is not a very spectacular landslide, but on closer examination it reveals lengths of wooden sleepers and the occasional chair and short length of rail. Nearing Lochearnhead, the assorted buildings which make up the village are united by the viaduct which carried the branch to St. Fillans along the shores of the loch. For the photographer, every hundred yards or so a fresh vista is opened out, every one becoming the master shot to end all master shots, until the next vista is reached. The Callander and Oban main line contours high around the hillside above Lochearnhead, forcing the walker seeking refreshment, accommodation or transport, to leave its course and descend the hillside into the village.

Following the railway, the descent continues towards **Balquhidder Junction**, passing through a cattlepen which has been built across the trackbed, before the remains of the junction and the station are reached.

135

Road improvements and the siting of a council roads' depot have removed many relics of the railway in this area. Of the station only the island platform and the steps leading down to the entrance subway remain, surrounded by a sea of weeds and neglect. From the roadside below, the brick built retaining wall and arched entrance passageway survive to remind passers by of the former existence of the railway.

Continuing on towards Callander by passing underneath the overbridge at the south end of the station, it is a short walk to **Kingshouse Station**. Recent roadworks have removed many traces of the railway by removing the need for the road overbridge with its tight and dangerous approach corners. Beyond the station, an overbridge across a minor road has been removed and a small forest planted on the Strathyre abutment. Although it is only a few miles from Strathyre, the close proximity of the main road makes it a very dull stretch of the railway, especially after the scenic delights of Glen Ogle.

Entering the village of Strathyre, the trackbed becomes the local dumping ground, before it reaches the filled-in road overbridge to the west of the station. The only remains of **Strathyre Station** consist of the platforms which are now used as fences for the adjacent car park. No longer can one obtain refreshment from the ornamental fountain that once stood on the platform. Beyond the station, the railway passes the Forestry Commission information office. Apart from the provision of toilets nearby, the information office is well worth the detour, for its interesting exhibition about the uses of a modern forest.

Although the bridge over the River Balway has been removed, army engineers have constructed a footbridge on the site of the old bridge, making it possible to cross the fast flowing river. Having endured the noise of the road to Strathyre, the railway now heads for the opposite bank of Loch Lubnaig for a pleasant lochside walk of four miles. At the head of the loch by the bridge near Kipp Farm, the trackbed is used for the cultivation of a fine crop of kitchen sinks; the old fashioned white glazed earthenware variety.

So the solitude and tranquillity of the lochside returns, as the Strathyre forest gradually descends to the shores of Loch Lubnaig. The beauty of this sylvan stretch is broken in one place by an extreme case of car dumping. Miles from the nearest road, a car rests on the trackbed undergoing its final decay surrounded by fairly healthy saplings. Nearing the Stank Farmhouse the trackbed becomes a forest road serving several forest cottages before it enters a car park at the south end of Loch Lubnaig. From the carpark to Callander there are several missing bridges including the two major viaducts over the River Balway, which is crossed and recrossed by the railway near the Falls of Leny. The best plan is to try to follow the railway as close as practicable on the west bank until the missing bridge near Callander is reached.

## VII/1c:  Balquhidder Junction to St. Fillans

Leaving the derelict site of Balquhidder Station in a northerly direction, the main line of the C&O veers off towards some nearby cottages. The St. Fillans branch having negotiated a council road depot continues its progress sandwiched between the main road and the forest. After a further ¾ of a mile it crosses the main road then emerges from a short wooded stretch at the dismantled viaduct over the wide Kendrum Burn. On the opposite bank the trackbed continues through further woods to emerge at the site of **Lochearnhead Station**, with its island platforms. Now the property of an English Scouting Group, the tastefully restored buildings and the general tidy appearance of the site must make it a prime candidate for a best-kept disused railway station award! Complete with the correct railwayana, it takes only a little imagination to see a Caley tank arriving from Comrie at the station. Sadly, the sounds of human voices are those of the scouts and not the passengers disembarking from the long gone passenger train. The subway only echoes to the feet of a scout fetching logs from the logpile in the original underground entrance to the station.

Across the main road, the embankment marking the remains of the overbridge across the A85 may be scaled giving access to the curving viaduct which spans the entrance to Glen Ogle. Sadly, a modern house mars continuation beyond the viaduct, return being by means of the original ascent. To regain the trackbed entails making a detour through the small settlement of Lochearnhead, possibly calling in at an hotel to refresh the necessary systems for the final assault towards St. Fillans. The trackbed between Lochearnhead and Drumveich, approximately 1.5 miles eastwards, is very overgrown, usually near missing bridges which slows down progress.

Beyond the missing bridge over the lane leading up to Glenbeich Lodge conditions dramatically improve, with the trackbed being used as a forest access road. This has resulted in the trackbed becoming a grassy track, interrupted by the occasional gate as it passes alongside or through an assortment of coniferous and deciduous plantations. The woodland muffles any traffic noise from the road below, following the shores of Loch Earn, whilst across the silvery waters there are glimpses of the twin Callander Munros (hills of 3,000ft plus) of Ben Vorlich and Stuc na Chroin through the hills of the southern banks. Nearing St. Fillans the viaduct across the Ault na Phionn, in the murky depths of Glentarken Wood has been dismantled, necessitating a scramble down and back up from the main road. Beyond this obstacle the trackbed though overgrown in places can be followed through a short tunnel before emerging at the site of **St. Fillans Station** and the end of the walk. The station site has been landscaped and converted into a mixture of log cabins and a caravan site. Amazingly the signalbox and station buildings remain intact amidst all of these modern holiday developments as a final memorial to the passage of the railway.

# The Forth & Clyde Junction Railway

In 1845, the first plans were mooted for a railway from Stirling to Loch Lomond. Although these plans were thwarted by the collapse of the Railway Mania, they were revived in 1851 under the guise of the "Forth and Clyde Junction Railway". The promoters having gained running powers over the Stirling and Dunfermline Railway at Stirling and the Caledonian Railway from Bowling to Balloch, had visions of their railway becoming a major carrier of through freight from Fife to the Clyde. The railway passed through pastoral country, avoiding many of the villages that it purported to serve and was largely without any major engineering works. The line was initially opened from Stirling to Buchlyvie on the 18th March 1856 and throughout on the 26th May 1856.

On 1st August 1882, the "Strathendrick and Aberfoyle Railway" was opened, using the metals of the F&CJR from Gartness Junction to Buchlyvie Junction. Aberfoyle was soon being promoted as a key point for access to the "Trossachs", made popular by the writings of Sir Walter Scott. It was also the site of several quarries which provided a useful source of goods traffic for the railway. Although the S&AR became part of the North British Railway, the F&CJR remained an independent concern, forming part of the LNER at the 1923 grouping.

With the lack of passenger traffic, the LNER withdrew the passenger service from Stirling to Balloch on the 1st October 1934. Balfron and Buchlyvie Stations remained open for passenger traffic, being served by the Aberfoyle trains until their withdrawal on the 29th September 1951. Freight services from Gartness Junction to Drymen and from Buchlyvie Junction to Port of Mentieth were withdrawn on the 1st November 1950. On 5th October 1959 the freight service from Aberfoyle to Gartness Junction was withdrawn and the final freight service on the F&CJR was withdrawn on the 1st September 1964 from Jamestown to Balloch.

*Mileages*

| | |
|---|---|
| BALLOCH CENTRAL | 0.00 miles |
| JAMESTOWN | 0.75 miles |
| CALDARVAN | 3.00 miles |
| DRYMEN | 5.75 miles |
| GARTNESS | 7.00 miles |
| BALFRON | 9.00 miles |
| BUCHLYVIE | 13.25 miles |

| | |
|---|---|
| BUCHLYVIE | 0.00 miles |
| GARTMORE | 4.00 miles |
| ABERFOYLE | 5.75 miles |

| | |
|---|---|
| PORT of MENTIETH | 16.00 miles |
| KIPPEN | 20.00 miles |
| GARGUNNOCK | 23.00 miles |
| STIRLING | 27.00 miles |

*Ordnance Survey 1:50,000 map numbers:– 56, 57, 63, 64*

*Public Transport*

Balloch Central is served by electric trains from Glasgow and Dumbarton. Aberfoyle is served by buses from Glasgow and Stirling, which also serve many of the former stations on the former Forth & Clyde Junction Railway. Stirling is served by trains and buses to Glasgow, Edinburgh and Perth.

## VII/2a: Aberfoyle to Balloch

**Aborfoyle Station** has suffered the ignominious fate of many a closed station, by being converted into a car park. Very little railway remains survive, apart from the trackbed which has been converted into a footpath for about one mile from the station site. The trackbed remains obstacle free until the site of **Gartmore Station** is reached. A platform and loading platform remain as the trackbed continues underneath the A81 by means of an impressive concrete skew bridge. Although the trackbed beckons on invitingly, the bridge carrying it over the River Forth at Grid Reference 544980 is missing. Apparently the Forestry Commission, who own the trackbed, had sold off its "iron parts" before realising how useful its retention would be. The intending walker has to make a detour along the main road, to cross over the river before regaining the trackbed.

From the south abutment of this bridge, the trackbed is used as a forest access road all the way to Buchlyvie Junction. In the early 1980s the trackbed was resurfaced providing a pleasant obstacle-free walk of nearly three miles across Flanders Moss. The only obstructions encountered are the occasional gate. Across the moss the railway was built using the time honoured method of sinking brushwood mats into the moss, until a firm enough base was available for the railway line. With the railway effectively floating on the moss, this resulted in the trains vibrating much of the surrounding country in their passage. Nowadays the trackbed is the firmest land in the surrounding landscape. **Buchlyvie Junction** stands forlorn, where the S&AR gained the metals of the F&CJR, shortly afterwards the site of **Buchlyvie Station** is reached. Now in private ownership, the station buildings and platforms survive, although a short detour is necessary to regain the trackbed. Saplings and trees growing in the trackbed make for slower progress even on embankments, though the occasional relic such as chairs and signal bases reward the intrepid explorer. Nearing Balfron Station a series of bridges carry the water pipeline from Loch Katrine to Glasgow over the trackbed. This pipeline will prove a blessing later on this walk.

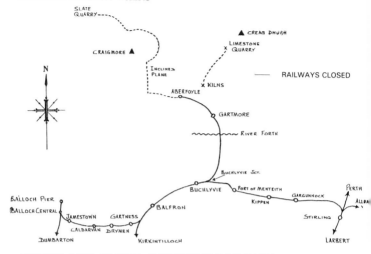

# FORTH AND CLYDE JUNCTION RAILWAY
## and the Aberfoyle Branch

**Balfron Station** is also privately owned, a stable block occupies part of the platforms, the trackbed between which has been filled-in. Some of the station's furnishings have been reused as flowerpots on the grassed-over platforms. Over the lane leading to the village of Balfron, the trackbed passes the farm of "Indians" (the natives are friendly) remaining relatively clear, albeit waterlogged in parts. The bridge over the A81 has been removed by road widening operations but the landscaping of the embankments provides a gentle slope down to the road.

Over the road the initially clear trackbed disappears in a dense collection of saplings, before emergng at the site of **Gartness Junction**. This location provides a rich assortment of relics, from assorted bolts, bullhead track keys to even the remains of a wagon's axlebox cover. The route of the S&AR towards Kirkintilloch is soon blocked by the dismantled viaduct over the Endrick Water. The F&CJR leaves the junction in a cutting which is waterlogged in wet weather, before opening out at the site of **Gartness Station**. Here the derelict crossing gates remain permanently closed against the railway whilst they slowly disintegrate. Whilst the trackbed can be followed (in places only just) the nearby minor road may provide a more attractive alternative.

Although an overbridge near Dalnair Farm has been removed, the trackbed suddenly opens out at the site of the former western bridge abutment as it is joined by the water pipeline. Instead of fighting

*Endrick Viaduct, east of Drymen*

through dense saplings, the walker now embarks on a walk along a grassy path for about three miles, interrupted by the occasional gate across the trackbed. This pipeline also allows one to cross the Endrick Water, where it crosses the piers of the former railway viaduct, with a footpath being provided on top. Once over the water, **Drymen Station** is reached. The Goods Yard provides a healthy crop of containers whilst some of the station buildings have been converted into a private house. The pipeline re-uses the trackbed as far as the crossing at Milford, making the walking very easy, with fine views of Ben Lomond to the North. At Milford, the former crossing keeper's cottage survives along with a goods van body. From this point the trackbed becomes a jungle of saplings once again. Where the line crosses fields, it has been landscaped in places.

At **Caldarvan Station** the railway is separated from the road by a high fence adorned with private property notices. Of the station a wooden sided platform survives, whilst the railway has been used as an access road to some houses. If the minor road is followed to Auchencarroch Farm, shortly before the farm is reached, the route of a tramway from a quarry on the slopes of Blairquhomrie Moor to interchange sidings with the F&CJR can be seen passing underneath the road. Nearing Alexandria the trackbed clears once again before its route has been landscaped on the outskirts of the town. Here the peace is broken by the mating cries of the lesser horned ice-cream van and a tour of a council housing estate is needed to enable the transport at **Balloch** to be reached, at the end of the walk.

## VII/2b:  Buchlyvie to Stirling

Returning to **Buchlyvie Station**, access to the trackbed can be gained either at the station or at an underbridge where the lane leading to Woodend passes beneath the railway. This bridge clearly shows that it was widened at some date, probably when the branch to Aberfoyle was opened. Although the two lines met at Buchlyvie Junction, they ran as a double track to the station, a further quarter of a mile to the west. Rather than continuing along the forest road, which utilises the trackbed of the Aberfoyle Branch, the original route of the F&CJR is followed from Buchlyvie Junction, initially in a dense undergrowth of wild flora.

The section of the trackbed of the Forth & Clyde Junction Railway from **Buchlyvie Junction** to Mey's Siding was abandoned in 1951 and has long since reached the steady state as nature reclaims back her land. The undergrowth diminishes as cattle and sheep have gained access to the trackbed in parts where the lineside fencing has decayed. Central Regional Council are understood to have purchased the trackbed for possible conversion into a "medium distance footpath". This has left the trackbed to wallow in a planning limbo, whereby adjacent farms can unofficially use the land but are prevented from purchasing the land and using it officially. More conscientious farmers maintain their lineside fencing, allowing the trackbed to become an unofficial nature reserve untouched by modern chemicals. In other cases the fencing has collapsed, allowing the trackbed to merge into the surrounding field systems.

At **Mey's Siding** the level crossing remains remarkably intact, with its gates permanently closed against the railway and their metal diamond plates still showing traces of their final coat of red paint. Shortly afterwards the missing bridge over a burn at grid reference NS588953 is reached. Rather than trying a standing long jump, burn plodging is required. Fortunately in summer the burn is normally low and it can be forded without the need for removing one's footwear. Nearing **Port of Mentieth Station**, a detour around the back of the station building is required. The station house has been converted into an attractive dwelling house with whitewashed walls and a small mural depicting various steam locomotives on one wall.

Continuing on towards Kippen, although the OS map goes to great pains to mark two bridges near Newburn Farm, both have been removed. The first bridge had been a large double-span over a small stream (fordable again) whilst the second bridge had been a small bridge over a large bed of nettles (where the penalties for a missed long jump are somewhat stinging). Having negotiated the bridges, a short walkable stretch allows the system to gather its strengths for a jungly part of the trackbed in a small wood before it emerges at the A811 which uses part of the trackbed for the Kippen bypass. The trackbed eventually emerges from out of its tarmac tomb heading towards Middle Kerse Farm, where crops are grown on the trackbed, forcing a further roadside detour. In the short walkable piece of the trackbed, a quarter milepost remains in the trackside verge, as it is attached to a long length of rail its remaining there seems relatively assured.

**Kippen Station** has also been converted into a private house, the signal box being used as a glorified garden shed. On the other side of the road crossing, the trackbed is decorated by the usual car dump. However, the missing bridge over the Boquhan Burn brings an end to these eyesores. The bridge had been a large span over a seemingly small burn, easily forded in dry weather conditions. The trackbed towards Gargunnock varies between a pleasant grassy lane to a dense assortment of undergrowth with a rich collection of willow-herb, vetch, cow parsley, grasses, thistles and nettles. Two crossing keepers' cottages, one abandoned, add a modicum of railway interest to the rural scene. Examination of the trackbed reveals sawn off bolts and other iron detritus from the demolition of the line in the early 1960s.

Nearing **Gargunnock Station**, the trackbed emerges into a timber yard before crossing a minor road and reaching the site of the former station. All that is left apart from some railway cottages are parts of the wooden facing to the platform edges. Beyond the station, the trackbed disappears into a small wood, in the gloomy depths of which a missing bridge over the Gargunnock Burn lurks to trap the optimistic walker. A roadside detour is advisable to use the adjacent road bridge over the burn.

Beyond this obstacle the trackbed is walkable, albeit at times through waist high undergrowth, until a dense band of trees beyond West Carse Farm effectively block onward progress. It is possible that a bridge is missing in the woodland, but without machetes this cannot be verified. Eventually the trackbed emerges and can be followed towards the M9, although missing bridges slow down the walker. Nearing the motorway its course disappears and beyond the motorway embankment which straddles the railway, only faint traces of the trackbed can be discerned in fields before all hope is abandoned as the railway enters the Raploch Housing Estate on the outskirts of Stirling.

# The Aberfoyle Mineral Railways

Although Aberfoyle is thought of today as a tourist centre, lying as it does near limestone and slate strata, it was once an important quarrying town. A limestone quarry to the north-east of the town, below the summit of Creag Dubh, had its own mineral railway system, whilst the main railway led to a slate quarry on the north face of Craigmore, to the north west. This latter involved the construction of an inclined plane from behind the school, rising on a gradient of 1 in 8 to reach a level of nearly 750 feet beneath the summit of Craigmore. From this point the track contoured round the hill to reach the slate quarry.

The inclined plane was double tracked, full wagons descending were used to haul the empty wagons back up the incline. On the level, horse haulage was employed, each horse being capable of hauling six loaded wagons of 500 full or 1,000 undersized slates. Within the quarries, there were a further four inclined planes. These connected the various quarries to the start of the mineral railway. Aberfoyle Slate Quarries opened before 1750 and finally closed in 1958. The mineral railway and the main incline were abandoned in 1947 when the road was constructed from Aberfoyle over the Duke's Pass. Some of the final slates quarried were used in the construction of the David Marshall Lodge near Aberfoyle.

## VII/2c:   The Aberfoyle Slate Quarry Line

The base of the inclined plane can easily be reached by taking the B829 (Inversnaid) road out of Aberfoyle. It starts behind the former school on the north side of the road. A footpath starting to the west of the school leads to the base of the plane. Although it has initially merged into the surrounding woodland, as it ascends the hill its course becomes more distinct. About one third of the way up the incline a level track crosses its course heading to a nearby abandoned limestone quarry. The bed of the incline varies from embankment to cutting, being very grassy and wet in the latter places. Care should be taken ascending the incline due to its steep and slippery gradient. At the summit very little remains of the "engine house" which would have controlled the operation of the incline. The route of the mineral railway now levels out and contours round the hill for a distance of 2–3 miles before it reaches the slate quarry.

Initially the route lies in open country but then it enters the forest, where fortunately the Forestry Commission have retained the route of the railway as a ride, thus allowing the course of the railway to be followed. In places it is indistinct but in other places it consists of snaking embankments threading their level way through the trees. Near the main quarry three smaller quarries have removed parts of the trackbed, but it is possible to make a detour around these. Once past the final obstruction and back onto the trackbed, the rusty remains of the original rails still in situ reward the walker.

They mark the entry of the trackbed into the main quarry; a lunar landscape with mounds of abandoned slate detritus amidst the lush green of the surrounding forest. Inside the quarry, the surviving stone building is a smithy, whilst lower down in the workings a bothy can be inspected by the more intrepid and careful explorer. Everywhere though, there are the remains of the defunct slate industry, gradually being hidden by the encroaching green of nature.

Returning to Aberfoyle, a detour to the nearby David Marshall Lodge will prove most rewarding. A small exhibition outlines the history of the area and the everyday work in the forest. There is also a café to refresh any weary traveller.

# VIII:
# WALKS IN
# STRATHCLYDE REGION

## Railways of the Blane Valley

The Campsie Glen branch was opened from a junction with the Edinburgh & Glasgow Railway, at the east of Lenzie Station, to Lennoxtown on the 5th July 1858. It served the industrial town of Kirkintilloch, where it passed underneath the Forth & Clyde Canal, as well as numerous industrial concerns at Milton of Campsie and Lennoxtown. Eight years later, on the 5th November 1866, an extension from Lennoxtown to Killearn was opened for goods traffic. Passengers had to wait until the first of July of the following year, before they could travel by train to Killearn, using the rails of the Campsie Glen branch and the Blane Valley Railway.

North of Kirkintilloch, the line was crossed by the Kelvin Valley Railway, which opened a passenger service from Glasgow to Kilsyth via Kirkintilloch, on the 1st June 1878. The railway used a connecting spur onto the Campsie Glen branch, to reach Kirkintilloch. The Blane Valley Railway was used by the Strathendrick and Aberfoyle Railway, which opened their line from Killearn to Aberfoyle on the 1st August 1882. This company also used part of the Forth & Clyde Junction Railway (which ran from Balloch to Stirling, along the northern foothills of the Campsies), from Gartness Junction to Buchlyvie Junction, in their route to Aberfoyle.

The lines along the foothills of the Campsies, became part of the North British Railway, which in turn became part of the London & North Eastern Railway, after the 1923 grouping of the railway companies. In spite of its tourist potential, the line from Kirkintilloch to Aberfoyle was not very profitable. The LNER operated steam railcars on some services in an attempt to reduce operating costs. It is perhaps due to the outbreak of the Second World War, that the passenger service to Aberfoyle survived, to become a loss making service for British Railways, after the 1948 nationalisation.

British Railways soon sought the withdrawal of passenger services north of Kirkintilloch, closing all services during 1951. The first casualty was the service along the KVR which ceased on the 4th August, although a vestigial service from Kilsyth to Kirkintilloch remained for a further two days. Finally the passenger service from Kirkintilloch to Aberfoyle was withdrawn on the 1st October. The passenger service from Lenzie to Kirkintilloch survived for a further decade, it was finally withdrawn on the 7th September 1964.

Although passenger trains had ceased, Aberfoyle maintained a goods service, on account of its nearby slate industry, until the 5th October 1959 when the line was cut back to Lennox Castle Siding. A further reduction took place on the 28th September 1964, with the closure of the goods service from Lennoxtown to Lennox Castle Siding. The final closure took place on the 4th April 1966, when goods services on the original Campsie Glen branch and its associated connections were withdrawn. The goods service along the KVR had ceased ten years earlier, when the line from Torrance to Kelvin Valley East Junction was taken out of use by the 24th June.

*Mileages*

| | |
|---|---|
| LENZIE | 0 miles 00 chains |
| Campsie Branch Junction | 0 miles 04 chains |
| Monkland Junction | 1 mile 00 chains |
| KIRKINTILLOCH | 1 mile 59 chains |
| Kelvin Valley South Junction | 2 miles 35 chains |
| MILTON OF CAMPSIE | 3 miles 37 chains |
| LENNOXTOWN | 5 miles 20 chains |
| CAMPSIE GLEN | 6 miles 16 chains |
| STRATHBLANE | 9 miles 40 chains |
| BLANEFIELD | 10 miles 36 chains |
| DUMGOYNE | 13 miles 35 chains |
| KILLEARN | 14 miles 72 chains |
| Gartness Junction | 16 miles 22 chains |

*Ordnance Survey 1:50,000 map numbers:– 57, 64*

*Public Transport*

Lenzie is served by the local DMU service from Glasgow to Stirling and Falkirk, on all days except Sunday. Kirkintilloch is served by buses from Glasgow, Stirling and Falkirk, as well as a local service to Lennoxtown. Strathblane is served by buses to Glasgow, which pass by Milngavie Station, on the Glasgow Electric suburban service. Buses from Glasgow to Stirling via Balfron, pass close by the route of the railway from Strathblane to Gartness Junction. The frequency of this service is limited, especially on a Sunday.

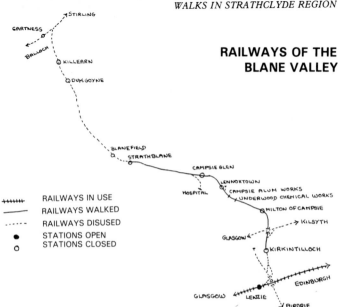

**RAILWAYS OF THE BLANE VALLEY**

+++++ RAILWAYS IN USE
―――― RAILWAYS WALKED
----- RAILWAYS DISUSED
● STATIONS OPEN
○ STATIONS CLOSED

## VIII/1: Lenzie to Strathblane

Having arrived at Lenzie Station, the walker should gain the B757 which passes to the east of the station, turning north to reach the nearby crossroads. Turning right, along the road signposted to an industrial estate, one will find oneself walking parallel to the Edinburgh and Glasgow Railway and the start of the Campsie Glen Branch. Half a mile down this road, the trackbed of the Monkland & Kirkintilloch Railway once crossed over the road, having passed underneath the Campsie Glen Branch. Landscaping of these lines and the nearby site of Woodilee Colliery, has eradicated many traces of the former use of the land. Whilst it is possible to follow the Campsie Glen Branch, the walker may elect to follow the M&KR route, which has been converted into an illuminated public footpath, to the site of **Whitegates Crossing**, where it crossed the B757 between Lenzie and Kirkintilloch. The walk passes the site of the connection with the Campsie Glen Branch, at the site of Woodley Junction. A path follows the route of the connection, to reach the landscaped expanse of the former Monkland Junction.

If the walker is still following the M&KR, the path ends at Whitegates Crossing, where the history of the railway is recorded by a commemorative plaque. Beyond the road, the trackbed is built upon, by modern council offices behind which it emerges into playing fields and the landscaped site of the railways **Townhead Terminus**. Here the M&KR had interchange facilities with the nearby Forth & Clyde Canal. The canal can be used to reach the site of Kirkintilloch Station. However, if the walker had used the connection to Monkland Junction, the route emerges from the landscaping to pass the site of **Townhead Halt**, before passing under the B8048.

The trackbed having passed underneath this road, emerges into what was an attractive park on the site of the connection to Meiklehill Colliery. This pleasant expanse of green was far too much for the modern highway "engineers", who have decided to run the Kirkintilloch Bypass through the site, on a lofty embankment. Emerging from underneath this tarmacadam burden, the trackbed reaches the famous bridge over water (the Luggie Water) and under water (the Forth and Clyde Canal), at the far end of which is the site of **Kirkintilloch Station**. Very little remains apart from traces of the former branch which served the nearby Lion Foundry (where many telephone and pillar boxes were cast) and a goods shed, which is now used by a haulage contractor.

Further progress along the railway is marred by the removal of the bridge over the Glazert water. One should follow the B757, signposted to Lennoxtown, to cross over the water and regain the trackbed by turning right into the nearby industrial estate. Where the access road turns back towards the Glazert Water, a muddy path cuts across to the nearby trackbed. Soon, one passes the site of Kelvin Valley South Junction, where the connecting spur onto the KVR turns away eastwards. Ahead lies the course of the KVR, passing over the trackbed, including an impressive two arched stone viaduct over the Glazert Water. This is the sole surviving railway crossing over this water course in the Kirkintilloch area, as the bridge on the connecting spur has also been removed. Unfortunately the bridge which carried the KVR over the Campsie Glen Branch has also been removed, preventing access onto the river bridge from the lower trackbed, except by the most devout of rock climbers.

Beyond this location, the Campsie Glen branch has been converted into an official walkway, to the site of Campsie Glen station. There are also signs that the KVR towards Torrance is also being converted, so perhaps someone will put in one of the missing bridges, to permit access along the KVR towards Kilsyth. The muddy track that the trackbed has become soon ends, being replaced by a ballast of fine chippings providing the walker with a pleasurable walk alongside the burbling Glazert Water. Seats have been provided at frequent intervals, usually of metal, although a rather fine stone built one records the efforts of a manpower services team's efforts in 1986. Approaching Milton of Campsie, the trackbed curves westwards, to run alongside the foothills of the Campsie Hills. The site of sidings which served the Kincaid Print Works is passed, before the walker reaches the site of **Milton of Campsie Station**.

Although the original buildings have been removed, the former platforms remain, to mark the station site. The station was on either side of the bridge which carried the B757 over the railway. The original stone built bridge has been strengthened, by filling in most of the original arch, leaving a corrugated iron clad tunnel to permit access along the former trackbed. Beyond the station, traces of trackbeds which served industrial complexes on the north side of the Glazert Water can be found on the right hand side. These include the remains of three bridges which served the Lillyburn Works. Although these are semi derelict, the bridges are well and truly fenced off, to prevent unwanted incursions from the south. The trackbed continues towards Lennoxtown, as a pleasant country lane, well frequented by locals walking their dogs.

The railway crossed the Glazert water three times before Lennoxtown. The first two bridges have had new timber decking placed on some of the original girders. Traces of milepost and gradient post bases bring the walker past the crossing of the B822 near Rowantreefauld Cottages. The line is now out in open country, and one is rewarded with impressive views of the Campsies. Near Lennoxtown there were sidings for the Underwood Chemical works and the Campsie Alum Works before the line crosses the Glazert Water. When the extension to Blanefield was opened, the original final section into Lennoxtown was bypassed and a new river crossing and station were provided. The original station became the town's goods station. Whilst both bridges have been removed, the older bridge's masonry piers now support a modern replacement timber bridge, leading on to the landscaped site of the original **Lennoxtown Station**.

Cutting across these fields, there is very little trace of the railway, or of the new station apart from the bridge which carries the access road to Muirhead Farm over the railway. The pleasant track continues westwards, passing underneath an ornamental bridge, at the entrance to the Lennox Castle estate, to reach the site of **Campsie Glen Station**. Apart from a short stone-sided platform, which may have once been a loading dock, no other trace of this station survives. The station served the nearby Lennox Castle, the grounds of which were adapted and extended to form a military/psychiatric hospital. A branch was built into the hospital grounds during the First World War, to bring in supplies and wounded troops. The trackbed beyond the station is obstructed by the gardens of the nearby entrance lodge, and one should divert into the grounds of the hospital.

The entrance drive reaches a T-junction, and a right turn should bring the walker to the brick built weigh-house and adjacent weigh bridge, alongside the hospital branch. Turning back towards the junction along the trackbed, one crosses onto the north bank of the Glazert Water, by means of an early railway concrete bridge. Hopefully the men in the white coats have not followed, as the walker regains what is now the trackbed of the Blane Valley Railway, heading westwards towards Blanefield. Unfortunately the final bridge over the Galzert Water has been removed, as the river turns northwards towards the Campsie Hills. A kind-hearted farmer has provided a crossing of the water, a hundred yards north of the former railway crossing, using recovered railway sleepers.

Returning to the trackbed, the walker passes through a short overgrown section, emerging into the open to run alongside the Pow Burn. The railway had very little earthworks in this section, and with the help of some landscaping, it is very difficult to visualise that a railway once passed through the grassy fields. Only the occasional remains of telegraph poles and grass covered mounds, indicate the route of the railway, whilst inquisitive cows follow one through the fields. The prominent shape of Dunglass Hill is passed, along with traces of the sidings which served the nearby quarry, before one reaches a boggy cutting on the outskirts of Strathblane. Unless wellingtons are worn, the advised course is to head up and follow the railway from the nearby cutting sides, rather than wading through this watery obstruction. At the far end of the cutting, a notice proclaims the railway is now a bridleway!

**Strathblane Station** has been adapted to provide the gardens of a private house, that presumably was once the former station master's accommodation. A nearby lane will take one up to the nearby A891, the main road from Strathblane to Lennoxtown. A short distance (left) along the road, the walker will find a large public house and the nearby bus stop, for buses to Milngavie and Glasgow. The trackbed through the village and the continuation towards Blanefield, has been landscaped and is now built upon by a linear housing estate, forcing the walker onto the nearby main road, to reach Blanefield.

# Dalry to Kilmarnock

*(For the following history I am indebted to S. W. Rankin, courtesy of the G&SWRA)*

The Dalry – Kilmarnock line experienced several differing phases in its life, varying between branch and through traffic routes. In civil engineering terms it was undoubtedly a main line with near level grades, maximum 1 in 500, combined with good alignment, the sharpest curve being about 1.75 miles radius. There was double track throughout and there were major goods loops on both sides at Montgreenan and Crosshouse, also at Dalry Junction. The only speed restrictions on the 10.5 mile length were at the extreme ends, 30 mph at Dalry and 15 mph at Kilmarnock.

Inaugurated in 1837, the line was opened on 4th April 1843 as the Kilmarnock branch of the Glasgow, Paisley, Kilmarnock & Ayr Railway and it was joined on 22nd May 1848 by the Busby or Busbie branch from

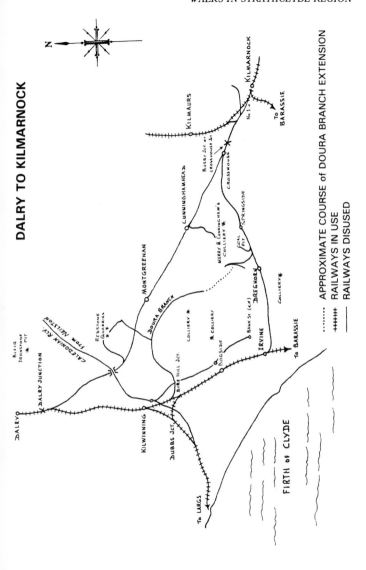

**DALRY TO KILMARNOCK**

N

........... APPROXIMATE COURSE of DOURA BRANCH EXTENSION
++++++ RAILWAYS IN USE
———— RAILWAYS DISUSED

To KILMARNOCK

KILMAURS

Busby Jct
Crosshouse Jct

No 1 ——
To BARASSIE

CROSSHOUSE

CUNNINGHAMHEAD

STRINGSIDE

MERRY & CUNNINGHAM'S
COLLIERY

COAL
PIT

MONTGREENAN

DREGHORN

DOURA BRANCH

COLLIERY

BLAIR
IRONSTONE
PIT

CALEDONIAN RLY
FROM NEILSTON

REDSTONE
QUARRIES

BYRE HILL JCT

COLLIERY

COLLIERY

DRONGSIDE

BANK St (LP)

IRVINE

To BARASSIE

DALRY JUNCTION

DALRY

KILWINNING

DUBBS JCT

FIRTH of CLYDE

To LARGS

151

Irvine, which was closed after less than two years' service on 15th April 1850. On 28th October 1850 the main line was opened throughout to Carlisle and the G&SWR was formed from the constituent companies. The Dalry – Kilmarnock line now enjoyed the status of being part of a main Anglo-Scottish route for all types of traffic. In passenger terms, this lasted until the opening on 26th June 1873 of the Glasgow, Barrhead & Kilmarnock Joint Line. This route was some 9 miles shorter than via Paisley & Dalry and the main line passenger trains thereafter used it, although the grades were much heavier. Local passenger trains continued to serve the Dalry route.

Through goods traffic also stayed on the easily graded Dalry – Kilmarnock line; in addition, the original route was also convenient for exchanging Greenock and local freight at Elderslie, two miles west of Paisley. The run from Glasgow (College) to Carlisle was universally known as the "Long Road Goods" and the various G&SWR 0-6-6 classes from Patrick Stirling's 58 class right down to Drummond's "Pumpers" served in long succession until the 1930s, the 2-6-0s carrying on into the 1940s.

Local passenger trains from Glasgow to Dalry and Kilmarnock had a choice of the Paisley Gilmour St. or Canal (usually Canal), and the Lochside or Kilbirnie routes. These continued until June 1966 when the Kilbirnie loop was then closed to regular passenger services. St. Enoch was closed simultaneously and all remaining services were diverted to Glasgow Central. Dalry – Kilmarnock remained open, with one or two trains to Carlisle per day, as the Barrhead – Kilmarnock line was under some threat from the Beeching Plan of 1963. It eventually transpired that the Barrhead route was used to by-pass the West Coast Main Line during electrification works, after which it was singled and the Dalry – Kilmarnock line was closed. There was a Glasgow Central – Euston sleeper nightly via Paisley (where it picked up) and Dalry which ran until May 1974, usually hauled by a Class 47 diesel. This would be the last regular passenger train to use this route.

Individual stations on the line succumbed to closure at various dates. Dalry Junction, or Kilcush Junction, which lay in the vee of the Junction, was closed on 31st December 1859. Montgreenan station opened on 1st February 1878 and was closed on 7th March 1955. The station house is now a private house and is the only extant station building on the line. Cunninghamhead was an original station on the line, opened as Stewarton (although it was four miles from the village) and was renamed on 1st September 1873, two months after the opening of the Barrhead line. It was closed on 1st January 1951 and virtually nothing can be seen of it today. The final station, Crosshouse, in the vee of the junction with the line to Irvine via Busby, was opened on 1st September 1872 on the site of the earlier Busby Station. The signalbox at this site, was named Busby Junction until 10th March 1924. Crosshouse Station was closed on 3rd March 1969, the final station to be closed on the line.

Although overshadowed by the main line traffic, there would have been a fair amount of local goods traffic in the earlier years. Travelling from Dalry Junction, immediately on the left a branch about 1.25 miles in length, trailed in from Blair Pits (ironstone) numbers 2, 9 and 10. After passing underneath the Caledonian Railway's Lanarkshire and Ayrshire line, there were the Redstone Coal and Stone Sidings. There was a facing branch off to the left, leading to the Redstone Quarries, ½ mile distant. The signalbox at this location was closed in 1918. At Montgreenan there is nothing special marked on Airey's 1898 map of the district, the 1896 gradient profile, or the 1906 Ordnance Survey 1 inch map, but there were the lay-by sidings. At Annick Lodge, 1 mile 10 chains east of Montgreenan Station, a short branch on the south side facing west is shown on Airey's map.

Just east of Cunninghamhead station were the North and South Junctions of Merry and Cunningham's Warwickhill Colliery branch which was 1.75 miles long on the south side, facing east, of the main line. After another mile or so there was Busbiehead Signal Box, which controlled access via a siding to Busbiehead No. 3 Pit. Busbiehead No. 2 Signal Box was at the site of Crosshouse Junction. At Crosshouse Junction there was a small goods yard with a wooden shed that still exists. Between Crosshouse and Kilmarnock No. 1 signal box (where the line joined the older Kilmarnock and Troon Railway) there were three more named sidings. In the early years, all three sidings (Fardlehill, Bonnyton and Woodhill) were all controlled by their own signal boxes. The Woodhill siding, at least, was also a mineral branch.

The Montgreenan area in particular was intensively worked for coal and ironstone. There were also several brickworks in the area. Running parallel to the main line for two miles, and only ½ mile distant from it, ran the purely mineral Doura Branch. This provided a direct link to the Eglington Iron Works and Ardrossan Harbour. This branch allowed the main line to be freed from a substantial amount of slow local freight. With the decline of the pockets of heavy industry and the gradual extinction of its links, the area has now returned to its earlier rural peace.

Fardlehill and Bonnyton, though receiving only brief mention earlier, seem to have been the only locations on the line where private industrial engines could be seen. Archibald Finnie & Son worked pits at Fardlehill until 1927 and used an 1883 Grant Ritchie and an Andrew Barclay engine. The Bonnyton Colliery and Fireclay Works has three Barclay pugs, two of which survived until 1962. These engines were all standard gauge 0-4-0STs.

*Mileages*

| | |
|---|---|
| DALRY | 0.0 miles |
| MONTGREENAN | 5.00 miles |
| CUNNINGHAMHEAD | 7.25 miles |
| CROSSHOUSE | 9.50 miles |
| KILMARNOCK | 11.25 miles |

*Ordnance Survey 1:50,000 map numbers:–* 63, 70

Public Transport

Dalry is served by electric trains from Glasgow Central to Largs and Ayr, whilst Kilmarnock is served by an hourly train service to Glasgow Central, as well as a limited service to Ayr and Carlisle. There is also a regular bus service from Kilmarnock to Ayr and Glasgow. The frequency of these services is reduced on a Sunday, especially the rail service during the winter months.

## VIII/2: Dalry to Kilmarnock

Like Railway Historians, devotees of Railway Rambling tend to concentrate on the branch lines at the expense of the main lines. Sometimes the latter provide a better training ground for the novice walker. Disused main lines generally maintain a greater semblance of a former railway route and less of a semblance to the Amazonian Rain Forest. The route of this walk is a typical example – opened in 1864, it served as a main line until abandonment in the early 1970s. Although it provided a longer route from Glasgow to Kilmarnock, its easier gradients counteracted the distance advantage of the joint route via Barrhead. Since closure, however, it has slipped into a forgotten state. Many people (including the Ordnance Survey) believe the line still to be open and it is rumoured that British Rail are considering its reinstatement. Should this happen, Kilmarnock trains will once again serve Paisley at the expense of the sprawling metropolis of Barrhead.

The walk starts at **Dalry Station**, a functional shadow of its former rambling size, served by trains from Glasgow to the Ayrshire Coast. The "Ayrshire Electrification" was responsible for the station's modernisation and improvement. By following field paths, that once formed part of a system of lines serving a local works, it is possible to reach the Kilmarnock line at **Dalry Junction** where it leaves the extant Costal line. Nowadays this area provides a haven for local bikers and possibly glue sniffers. The more caring natives become friendly when they learn that you are only there to follow the disused railway line. Maybe by creating a greater public awareness in the fate of these disused lines, there will be a greater pressure to convert them for recreational purposes.

At the junction site, the shell of a rather attractive limestone building stands forlorn. From its appearance it would seem to have been the base of a water tower. Leaving the junction, the line gradually climbs to attain a summit near to where it passes underneath the abandoned line from Kilwinning to Barrmill. The trackbed remains distinct with well-bedded ballast providing a reasonable walking surface. The bridge carrying the abandoned line from Kilwinning is a rather attractive three-arched structure. Now it stands neglected but intact, seen only by those walking this trackbed. To the west a final view may be seen of the current line to Kilwinning before our line embarks on a gentle downgrade. The trackbed remains in good condition although it would appear that the line had been singled before it was finally abandoned. Nearing the missing overbridge across the B778, the trackbed displays an abundant crop of fishplates, chairs, pieces of rail and even the girders of the missing bridge.

Having negotiated the missing bridge, a gentle descent takes the line to the viaduct over the Lugton Water, followed by a gentle rise to the site of the first station on the line at **Montgreenan**. Now a private house, the brick built extensions blend in well with the warm red sandstone of the original buildings. The building still betrays its ancestry, fronting onto a lush green lawn formed from the trackbed between its platforms. Beyond the station overbridge, although the line is thought to be owned by Strathclyde Regional Council, all is not well. The trackbed is being used as a hideous rubbish dump for unwanted materials from a house renovation. Past this eyesore, rural serenity descends once again. In places the boundary fence is composed of limestone walling – possibly at the insistence of a local landowner during the construction of the line. Before reaching the next station, the other missing bridge is reached. Its absence over the A736 presents no major difficulty as gentle slopes have been provided down to the road from both embankments. The bridge abutments indicate that the bridge had possibly been constructed as a stone arched bridge and was converted into a standard girder bridge at a later date.

Very few remains can be found of the site of the former **Cunninghamhead Station**: only a short piece of stone walling from a cattle dock or goods platform remains visible. The grass covered site reveals on closer examination a rich flora thriving in the tranquil atmosphere. Many varieties of wild flower are supplemented by wild strawberries and brambles which could provide a useful source of refreshment in the right season. Only a few fences across the trackbed impede the progress towards Crosshouse. However, as compensation a fox may accompany the lucky walker. The rich flora bears witness to a land untouched by weedkillers and other chemicals since closure. In the nearby fields cattle try to climb through the boundary fencing to feed off the railway land.

**Crosshouse Station** was the junction of the line to Irvine which passed through Dreghorn. Near the junction it is used as a practice ground for trail-bikers, but high fencing prevents them from encroaching onto this trackbed. Continuing on towards Kilmarnock, the countryside gradually turns into an urban landscape and the trackbed becomes clothed in society's unwanted materials. A buffer stop looms into view, civilisation has returned, and a long siding infrequently used occupies the final half mile of the line. Approaching **Kilmarnock** its condition deteriorates. Concrete sleepers are replaced by wooden sleepers which in turn are replaced by an empty space. The time has come to leave the trackbed and head into Kilmarnock by road. The line itself continues on, passing closed factories and becomes double track in a final fling before emerging into a near empty yard on the north side of the railway station.

# Muirkirk to Coalburn

The railway line from Muirkirk to Coalburn raises an interesting question for the railway walker; when is a railway line not a railway line? The eight miles between the two places across the bleak, windswept Douglas Moor, is the route taken by perhaps the most enigmatic of disused Scottish railway lines. In the 1880s, the Caledonian Railway opened its Spryeslack branch to tap the immensely rich Douglas Coalfield round Galawhistle and Glenbuck. Early in the twentieth century, the C.R. planned to extend this route to Muirkirk, to give the Caledonian another route into the expanding coal and iron town, the other route being along the banks of the Douglas Water from Lanark. From the west, the Glasgow and South Western Railway had also reached Muirkirk, from Cumnock.

It was to be an expensive extension of the Galawhistle line, involving the construction of three major viaducts and a deep stone cutting in its short length. The line was signalled and finished in all respects, but it was never opened. The reason is said to be the G&SWR threatening to apply for running powers over the new route, deep into the heart of Caledonian territory. The Caledonian was not prepared to accept this risk, and never opened the new line. During World War 1, the tracks were lifted on the extension. The trackbed remained railway property until 1942, shortly after the Ponesk and Auldhouseburn viaducts were dismantled by demolition and bombing exercises during the Second World War.

Since then all of the railways which once served Muirkirk and Coalburn have been closed, adding further abandoned trackbeds to the enigmatic railway that never was. However, with recent developments to create a large open cast mine on Douglas Moor, the wheel could make a full revolution, with the reopening of a railway into the area, to carry away the fruits of the open cast development.

## VIII/3: Muirkirk to Coalburn

Muirkirk lost its passenger services from the west on September 10th 1951 and from Lanark in the east on 5th October 1964. Since then, the main public transport route has been from Cumnock in the west, with a minibus service providing a limited connecting service with the regular bus from Lanark to Glespin. However, it is the latter service which perhaps suits the motorised walker, leaving the car in Lanark to use public transport to reach the start of the walk, and return back from Coalburn at the end of the walk. Leaving Muirkirk by means of a minor road to Kaimes, the site of **Muirkirk Station** is reached, half a mile out of

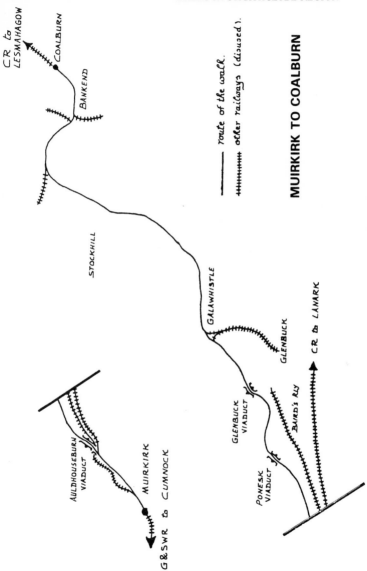

**MUIRKIRK TO COALBURN**

CR to LESMAHAGOW

COALBURN

BANKEND

STOCKHILL

GALAWHISTLE

GLENBUCK

CR to LANARK

GLENBUCK VIADUCT

PONESK VIADUCT

BAIRD'S RLY

AULDHOUSEBURN VIADUCT

MUIRKIRK

G&SWR to CUMNOCK

———— route of the walk.

++++++++ other railways (disused).

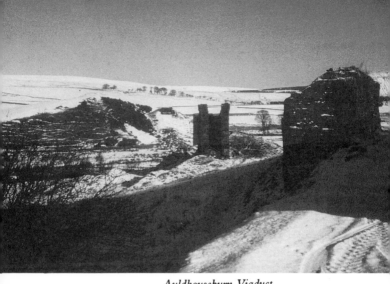

*Auldhouseburn Viaduct*

the town. Very little remains of the station, apart from an empty platform and a railway house. Immediately to the east of the station, the trackbed is blocked by an industrial establishment, that appears to have gone the same way as the railway. However, a nearby lane allows the walker to circumvent this obstacle to regain the trackbed of the CR line to Lanark.

The Caledonian line, opened to passenger services on 1st June 1874, follows the route of an earlier line, built by the Baird Iron and Coal Company towards Glenbuck. This earlier line can be seen in places, making for Glenbuck by a series of twists and turns, in marked contrast to the relatively direct course of the Caledonian Route. Very few obstacles impair the progress of the walker as he reaches the junction with the railway that never was, near Crossflats Farm.

Leaving the CR line, the trackbed of the Baird's line is crossed as it heads underneath the trackbed of the extension. Impressively massive brick walls would have supported this bridge, possibly wide enough to have allowed for a triangular junction with the Lanark line. Shortly afterwards, the trackbed would have crossed the Auldhouse Burn, by means of the first dismantled viaduct. If it is not possible to wade across this burn, a detour can be made via the access lane to Crossflats, regaining the trackbed as it crosses the A70 near Lightshaw. Of the viaduct, a few masonry piers still point defiantly skywards, watching over their fallen brethren. Once across the burn, the trackbed can be regained for a short stretch before the missing bridge over the A70 obstructs progress once again.

Across the road, the railway starts climbing for the crossing of the Douglas Moors. Considering its relatively early abandonment, the trackbed is remarkably clear of the usual dense undergrowth which impairs many similar railway walks. The railway alternates between cutting and embankment as it heads towards the Ponesk Burn Viaduct. Before the viaduct is reached a large quarry is passed, with perilous drops from the embankment into the workings of the quarry. A watchman is likely to approach the walker making tracks for Coalburn, but a short explanation about this strange hobby reassures him sufficiently to allow the walker to regain the trackbed for the short walk to the viaduct. It is a forlorn sight, the piers lying broken on the valley sides, with only their stumps marking their original position when they formed part of the viaduct.

The Ponesk Burn can be forded, followed by a scramble up the valley side, to regain the trackbed. In this desolate location, the walker suddenly comes across a working coal mine, complete with a narrow gauge rope worked inclined plane. This small private mine, known appropriately as the Viaduct Mine, is the last working remnant of the Muirkirk coalfield. Having spent some time exploring this unexpected discovery, the trackbed is regained for a pleasurable walk towards the final viaduct, across a burn flowing into Glenbuck Loch. The private mine uses the railway as its access road, allowing the walker to make rapid progress towards this viaduct. The railway curves onto the Glenbuck Viaduct, now marked only by its standing piers. Another valley side is descended, to gain an access road to a disused mine, where a bridge provides a dry crossing of the burn. Once over the burn, the valley side is climbed, and the trackbed regained for the final part of the unopened extension from Muirkirk.

Perhaps once back onto the trackbed, the walker will take a short break for lunch. Certainly a break is welcomed after the three bouts of descending and ascending of valley sides. The final views of Glenbuck are obtained, before the trackbed enters a long cutting, climbing further up into the Douglas Moors, for the junction with the Galawhistle branch. The junction site is an amazing location, suddenly the solitude of the trackbed is broken by a series of lines heading towards Coalburn and back down the valley to Glenbuck. The three lines would appear to have formed a triangular junction, amidst the loneliness of the moors still strewn with the spoil heaps of long closed mines. Strangely, the extension appears to have made a dog-legged junction with the Galawhistle Branch, for although the earthworks exist for the direct connection, the trackbed turns right and then left to gain the continuation of the branch towards Glenbuck.

The next few miles along the Galawhistle Branch have at times an oppressive air in the loneliness of the moors. Initially the line descends towards the confluence of the Monks Water and the Galawhistle Burn. The trackbed is used as an access road passing through empty moorland, with only the occasional sighting of sheep to remind the walker of the fragmentary impact of mankind on these lands. At the confluence of the two streams, the trackbed turns north-westwards, crossing a saddle between Hagshaw Hill and Meikle Auchinstilloch, before dropping towards South Cumberhead and the Scots Burn. The sudden sighting of habitation comes as a relief, although there is still nearly three miles to go before reaching Coalburn.

Tracked vehicles that have been using the trackbed as a road, now leave the railway behind, as it crosses over the lane leading up to South Bankend. Although the bridge has been dismantled, it can be easily detoured, allowing the trackbed to be regained as it makes a sweeping semi-circular arc towards Coalburn. Having passed Stockhill Farm, the walker starts to encounter fences, both across the trackbed and running down the centre of it, that are usually topped by a couple of strands of barbed wire. At the northernmost limit of the line, the trackbed enters a shallow waterlogged cutting, at the end of which is a junction with a branch that trails in (L) from mines near Dalquhandy. Suddenly the landscape is marred by dumped heavy earth-moving equipment, that have left their mark on the trackbed as it turns towards Coalburn. The trackbed turns SW then skirts a large spoil heap, before it joins the branch (R) from further mines in the area of Bankend.

Beyond the junction, most traces of the trackbed have been removed by landscaping operations. These have left behind a very marshy land, beyond which the trackbed has a final fling before reaching the terminus of passenger services at Coalburn. A few rotting sleepers along with occasional pieces of ironwork, act as silent memorials to the station. The actual station site has been partially built upon by a stone faced house, that may have once have been part of some railway building. Sadly the walker is not greeted by a welcoming blast on a steam engine whistle, the only whistling is that of wind passing through the wires of the telephone system, whilst the walker waits for the bus back to the main transport hubs of this area. Coalburn, apart from the regular Central SMT service to Glasgow, is also served by an independent operator with a round-about route via Lesmahagow to Lanark. Maybe there is time to seek refreshment in a warm café or hostelry, and perhaps reflect on the railway that never was, before starting on the journey home.

# The Maidens & Dunure Railway

In 1902 the Glasgow and South Western Railway started construction of a railway from Alloway Junction, on the Ayr to Stranraer line. The new route was to pass through the heart of Burns Country, running 600 yards south of his birthplace, 230 yards to the north of the monument and the Auld Brig o'Doon. It also ran a few yards beneath the graveyard of the Auld Alloway Kirk. To avoid the land being spoiled by the passage of the railway, it passed through the hallowed square mile, by means of a cutting and a tunnel beside the kirkyard. The line, known as the Maidens and Dunure Light Railway, then wound its way along the Ayrshire Coast, rejoining the Stranraer line to the north of Girvan. Although the line was built to the light railways act of 1896, there were considerable engineering works, including the lengthy viaducts, over the Croy and Rancleugh Glens. The latter of these viaducts rising to a height of 125 feet.

The railway passed Croy Electric Brae, where an optical illusion made the downhill slope of the line appear to be an uphill gradient. Engines apparently appeared to climb this gradient with very little effort. One of the main reasons for the construction of the railway was to serve the Turnberry Hotel and Golf Course. As the hotel was built by the G&SWR, its front entrance faced the railway, whilst the rear entrance opened out onto the Golf Course. Special arrangements were provided by the railway, to ensure the passengers reached the hotel with a minimum of delay.

The line was never profitable and the LMSR withdrew the passenger service from Turnberry to Ayr on 1st December 1930, although it was later reinstated from 4th July 1932 to 31st May 1933. A passenger service from Girvan to Turnberry, to serve the hotel, continued until 2nd March 1942. The line remained in use for goods, and in conjunction with the opening of Butlins Holiday Camp in 1947, a new passenger service was provided from Alloway Junction to a new Heads of Ayr station. This was withdrawn on the 12th September 1968.

In retrospect the railway closed before its time. Had it survived it would have been a great asset to the tourist trade of the area. It would have provided a link for the Turnberry Hotel, Culzean Castle, Alloway and Butlins Holiday Camp at Heads of Ayr.

*Mileages*

| | |
|---|---|
| AYR | 0 miles 00 chains |
| ALLOWAY | 3 miles 00 chains |
| HEADS OF AYR (Original) | 6 miles 20 chains |
| DANURE | 8 miles 00 chains |
| KNOWESIDE | 11 miles 00 chains |
| GLENSIDE | 13 miles 00 chains |
| MAIDENS | 15 miles 20 chains |
| TURNBERRY | 16 miles 60 chains |
| GIRVAN | 21 miles 60 chains |

*Ordnance Survey 1:50,000 map numbers:– 70, 76*

*Public Transport*

Ayr is served by regular rail and bus services to Glasgow and a limited rail service to Kilmarnock and Carlisle. Girvan is served by trains to Ayr and Stranraer. There is a limited bus service from Ayr to Dunure, as well

161

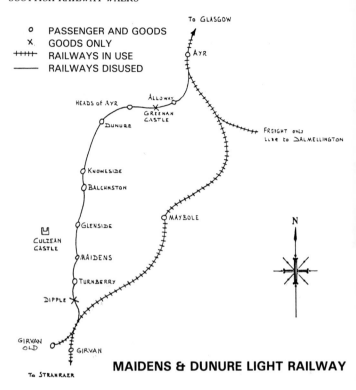

To GLASGOW

o   PASSENGER AND GOODS
x.  GOODS ONLY
++++  RAILWAYS IN USE
─────  RAILWAYS DISUSED

AYR

ALLOWAY

HEADS of AYR

GREENAN CASTLE

DUNURE

FREIGHT only
line to DALMELLINGTON

KNOWESIDE

BALCHNSTON

MAYBOLE

GLENSIDE

CULZEAN CASTLE

N

MAIDENS

TURNBERRY

DIPPLE

GIRVAN OLD

GIRVAN

**MAIDENS & DUNURE LIGHT RAILWAY**

To STRANRAER

as a limited bus service from Ayr to Girvan that serves Culzean Castle (Glenside Station) and Turnberry.

## VIII/4a: Dunure to Alloway

The railway passes underneath the minor road to the south of Dunure in a steep rock sided cutting, that is very waterlogged. Standing on the bridge, the walker can view the trackbed as it curves away south towards Knoweside Station. By following a path which serves the nearby TV/Radio Ariel to the west of the railway, the trackbed can be gained to the north of the cutting and the nearby silage pit. The route soon becomes a dry embankment, used by sheep, as it skirts the eastern side of the 1930s council housing of Dunure village. Beyond the village there is a good view of the ruins of Dunure Castle and the warm waters of the Ayrshire coast. Having passed the village, several tracks join up

*Track bed to the south of Dunure*

with the railway as it heads towards the remains of Dunure Station.

The trackbed crosses the Dunduff Burn on an impressive lattice girder bridge, high above the twisting torrent of the burn. Surprisingly these girders have remained in situ, although some of the original lattice work has been removed. A path on the north side of the burn provides a limited view of the bridge in winter. Perhaps the large number of trees have helped to hide the bridge from the eyes of the phantom removers of old railway bridges. Another rock-sided waterlogged cutting that is overgrown with brambles and unwanted human refuse has to be negotiated before the empty platform of **Dunure Station** is reached. The trackbeds on either side of the original island platform are very overgrown, although a path can be made along the moss covered platform. Traces of the foundations of the small station buildings and the once well kept flower beds, may still be found amidst the undergrowth.

Leaving the station behind, the walker passes a small wooden stable, before joining a path which weaves its way through the gorse and broom, which are slowly reclaiming the land for Mother Nature. Nearing Drumbain Farm, two low brick built buildings are passed, which appear to have been built on the original trackbed. Beyond these buildings are the remains of bridge 21, that once carried the railway over the farm lane and nearby stream. A convenient plank over this stream allows the walker to regain the trackbed for a short section that ends in the landscaped cutting to the north of the lane leading to Fisherton Cottage. The nearby fields provide a convenient grassy detour, to return to the railway as it starts curving round the headland into Bracken Bay. Gorse starts to encroach onto the trackbed, although a good man/sheep-made path allows the obstacle to be passed without any major difficulty. A muddy cutting, spanned by a wooden overbridge, guides the walker into the Bay, with its views of the nearby Heads Of Ayr and along the coast of Ayr, Irvine and even the tall chimney of the Inverkip Power Station to the north of Wemyss Bay. This lonely spot, far away from the roar of modern society, provides a pleasant lunchtime stop for the walker.

The trackbed soon becomes a long, straight embankment, that can be very windswept at times. One is advised to hold onto one's hat, in case the wind decides that it is no longer required. A lane leading up to the A719 near Old Lagg, is still spanned by a series of planks resting on the original girders of the underbridge. Beyond this, the embankment has been partially landscaped to provide a play area for the caravan site built on the site of the old **Heads of Ayr Station**. Very little can be found of the former station; only traces of a concrete sided platform that may have once been the original station platform.

Leaving the caravan site behind, further landscaping guides the walker towards an overgrown cutting. A detour into the nearby field can be used to regain the trackbed as it becomes a wide embankment past Laigh Kyle Farm. If the Highland cattle behind the farm are a deterrent, the nearby lane leads up to the A719 instead. However, the cows are really very friendly, as they help the walker onto another embankment to reach the western edge of Butlin's Holiday Camp.

Butlin's opened in 1947, and countless thousands of holidaymakers have had a wonderful time there since. To avoid any problems, it is advised to head up the main access road, to reach the A719, which is used as a detour around the high fences of the camp. Looking along the trackbed, as it passes to the north of the main buildings, no trace can be seen of the concrete platform of the new **Heads of Ayr Station**. Once past the camp, a lane leads back to the trackbed alongside an attractive house with Dutch gables. The lane passes several farm cottages, ending alongside a hedge built on a concrete walling from the former station. It is difficult to know if this walling is in its original position, as landscaping of the railway after its closure, has removed most traces of its original route.

Turning one's back on Butlin's, the trackbed is partially overgrown, but it soon opens out into a pleasant country lane. A bridge which carried the railway over a small burn has been removed, providing the only obstacle on the way. Nearby can be found the remains of milepost 45, indicating the mileage from the former Glasgow St. Enoch Station of the G&SWR. Nearing the A719 the trackbed becomes boggy, caused by the filling in of the bridge under the main road. Beyond the main road, the trackbed is owned by the Kyle and Carrick Council, forming an unofficial footpath to Ayr, well used by the dog owners of Alloway. The line skirts the southern edge of the village, which has become a dormitory town for Ayr and Glasgow. Beyond the bridge which carries the minor road that links the A719 and B7024, the route enters the square mile that forms the heart of Burns Country. The next bridge is a spectacular brick and stone cladded concrete bridge, which carries the railway over the River Doon, complete with mock castellations and lookout towers.

A path heads down to the riverside, which allows the walker to have a closer look at this impressive bridge. Over the bridge, the trackbed enters a tunnel, which allowed the railway to pass beneath the graveyard of the Auld Alloway Kirk. In some ways, it is more a long bridge than a genuine tunnel, at the end of which was **Alloway Station**. The original island platform is very overgrown, although traces of the concrete bases of the footbridge and a small brick building (lamp room) may be found on the platforms. The former extensive goods yard is now used by a sports hall and Burns Visitor Centre. Few will be able to pass without learning something about Scotland's most famous poet.

Beyond the boggy site of the station, the trackbed becomes a firm dry path, for the final mile or so towards Alloway Junction. The official walkway ends at the site of the bridge which once carried the railway over the main road into Ayr. Road realignments, in connection with the Ayr Bypass were the cause of the bridge's removal and landscaping of the former abutments. The walker however, having negotiated the main road, no doubt will climb the eastern abutment's site, to walk the final section of trackbed to **Alloway Junction**. The track passes over a lane, which was once a through track to the Ailsa Hospital, which forms the last exit point from the trackbed.

Once across the bridge, the line skirts a modern housing estate. The owners of some of the houses are starting to "claim" sections of the trackbed. Several telegraph poles, with their insulators still attached, act as a guide as one reaches the former junction with the Stranraer Line. A high security fence prevents a close inspection of the junction, and the walker has either to return to the lane or the main road, to seek an exit from the railway. Ayr is about a mile down the main road, which is one of the main bus routes into the town. It is a busy seaside town, that offers a wide variety of accommodation and places of refreshment, to the tired walker.

## VIII/4b:  Culzean Castle to Girvan

The starting point of this section of the walk, along the former Maidens and Dunure Light Railway, is the main entrance to Culzean Castle. It is served by a limited bus service from Ayr to Girvan. Although there is a regular service between these two towns, the majority of the services use alternative routes inland, by-passing the Castle. The main drive to the castle crosses the trackbed, but it is easier to continue along the drive, until it makes a right handed turn to head down towards the castle. On this bend a path which is signposted to the picnic site should be followed, as this turns back towards the railway. It crosses the trackbed, to the south of the site of **Glenside Station** by means of an attractive stone overbridge, on the other side of which steps lead down the cutting's side onto the trackbed. In the case of a railway walker suffering from loss of memory, or disused trackbed withdrawal symptoms, a signpost indicates that the path is now a "disused railway".

Although the trackbed forms part of a nature trail in the grounds of the castle, very little clearance work has been done to the rich growth by the present owners, the Natonal Trust for Scotland. Apart from repairing the drainage system, a limited amount of tree/undergrowth clearance has been performed to permit passage along the trackbed. Initially the trackbed in the cutting is slightly waterlogged but conditions rapidly improve as the walker starts on the southbound journey to Girvan. The section in the care of the NTS makes for an enjoyable walk, conditions generally being dry underfoot. Two dismantled bridges have been replaced, making for an obstacle free walk. The rich assortment of trees are matched by a wide variety of flora, pink and red campion, primrose, daisy and even the humble dandelion, adding a rich splash of colour to the restful shades of green. The background rumble of traffic is kept low and easily drowned by a medley of bird songs. In the surrounding field a pair of hares may celebrate the arrival of spring, whilst cows and sheep munch away at the grass.

Leaving the care of the NTS, the trees and undergrowth close in, although passage can be made along the trackbed. There is evidence of a limited amount of clearance work being undertaken, possibly to extend the walkway. Approaching the site of **Maidens Station** the walker encounters a caravan site, which has removed most if not all traces of the station. Where the railway crossed over the A719 (bridge removed) the caravan site ends. Possibly the only visible remains of the station, which once had an island platform, is a concrete flight of steps leading down to the main road from the northern embankment of the former railway bridge. Across the road, a path leads one back up to the railway, to the east of the former bridge abutment. After enjoying a brief woodland sojurn, the trackbed emerges into farmland amidst signs of clearance of unwanted saplings. Only a short section has been totally ploughed into the adjoining field system, luckily the adjoining field remains in pasture, allowing progress to be made without an unwanted detour. Mostly the trackbed has merged into the pastures that are grazed by a mixture of Ayrshire and Jersey cows, more interested in the luxurious grass than a mere railway rambler.

The trackbed is only marked by the occasional shallow cutting or embankment, making a level track through the fields. Nearing Little Turnberry another caravan site is espied. Initially it can be detoured by means of the adjacent fields, but the walker is eventually forced to wander through the site, much to the amazement of its inhabitants. In this stretch the trackbed is wider than usual, probably to accommodate sidings for military traffic to the nearby disused airfield. Beyond the caravan site, the trackbed narrows and after short agrarian and arboreal sojurns, merges into the primeval jungle that marks the site of **Turnberry Station**.

Whether the trackbed has been filled in up to the original platform height by natural or human means, it is difficult to say. The only visible relics of the station are the large slabs that formed the edging of the single platform. Nearby stand the cream buildings with red-tiled roofs of the Turnberry Hotel, which was originally connected to the station by a covered way which led through a large conservatory into the main entrance of the hotel. This covered way, along with the station buildings and glass canopy, have all disappeared. So have the trains that once brought golfers to the attractive links course. A road detour is now required, initially down the goods access road for the hotel, then via the A77 and a minor road leading to High Drumdow, in order to regain the trackbed on the opposite side of the Milton Burn. The removal of the bridges over these roads has resulted in a short isolated section of trackbed remaining, which may be further severed if the bridge over the Milton Burn has been removed.

Continuing on towards the site of **Dipple Station**, the trackbed remains clear of most obstructions. This is largely the result of the decay of the railway fencing, allowing cattle and sheep access to the trackbed from the adjoining fields. Where this has not happened conditions are very different, the undergrowth of gorse and brambles acting as a strong deterrent, especially to anyone foolish enough to be wearing shorts or other unsuitable jungle attire. Passing Matthew's Port, the final caravan site of the day is encountered.

This site is split in two by means of a concrete overbridge, which carries the minor road to Townhead over the railway. Nowadays the only wheeled traffic passing under the bridge are cars bringing occupants to the many caravans. It is interesting to wonder how many of these motorists realise that the bridge predates the caravan site by a considerable number of years. Having left the caravan site behind, the walker faces another major obstacle at the aptly named Dunnymuck Farm. Since Dun is a gaelic name for hill, this may give some insight about the obstacle, which is a large rubbish heap straddling the trackbed.

Beyond the farm conditions become impossible. A dense growth of nettle, gorse and brambles have totally blocked the railway. The fields of the eastern side of the railway provide a preferable alternative to the hazards of the A77, even if some fording of streams is required. Once the walker reaches Burnside Farm, the trackbed clears, thanks to the voracious appetite of the farm's cattle. The next mile or so of the route makes for a pleasant walk, passing the ruined remnants of a chapel near the buildings of Chapeldonan, before the Girvan rubbish tip is found. This refuse tip occupies a cutting adjacent to the former Ministry of Defence depot of Grangeston.

The depot was originally rail connected, but the modern industrial estate that now occupies the site relies on the heavy lorry for the transport of goods. The infilled cutting emits an evil coloured liquid, into evil smelling pools in various lurid hues of green, blue and ochre. Beyond the cutting the trackbed is very overgrown with gorse and brambles. The time has come to head towards the Girvan Bypass by means of fields leading onto a farm access lane. Perhaps the walker will make a short detour to view the remains of the junction of the M&DLR with the main Stranraer line, before continuing into the town.

The farm lane leads underneath the new road bridge, which forms the northern end of the Girvan bypass, to reach the route of the former main A77 out of the town. A minor road which is signposted to the "golf course" can then be used, to reach the site of the original **Girvan Station**. The railway from Ayr to Girvan, which eventually reached Stranraer, was opened on 24th May 1860. With the opening of the Girvan to Portpatrick Railway on 5th October 1877, the present Girvan Station was opened, to the north west of the town. The old station remained in use for some passenger services until 1893, when it became the town's Goods Depot. Opposite the old station is a grassy embankment, which was a continuation of the lines to serve the nearby harbour. This extension has been landscaped to provide a park and small camp site. The site also supports a handy public convenience. Girvan is well served by cafés and a wide variety of accommodation. There are also regular bus and rail services to Ayr and Stranraer from the town.

*Ornamental overbridge near Lennox Castle*

# IX:
# WALKS IN DUMFRIES
# & GALLOWAY REGION

## The Port Road

The short sea crossing from the Mull of Galloway to Northern Ireland, has always been a lure for transport schemes. The Victorian railway promoters were no exception, and the first tentative approach of the Iron Road was made by the promotion of a railway from Dumfries to Castle Douglas, which received its act of Parliament in 1856. The next year, on the 17th August, a further act of Parliament authorised the construction of a line from Castle Douglas to Portpatrick, with branches to serve the harbours of Stranraer and Portpatrick. Construction was soon under way on both schemes, and the Castle Douglas to Dumfries line was opened on the 7th November 1859. The railway from Castle Douglas to Stranraer opened on the 11th March 1861, although the public service started on the next day. Four months later, the construction of the extension to Portpatrick received a setback, when two arches of the viaduct being constructed near Colfin collapsed. In spite of this setback, the extension to Portpatrick was opened on the 28th August 1862.

This opening allowed the operation of through trains from London for the ferry service from Portpatrick. The railway promoters then started to look at providing branch lines to some of the towns which were bypassed by the main line. The first branch to open, was from Castle Douglas to Kirkcudbright, which opened on the 17th February 1864. However, the ferry service from Portpatrick to Donaghadee was not living up to the hoped for demand. The government were forced to subsidise the service, but their support was withdrawn in 1868. Three years later, the South Pier Lighthouse at Portpatrick was removed, and transported to Colombo Harbour in Ceylon. At the same time an Act of Parliament was sought by the promoters of a railway from Girvan to Portpatrick, with a separate terminal station in St. John Street, Stranraer. In 1872 two Acts of Parliament authorised the construction of railways from Newton Stewart to Wigtown and from Girvan to Challoch Junction (near New Luce). The latter line having running rights over the

Portpatrick line, from Challoch Junction to Stranraer.

Whilst these lines were being built, the fortunes of Portpatrick continued to decline. In 1873 the harbour was officially abandoned and two years later the railway from Portpatrick Town Station to the harbour was closed. After failing to persuade the Caledonian Railway to operate the new line to Wigtown, the directors of the Wigtown Railway opened it for goods traffic from Newton Stewart to Wigtown on the 3rd March 1875. Passenger services started one month later, on the 3rd April. The line was extended to a terminus called Garlieston (although it was one mile from the harbour, at a site which was renamed Millisle) on the 2nd August. A tramway was opened from this terminus to Garlieston on the 3rd April 1876, although the goods service started a few days earlier. The WR gained a second Act of Parliament in 1876, authorising the extension of the railway to Whithorn and retrospectively authorising the construction of the Garlieston Tramway.

The railway construction in the area came to an end in 1877, when the remaining lines were opened over a period of three months. The Whithorn extension was opened on the 9th July, whilst the Girvan & Portpatrick was opened to New Luce on the 19th September. Having sorted out access problems, through running to Stranraer started on the 1st October. Even with the opening of the branches, traffic still failed to provide a return on the investment. In 1885 the independent Wigtown and Portpatrick lines were merged to form the Portpatrick and Wigtownshire Joint Railway, operated by the Caledonian and the Glasgow and South Western Railways. The G&SWR was already operating the lines from Castle Douglas to Dumfries and from Challoch Junction to Girvan, and the Kirkcudbright branch. The railways then settled down to provide a valuable service for the countryside, as well as providing a connection from England to the Northern Ireland ferry service, which was now firmly based on the sheltered harbour of Stranraer.

The Portpatrick Harbour branch was lifted soon after its closure, whilst the platform of the Harbour Station was reused to extend the platforms at Newton Stewart. In 1902, the girder bridge which carried the branch over Main Street were removed, although the abutments remained in situ. The PP&WJR became part of the London Midland and Scottish Railway, after the 1923 grouping of the railways, and became part of the Scottish Region of British Railways, after the Nationalisation of the Railways in 1948. Sadly, closures soon started to cut back the system. The first casualty was the line from Stranraer Town to Portpatrick, which was closed to passengers on the 6th February 1950, although a goods service continued to operate from Stranraer to the creamery at Colfin. The same year brought about the withdrawal of the passenger services on the Whithorn branch, on the 25th September.

The goods service to Colfin Creamery ceased on the 16th May 1959, whilst the Whithorn branch lost its goods service on the 5th October 1964. The final closures were not far away, the Kirkcudbright Branch lost its passenger services on the 3rd May 1965, whilst on the 14th June of the same year, the line from Dumfries to Challoch Junction was closed to all traffic, apart from goods services from Dumfries to the ICI factory at Maxwelltown. This closure also brought about the total closure of the Kirkcudbright branch. The last closure was the withdrawal of passenger services to Stranraer Town, which took place on the 7th March 1966.

Thus in a period of just over sixteen years, the efforts of the Victorian railway builders were thrown on the scrap heap; sacrificed to the voracious appetite of the internal combustion engine. The bones were picked clean during 1967 and 1968, when all tracks were lifted; leaving only the empty embankments and cuttings to echo to the roar of the traffic, rushing along the narrow roads, to reach the ferry terminal at Stranraer. Nowadays, passenger and goods services operate from Girvan to Stranraer Harbour, whilst goods services remain on the stubs to Maxwelltown and Stranraer Town.

*Mileages*

|  |  |  |
|---|---|---|
| DUMFRIES | 0 miles | |
| Maxwelltown | 1¾ miles | |
| Lochanhead | 6 miles | |
| Killywhan | 8¼ miles | |
| Kirkgunzeon | 10½ miles | |
| Southwick | 12½ miles | |
| Dalbeattie | 14¾ miles | |
| CASTLE DOUGLAS | 19¾ miles | |
| Castle Douglas | | 0 miles |
| Bridge of Dee | | 2¾ miles |
| Tarff | | 6¾ miles |
| KIRKCUDBRIGHT | | 10¼ miles |
| Crossmichael | 23½ miles | |
| Parton | 26½ miles | |
| New Galloway | 28¾ miles | |
| Gatehouse of Fleet | 38¾ miles | |
| Creetown | 43¼ miles | |
| Palnure | 46¼ miles | |
| NEWTON STEWART | 49½ miles | |
| Newton Stewart | | 0 miles |
| Wigtown | | 7 miles |
| Kirkinner | | 9¼ miles |
| Whauphill | | 11 miles |
| Sorbie | | 13½ miles |
| Millisle | | 15¼ miles |
| WHITHORN | | 19¼ miles |

| | |
|---|---|
| Kirkcowan | 58 miles |
| Glenluce | 64¼ miles |
| Dunragit | 67½ miles |
| Castle Kennedy | 70½ miles |
| STRANRAER Harbour | 73¾ miles |
| Town | 73 miles |
| Colfin | 77½ miles |
| PORTPATRICK TOWN | 80½ miles |

*Ordnance Survey 1:50,000 Map Numbers:– 82, 83, 84*

*Public Transport*

With the relatively sparse population of the area, it is not surprising that public transport is very limited. Stranraer and Dumfries provide links into the railway network, whilst the Galloway Rail-Link given in the BR passenger timetable, gives details of some of the buses from Dumfries to Stranraer. Castle Douglas provides buses to Ayr (not on a Sunday) as well as the main Dumfries to Stranraer service via Kirkcudbright. At Newton Stewart, this service connects with the Whithorn and Girvan services, whilst at Stranraer there is a service to Portpatrick (again there is no Sunday service on this route).

## IX/1a: Portpatrick to Stranraer

Portpatrick is a small, sleepy town on the western side of the Mull of Galloway, facing across the narrows of the North Channel to the Antrim coastline of Northern Ireland. Its proximity to this coast made it a tempting candidate for ferry services. However, it never lived up to its promise and after the failure of the Victorian schemes, settled down as a quiet fishing port, frequented by tourists in search of peace and tranquillity. Recently the town was selected as the western terminus of the Southern Upland Way, the long distance path stretching from the North Sea at St. Abbs (on the Berwickshire coast) to the Irish Sea. The railway rambler, may thus cause some confusion amongst the natives, who direct one onto the Southern Upland Way, as the way to reach Stranraer.

Very little remains of the harbour extension, the site of **Portpatrick Harbour Station** having been landscaped to form the town's bowling green and tennis courts. Beyond these green spaces, the line has been merged into the adjacent gardens, leaving only the abutments of the former bridge over Main Street, to mark its climbing course up to the Town Station. Beyond these stone monuments, further landscaping leads onto the site of **Portpatrick Town Station**. This has been converted into a caravan site, and the former station buildings have been adapted to provide the toilet block. This conversion has been achieved with very little external alteration to the attractive single storey building. The station platform remains, breached in one place by what is presumably the house for the owner of the caravan site. Considering

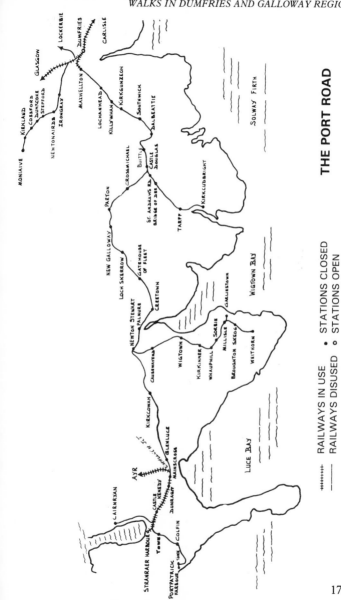

**THE PORT ROAD**

+++++++ RAILWAYS IN USE   •  STATIONS CLOSED

———— RAILWAYS DISUSED   o  STATIONS OPEN

this house must date after 1950, its style is more of the 1930s than the 1950s. The other main relic from the railway which has survived, is the former Station Master's House, which has become a private house, fenced off from the caravan site.

Photography of the station remains should be done with care, in case one of the residents emerging from the "station buildings" is not versed in the former use of their toilet facilities! The railway leaves the shelter of the Town Station, and starts on an unbroken 1 in 57 climb, to Colfin Summit. The route passes through a curving, rock-sided cutting, that funnelled the winds off the Irish Sea, increasing the effort required for a train to leave the town. On one notable occasion, when a train was experiencing difficulties on the grade, the driver instructed his fireman to split the train. The fireman replied "H'ye a saw?", because the train only consisted of one coach behind the struggling engine! On leaving the station, the trackbed passes behind a new school, where a path can be followed, to reach the trackbed as it emerges from a bout of in-filling (possibly from the construction of the school) at the start of the rock-sided cutting. On a windy day, progress can be slow as the route curves round Castle Point to reach the valley of the Pinminnoch Burn.

Leaving the cutting, the trackbed turns inland, alongside the remains of Dunskey Castle, the walker being faced with negotiating two electric fences to reach the safety of another caravan site. The first fence is not too bad, as it is a wire above a gate, allowing one to slide over the gate and pass beneath the overhead electrification. The second fence is more of a problem, especially if it is live. Beyond this resistance, the trackbed widens out, possibly where a siding had been provided for the nearby quarry. The caravan site is very well maintained, keeping the trackbed as a grassy covered playground for the residents, even retaining the bridge which carried the railway over the access lane past Portree Farm. Unfortunately beyond the caravan site conditions rapidly deteriorate, as gorse and broom grow in great profusion on the trackbed.

The way follows a faint path that weaves through the undergrowth. The path is made by some animal, probably human, using the trackbed and the nearby fields. The only major problem is the bridge which once carried the railway over the Pinminnoch Burn, in the middle of nowhere.

Suddenly the site becomes all too obvious, as the walker is faced with either trying to ford the burn, or a shuffle on the length of rail that now crosses the burn. The rail provides a more tempting solution, albeit cold and rusty, as carefully one inches across the great void, taking care not to turn turtle and end up with a rather damp head or worse. Having negotiated this obstacle, conditions do not improve, although again a faint path gives a guide as to which part of the trackbed can be walked, and which parts have to be followed in the adjacent fields. Eventually by the access road to Lagganmore conditions deteriorate to total impenetrability, and one is forced to follow this access road to reach the A77. This road has been realigned to the north of its original route, so

*Colfin Station*

the walker is faced with the overgrown remains of the old road, before reaching the new road, slightly further uphill.

The walker on reaching the A77, should turn right and follow the road, to regain the trackbed at the site of the crossing with the B7042 to Sandhead. The trackbed is a pleasant well grazed track through the fields, as the gradient eases off for Colfin summit. A water trough is provided for the sheep and for the drivers of heavy lorries and buses, that have found the climb up to Colfin too great a strain on their radiators. The former creamery at Colfin, which retained a goods service after the closure of the passenger service, has been converted into a fish factory. The double storeyed Station Master's house remains in use as a private house. **Colfin Station** has been converted into a small house, the owner of which keeps several assorted animals. Opposite the former station buildings, a temporary shelter has been provided for these animals, who roam the grass covered remains of the extensive siding area at the station.

Beyond the station, a further section of trackbed can be walked, ending up at a waterlogged cutting. This can be detoured by means of the field on the right of the rock-sided cutting. The minor road which crosses over the railway, in the middle of the cutting, should then be followed, to regain the A77 for a second section of road walking. The course of this road has been altered by realignments, from when the railway was operating, leaving the former bridge over the railway isolated, from the modern course of the road. The A77 should be followed to the access road to Cairnpot, to regain the trackbed. By now

175

the walker is used to following the railway both on the trackbed or by means of the adjoining fields, dependent upon the penetrability of the undergrowth, as the line now drops down on a gradient of 1 in 72 towards Stranraer. One open section of the trackbed is very wide, possibly the site for a siding for agricultural traffic from the nearby farms. The trackbed is still crossed at this point by a wooden overbridge, giving access, over the railway, from the adjacent fields.

Hacking through the gorse and head-high nettles, the walker comes across another bridge (which has been removed) over a burn, near to where the railway crossed over a lane from Kilhilt Farm. Beyond this minor watery inconvenience, the walker comes across a cutting that though free of gorse and other undergrowth is used for the storage of farm slurry, which has a decidedly unpleasant smell. Further field walking eventually brings one to the remains of the viaduct which carried the railway over the Pittanton Burn.

When the goods service to Colfin Creamery stopped, the viaduct was demolished, leaving a narrow strip of rough ground to mark its former course over the boggy valley of the burn. The walker should use this rough ground, to find a safe crossing of the burn, regaining the trackbed on the northern embankment of the former viaduct. The trackbed is initially clear of undergrowth, leading into a further overgrown cutting alongside Whiteley's Farm. This is virtually the end of the walkable section of the railway. Although the trackbed survives alongside the A77, it is very overgrown. A dense growth of rose bay willow herb makes for very slow progress.

Although the bridge which carried the railway over the A77 has been demolished, traces of the abutments have survived the associated road realignments. In spite of the gap, the rose bay willow herb has collonised the trackbed, beyond the bridge, with total impenetrability. Once in Stranraer, modern developments have eradicated all traces of the railway, only near the entrance to **Stranraer Town Station** does the railway once again become a recognisable entity. The former station buildings remain in a reasonable state of preservation, finding use as a depot for the British Rail Civil Engineer for the Stranraer Area. The platform is still rail served, even though it is now over twenty years since it was last used by a regular passenger train. Walking down the main road to the town from the station, one passes a road named Station Place. Since this leads to neither of the two actual stations, could this have been a naming in anticipation of the Girvan & Portpatrick Railway terminus at St. John Street in Stranraer?

## IX/1b:  Kirkcowan to Stranraer

Kirkcowan is a pleasant little village, with the remains of the old village church making a worthwhile detour. The village has two pubs and three shops, and is served by buses to Stranraer and Newton Stewart. **Kirkcowan Station** lies on the western side of the B733, on the outskirts of the village. The buildings and adjacent road overbridge have been demolished, leaving a mound of stones amidst the grass covered remains of the two platforms and a small loading dock. Leaving the station behind, the trackbed is used as an access road, ending up in an overgrown cutting, alongside the minor road to Mochrum Loch. Dropping down to the road level, there is a short section of embankment that ends in another missing bridge, this time over the Ballochrae Burn. Not only is the bridge missing, but the burn is used for drainage from the nearby fields. Having negotiated this watery obstacle, a double-stranded electric fence provides the final obstruction, before the trackbed can be regained. These problems can be circumnavigated by following the minor road, up to its junction with the B733. A gate gives access to a bridge over the burn, and the burn can then be followed, to regain the trackbed, beyond the electric fence.

The trackbed now heads across an open moss, turning away from the A75, for an isolated crossing of the Tarff Water. Only sheep graze the grass covered track, with firm conditions underfoot. The walker has very few problems to overcome; only the occasional fence hinders progress. A section appears to have been converted into a private nature reserve, for the trackbed is swathed in a variety of wild flowers, whilst plastic tubes shelter young saplings, which have been planted on either side. Strangely, these saplings do not appear to be suitable for growing in these conditions, because the growth is very stunted compared with natural tree generation found on other sections of the line. A further electric fence guards the approach to the double stone arched bridge over the Tarff Water, fortunately a stile and section of rubber tubing on the relevant piece of the electrified strand makes crossing this fence a shock-free experience. No doubt the photographer will pause to capture on film a record of the very attractive bridge over the water, especially as one wonders all the time if the bridge is still in situ, until the welcome sight of it casts away the worries.

Once over the Tarff Water, conditions soon deteriorate. A firm embankment guides the walker towards a waterlogged cutting. The walker should turn up the northern cutting side, to gain the track which crosses over to reach the isolated farm of the Mark of Luce. This track, having crossed the railway, turns left to run alongside the southern side of the trackbed. Beyond the cutting, conditions remain decidedly wet, and one is advised to follow the track to reach the A75, passing alongside an unmarked forest and a small industrial site. The A75 has been realigned, leaving the former bridge over the railway, standing in isolation over a further boggy cutting, whilst the road runs on the level, north of the original alignment. Such has been the road alterations, that it is difficult to visualise the former route of the railway, through this bleak terrain.

A short walk alongside the A75 is required, before the railway can be regained, by means of the access lane to Blairderry. The railway is now crossing Dergoals Moss, and the trackbed in places is very waterlogged,

177

forcing detours via the adjoining fields, to avoid the more squelchy sections. Fortunately conditions improve as the trackbed turns away from the road and forms a long, straight embankment, crossing the moss. A silage pit blocks the cutting at the end of the embankment, which can be detoured by means of the fields on the south of the railway, returning to what is marked on the map as a featureless section of the line. Presumably the cartographer was in a hurry when the map was being prepared, as the line passes through a series of cuttings and embankments, alongside the Lady Burn. The walker is rewarded with the remains of a mile post, measuring 41 miles from Castle Douglas, as well as several telegraph insulators, which escaped the demolition team.

Only one obstacle has to be overcome, the missing bridge over the Lady Burn. The girders have been removed, leaving only the remains of a telegraph pole to span the gap. Fortunately the burn can be forded on the south side of the missing bridge. Further 'non-existent' cuttings and embankments alongside the vestigial remains of an old military road, to reach the minor road from Corscreugh, near to its junction with the A75. The bridge which carried the railway over the minor road has been dismantled, and although a track can be used down to the road, it is an uphill scramble to regain the trackbed. The trackbed in places is overgrown, although one can force a way through to reach an open space marking the site of some long disused quarry, on the northern side of the railway, with traces of a loading platform and siding alongside the main line.

The walker disappears back into the undergrowth as the line runs alongside the houses of Glenluce Village. A faint path becomes clearer, as the walker passes man-made steps down to the lane leading up to Glenjorrie; possibly indicating the start of a disused official walkway. **Glenluce Station** is passed, marked by traces of the platform and goods shed. The site is now used as a car park. Beyond the forlorn remains of the station, the trackbed becomes very clear, as it reaches the Luce Viaduct. The A75 still does a U-turn underneath the lofty arches, to cross over the River Luce by means of an apology of a bridge, compared to the impressive brick and stone arched railway viaduct. No fences guard the viaduct, which would seem to have been converted into an official footpath over the river. The viaduct provides a good space for a break, with fine views seawards to Luce Bay and northwards through the wooded valley to the Galloway Hills. The track continues past the remains of the 16th Century Castle of Park, ending up in the nearby woods.

The walker has to navigate through further gorse and bramble covered sections of the line, using detours into the adjacent fields for the worst sections. The railway is now on the final climb up to Challoch Junction, where it was joined by the Girvan and Portpatrick Railway for the last few miles to Stranraer. A final missing bridge over the minor road to Glenluce Abbey, blocks the last section up to the overgrown site of **Challoch Junction**. Perhaps one's thoughts will be disturbed by the sudden sight of shining steel rails, colour light signals and the sudden roar of a diesel-hauled passenger or freight train starting on the long climb to Glenwhilly. The walker leaves the gorse and brambles behind, to follow the minor road to regain the A75, possibly walking on to the nearby village of Dunragit before catching a bus to Dumfries or Stranraer.

## IX/1c:  Maxwelltown to Castle Douglas

After the withdrawal of the passenger service from Dumfries to Stranraer over the Port Road, the section from Dumfries to the ICI factory at Maxwelltown was retained for freight services. The walker can reach the start of the abandoned railway at Drumsleet (two miles from Dumfries), by either walking or catching a bus or taxi from Dumfries. Heading up the minor road to Lochfoot, the remains of the bridge which took the railway over the road act as a signpost to the explorer of these abandoned trackbeds. Initially the route forms the partially landscaped gardens of the nearby cottages, before it enters a deep cutting. The removal of the ballast chippings in this section has blocked the original drainage, resulting in the cutting becoming a watery grass covered track, passing through the rock sided cutting. The cutting only opens out where it crosses over a tributary of the Crooks Paw Burn.

The cutting turns the former double tracked railway, through a gentle "S" bend, emerging onto the impressive multi-arched stone viaduct over the Crooks Paw at Goldie Lea. Although visible from the nearby main road, the viaduct only betrays its true length to the walker who reaches its forgotten location. Luckily the viaduct remains passable although few will be able to cross it without pausing to admire the graceful construction. Beyond the viaduct, the line enters a narrow pass as the hills close in, to reach a summit near the former station of Lochanhead. The line is initially an embankment above the road, climbing less steeply than the road, to end up in a cutting below the continuous roar of the traffic on the main arterial road. Conditions underfoot vary from sections of original ballast, to forest access roads, to moss covered earth which provides a welcome relief to weary feet after the heavier ballasted sections.

**Lochanhead Station** was one of the early closures on the line, not surprising considering its isolated location. The original buildings have been converted into an attractive house, looking over the grass covered station site. An attractive stone overbridge, taking a minor road to Lochfoot over the railway, complements the rather pleasant picture. Beyond the station, the trackbed has been stripped of its original ballast, leaving the original underbridges standing high above the grass covered mounds that mark the former route of the railway. Passing through pastoral country, one has to negotiate the odd inquisitive cow or sheep, wondering why anyone other than farmers would be found in

179

these lands.

**Killywhan Station** near the village of Beeswing, marks an end to the pleasures of walking the old railway. The station now survives as a private house, although an ugly breeze block wall obscures the traditional view of the station buildings from the platform. The western end of the station site forms a modern silage dump. The grass has been bagged into "sealed" tubes of plastic, but an oily foul-smelling liquid oozing out onto the ground leaves one with no doubt about their contents. Once past the station site, the trackbed has been reclaimed for agricultural purposes, embankments and cuttings have disappeared with little trace. It is difficult to realise that the railway once passed through this rolling landscape.

The only surviving relic of the railway is the derelict remains of a crossing keeper's cottage, where the minor road from Blairshinnoch crossed the railway. Beyond this the railway still remains entombed beneath the agricultural reclamation, with some very unpleasant electric fences lurking on the assumed route of the railway, to trap the unwary walker. The railway finally returns to its proper state, where it passes under the easternmost minor road from Kirkgunzeon to the A711. Shortly afterwards it reaches the caravan site, which now occupies the site of **Kirkgunzeon Station**. Initially untidy, conditions rapidly improve as the walker reaches the station buildings, which have been converted into a shop and office for the site. A swimming pool now uses the gap between the former station platforms. The nearby village supports a pub, not marked on the OS map, which provides refreshment for the walker.

Beyond the station, the trackbed enters an overgrown cutting before reaching the "improvements" caused by the removal of the former rail bridge over the A711. Beyond the road, the trackbed maintains a fairly straight course, with very minor earthworks, passing through a bleak semi-moss landscape, grazed by a few cows and sheep. The walker is passing one of the few uninteresting sections, that ends in the watery remains of **Southwick Station**. Conditions here are terrible, the trackbed is flooded up to the original platform height, both of which are very overgrown. Careful navigation via the former sidings on the south-east side of the station, allows the worst of these obstacles to be avoided.

Southwick Station marks the northern end of the rail network which once served the nearby ammunition depot. The once bustling site is now left abandoned to the sheep, the high fences which deterred unwelcome visitors slowly decay whilst the wind blows through the flimsily constructed brick buildings dotted at suitably safe distances on both sides of the trackbed. A combined road-rail bridge runs alongside the main railway bridge as it crosses over the Kirkgunzeon Lane, which is a river in spite of its name. Beyond it an electrical substation has been built on the trackbed, providing electricity to some of the few former MOD buildings that remain in industrial use. It is not too great an obstruction, as a clear path passes to the eastern side of its fences. A short distance further on, an overbridge has been completely blocked by an iron fence, but a path leads up and over this obstacle as the railway leaves the forlorn remains of the depot behind.

A waterlogged cutting remains to be negotiated, before the walker reaches the town of Dalbeattie, landscaping and road improvements have removed virtually all traces of the railway from the town. Only a stone built goods shed remains to mark the site of **Dalbeattie Station**. The former route can be approximated by careful map reading, whilst the trackbed can be regained to the west of the B794 as it leaves the town. The trackbed albeit overgrown in places, now turns northwards to follow and cross over the valley of the River Urr. The bridge site is marked by a series of stone pillars; the circular pillars of Urr. In dry weather the river may be fordable, although a fisherman's path follows the eastern bank, to reach an unmarked bridge near Ford Knowe.

The modern girder bridge allows a safe dry crossing to be made of the river, permitting the trackbed to be regained as it follows the Buittle Burn towards Castle Douglas. This section which is far away from the bustle of the road traffic, is a very pleasant walk. Generally conditions are dry underfoot, with the trackbed being largely a grass covered track, albeit overgrown in places. The remains of **Buittle Station** are passed, another early closure, which seemingly once had fairly extensive siding accommodation. Presumably this was another station, located more for operating convenience rather than any desire to serve any real population. The nearest village, Haugh of Urr is a good three miles distant, and that is by means of a ford or a footbridge. Continuing on, the ballast has been largely removed, leaving a moss-covered trackbed that is often waterlogged in the cuttings. The pleasure of being away from the road is short lived, as the railway reaches the site of the bridge which carried the railway over the A745.

Road improvements have allowed the road to occupy the former route of the railway, as it turns towards the town of Castle Douglas. The walker is faced with a sojurn on the wide grassy verges of the road. Only the former skew bridge which once straddled the railway at the entrance to the town, remains of the former railway route. **Castle Douglas** has been more thorough than Dalbeattie in removing any trace of the railway. Only a goods shed, with its doors painted in a faded version of Day-Glow Orange, remains of the station buildings. It is well hidden in the industrial estate which now occupies the former station site. Amazingly, the Station Hotel has continued to keep its name, as a reminder of the town's once important railway location. Unfortunately, the junction of the main line to Stranraer with the branch to Kirkcudbright has been landscaped, to provide a park and housing estate.

# IX/1d:  Castle Douglas to Kirkcudbright

When the Kirkcudbright branch opened to passenger services, the trains were forced to terminate initially at a temporary station, short of the junction with the main line to Stranraer. This station, **St. Andrews Road (Street)**, was short lived as trains were soon allowed to run into the main station. Today these initial miles of the branch are difficult to follow. The removal of an important bridge over a drainage ditch on Carlinwark Moss means the first practical point to join the branch is by means of the access road to Kelton Mains Farm. The drainage ditch is very deep and can only be crossed during lengthy spells of dry weather. When the Castle Douglas Bypass is constructed, this situation may ease as the road might cross this ditch at a handy place before rejoining the A75.

The trackbed towards the River Dee is fairly easy going, the only awkward section is near to the Lodge of Kelton, where an overbridge is partially blocked, converting the trackbed into a swimming pool. The Dee was crossed by means of two girder bridges, onto a conveniently positioned island. This island has been converted into a nature reserve, with access by the easternmost girder bridge. Unfortunately the other bridge has been removed and a detour via the interesting nearby road bridge is required, before the trackbed can be regained by the former **Bridge of Dee Station**.

Bridge of Dee Station had a single platform, with a small two-road goods yard to the west of the station. After the closure of the signal box, in 1925, the yard was operated by means of an Annett's Key attached to the branch staff. The station itself closed in 1949, and now forms a well kept private house. A gradient post stands at the original station entrance, off the minor road to Netherhall. Leaving Bridge of Dee, the trackbed can be followed without any major obstacle. One section has been landscaped, leaving a pair of bridge abutments, spanned by two concrete girders, as a memorial to the passage of the railway. The scenery is unspectacular as the line turns south-westwards to reach the site of the bridge over the A75.

Before reaching this bridge, the line enters a waterlogged cutting, caused by the provision of a new access to Barncrosh, which blocks the original drainage. Although the original road overbridge remains, this access now crosses the railway on a raised causeway, which has presumably caused the blockage. Road realignments have removed the trackbed, requiring the walker to follow the main line for a short distance. The trackbed can be regained on the south side of the road, near to the junction of the road to Balannan. Initially the trackbed has been landscaped, leaving only a cutting, now used as a silage pit, as evidence of the former route. The trackbed eventually resurfaces, as it starts to climb up and round Green Hill, to reach the site of Tarff Station. In a cutting north of the station, may be found a relic of the Victorian industrial past, a machine that was once the proud product of William Haigh of Oldham.

**Tarff Station** originally had a signal box and goods yard, although the former was closed prior to the closure of the branch. It was the only passing point on the line. The station building provided accommodation for both staff and passengers, who would have climbed up from the village of Ringford in the valley of the Tarff Water. The station has been bought by an agricultural contractor who uses the buildings for his accommodation. The rest of the site is used for the storage of agricultural products as well as an incognito museum of old engines and lorries. Leaving the station behind, the trackbed can be regained beyond the remains of the bridge, which carried the railway over the access road to the goods yard. The line is gradually descending, with very few major earthworks and a lack of relics. Only the remains of milepost 26¾ along with the occasional gradient post, bear witness to the almost total removal of all traces of the railway, after its closure. The route is relatively easy walking, apart from the odd silage dump or electric fence.

Nearing the Tongland Viaduct, which carried the railway over the A711 and River Dee, the trackbed has been totally landscaped into the surrounding field system. A detour down the the A762, is required, especially since only the piers of the viaduct remain in the river. Even so they form a frame to the whitewashed hydro-electric power station, downstream of the rail and road crossings. The road bridge still bears a plaque, indicating it was designed by Thomas Telford in 1805. On the south side of the river, the trackbed can be regained for a short overgrown section to Ardendee. The trackbed then has to be left behind, as the walker heads along farm lanes, leading onto the A711, to enter the town of Kirkcudbright.

**Kirkcudbright Station** was the main curiosity of the branch; a terminus approached by means of a shallow cutting on a curve. The passenger accommodation comprised a single platform underneath an overall roof. The overall roof was removed in LMS days. The platform line, and adjacent siding, terminating in buffer stops, were only separated from the nearby A755 (Bridge Street) by means of a stone built wall. The Kirkcudbright Branch was unusual in having sheds (which were sub-sheds of Dumfries) at both ends of the branch. The Castle Douglas shed was a goods shed, whilst the Kirkcudbright shed was a passenger shed. The shed incorporated a dwelling house for a railway employee. Apart from this locomotive shed and passenger accommodation, the station boasted a goods yard and coal depot, in what was a very confined space. During the Second World War, the station was a busy place, trainloads of tanks were worked to the terminus nearly every day, for use on the nearby tank training area.

Nowadays the station forms a housing estate, with only a plaque remaining to remind the residents that this was once a bustling branch terminus. Very little remains of the original railway, and the walker is left with only photographs to give an impression of the scene in its heydays. The town itself is an attractive coastal town, which still sees some

183

fishing trade. There are several cafés and pubs, whilst there is a reasonable amount of accommodation for walkers wishing to stay the night in the town.

## IX/1e:   Whithorn to Kirkinner

Alighting from the bus at Whithorn Bus Garage, the eye scans the desolate site of **Whithorn Station** in a hope of seeing something of the former railway buildings. However, extensions of the bus garage and the nearby council depot have obliterated all traces of the railway. The trackbed passes the nearby creamery, which provided a useful source of goods traffic for the branch. The trackbed forms a well used path as it heads past the crossing keeper's derelict cottage, on the access road to Chapel Orton. The empty stone built building is the first major relic of the railway. Beyond this cottage, the walker has to negotiate the first missing bridge, an underbridge to the north-west of Chapel Orton. The trackbed beyond is very overgrown, fortunately clearing as one reaches the site of the goods siding and platform at **Broughton Skeog**.

The platform has become a grass covered mound, boasting a fine crop of daffodils in the right season. The trackbed resumes to the east of the crossing, traversing two attractive stone built underbridges, before the first major obstacle at NX460448 is reached. A bridge over a drainage ditch, to the east of Broughton Mains has been removed, leaving only a telegraph pole straddling the remains of the brick built abutments. To make the situation even worse, the drainage ditch has been widened, to deter any attempts at the long jump record. If the telegraph pole shuffle is not performed, a detour to the nearby muddy fields (to the east) may reveal a nail encrusted plank at the junction of the drainage ditches at NX461444, which provides an alternative "crossing" point. The only dry detour would be to return to Broughton Skeog, to follow the roads to regain the trackbed at Pouton. This may be preferred!

For the walkers who risk the shuffle, hopefully avoiding the tearing of clothing on the nails, the trackbed resumes its walkable condition until the cutting at Pouton is reached. This can be very waterlogged and a detour via the nearby farm paths may be required to reach the remains of the abutments of the bridge which carried the railway over the B7052, by the site of **Millisle Station**. Millisle was once the junction of the branch to Garlieston, which runs to the north of the B-road, as a very overgrown track. This can be followed alongside the B7004, until the road turns north, crossing over the railway. A small building to the west of this crossing may have been a railway building.

The first Millisle Station, which also served Garlieston before the opening of the branch, was to the south of the later junction. When the branch opened, an exchange platform was provided, to the west of the junction. The southern platform face was used by the Whithorn trains, whilst the Garlieston trains used the other platform face. The actual junction, a trailing connection, was to the east of the exchange platform, followed by a small goods shed. Approaching the station from the Garlieston branch, one climbs up to the level of the Whithorn branch, passing the original station buildings, which have been whitewashed and converted into a private house. A horse in a paddock on the site of the goods yard, welcomes the sudden presence of friendly humans, especially if they offer a few titbits. Continuing towards Sorbie, the site of the exchange platform is passed, as the trackbed resumes its single track width where it enters a small cutting.

At the other end of the cutting, a new drainage ditch severs the trackbed, requiring a short roadside detour, regaining the trackbed by means of the access lane to Inch. Recent clearing operations by a nearby farmer have resulted in the trackbed once again becoming a walkable proposition. One passes milepost 14, before the farmhouse of Low Blair is reached. Further on, a bridge has been removed from over a burn, however a nearby plank provides a means of access to the opposite bank. Shortly afterwards the trackbed passes alongside the pristine buildings of the Sorbie Creamery. Road realignments have removed many traces of the site of **Sorbie Station**, leaving only the station master's house and adjacent goods office as relics.

At Sorbie, access onto the trackbed by the original road overbridge is very difficult, enforcing a roadside detour along the B7052 to Whauphill. The waterlogged cutting near Little Airies leads onto the depressing vistas over the Airies Moss. **Whauphill Station** served not only the nearby hamlet, but also Port William, six miles away on the western coast of the Whithorn Peninsula. The platform and goods yard were on the west side, with a crossing loop on the east. The large stone built goods shed still survives, with traces of its original platform and office inside. The station master's house has been converted into a private house, as well as serving as a post office for the hamlet.

Leaving the station behind, one has to negotiate a dump, to enter a "dead" cutting, full of a mass of natural and man-made refuse. The trees have been stripped of their bark, leaving their lifeless forms to fall and block the trackbed. Conditions improve a little as the cutting is left behind, but the trackbed is still waterlogged and the bridge which carried the railway over the access road to Drumjargon has been removed. The next relic is an attractive overbridge, which carries the minor road to Knockann over the railway. Nearby can be found the remains of milepost 10, indicating the distance from the start of the branch at Newton Stewart, along with several white telegraph insulators of LMS origin.

The railway then turns north-eastwards to reach the grass covered site of **Kirkinner Station**. The single platform served not only as a passenger platform, but also as a loading platform for the nearby goods yard. This platform still remains in situ, devoid of buildings, whilst the muddy site is used as a cattle field and caravan park. Nearby the station master's house still watches for potential customers coming up from the nearby village. The village has a pub and is served by buses to

*Nith Bridge, Dumfries*

# USEFUL ADDRESSES

Railway Ramblers,
c/o Mr N. Willis,
"Dinorwic",
74 Charnwood Drive,
Thurnby,
Leicestershire LE7 9PB.

The Ramblers' Association,
1/4 Crawford Mews,
York Street,
London W1H 1PT.

British Rail,
Scottish Region,
Scotrail House,
Glasgow.

Scottish Sports Council,
1 St. Colme Street,
Edinburgh EH3 6AA.

The Ramblers' Association
Scotland,
c/o Mr B. Forsyth,
12 Mosspark Road,
Milngavie,
Glasgow G62 8NJ.

Countryside Commission for
Scotland,
Battleby,
Redgorton,
Perth PH1 3EW.

Scottish Wildlife Trust,
25 Johnstone Terrace,
Edinburgh EH1 2NH.

The Branch Line Society,
c/o The Secretary,
15 Springwood Hall Gardens,
Gledholt,
Huddersfield HD1 4HA.

Scottish Youth Hostels Assn.,
7 Glebe Crescent,
Stirling FK8 2JA.

National Trust for Scotland,
5 Charlotte Square,
Edinburgh EH2 4DU.

Nature Conservancy Council,
Scottish Headquarters,
12 Hope Street,
Edinburgh.

*Broomhill Station*

IF YOU LIKE ADVENTUROUS ACTIVITIES ON MOUNTAINS OR HILLS YOU WILL ENJOY READING:

# CLIMBER
## AND HILLWALKER

**MOUNTAINEERING/HILLWALKING/TREKKING ROCK CLIMBING/SCRAMBLING IN BRITAIN AND ABROAD**

*AVAILABLE FROM NEWSAGENTS, OUTDOOR EQUIPMENT SHOPS, OR BY SUBSCRIPTION (6-12 MONTHS) FROM HOLMES MCDOUGALL LTD., THE PLAZA TOWER, THE PLAZA, GLASGOW G74 1LW*

---

## THE WALKERS' MAGAZINE

# the great OUTDOORS

**COMPULSIVE MONTHLY READING FOR ANYONE INTERESTED IN WALKING**

Available from your newsagent, outdoor equipment shop or on subscription from:
Holmes McDougall Ltd., The Plaza Tower, The Plaza, East Kilbride, Glasgow G74 1LW

# OTHER RAILWAY BOOKS
## by CICERONE PRESS

### WALKING NORTHERN RAILWAYS
### Volume 1: East
*Charlie Emett*

In this companion volume to Vol. 2: West, the author
describes 37 defunct lines from the Humber to Nor-
thumberland. Full of historical detail, practical advice
and intriguing anecdotes.

*ISBN 0 902363 76 X    160pp*

---

### WALKING NORTHERN RAILWAYS
### Volume 2: West
*Charlie Emett*

Covers the western side of the Pennines from
Derbyshire to the Scottish border. Thirty-six defunct
lines are described with a blend of history, anecdote
and guide to the walking trails. A splendid book for
the railway enthusiast.

*ISBN 1 85284 006 4  240pp*

---

*CICERONE PRESS publish a wide range of books for the
outdoor enthusiast. Subjects include walking and climbing
guides to many places in Britain and Europe; books on
canoeing, birdwatching, ski-touring - and more general
books on Cumbria*

*Available from bookshops and outdoor equipment shops or
send for latest catalogue and price list to:*

*CICERONE PRESS, 2 Police Square, Milnthorpe, Cumbria.*